# The Challenge of
# Urban Reform

# The Challenge of
# Urban Reform
*Policies & Programs in Philadelphia*

# Kirk R. Petshek

Temple University Press
*Philadelphia*

Temple University Press, Philadelphia 19122
© 1973 by Temple University. All rights reserved
Published 1973
Printed in the United States of America

International Standard Book Number: 0-87722-058-1
Library of Congress Catalog Card Number: 72-95878

*To Evelyn*
with gratitude and love

# Contents

# Foreword

No municipal reform movement more captured the imagination of observers, both nationally and locally, than did that of Philadelphia during the mayoralties of Joseph Clark and Richardson Dilworth in the mid-fifties and early sixties. Kirk Russell Petshek, a distinguished civil servant and professor, was among its devoted participants.

After graduate study at Harvard University, Professor Petshek went on to an academic career at Middlebury College and Colgate University and then into government service. In the middle 1950s he became the city economist of Philadelphia, perhaps the first person in any American city to hold that office. His last post included teaching and research in urban affairs and business administration at the University of Wisconsin.

Shockingly, Kirk Petshek died this year long before his time. Had he not, his critical eye would have sharpened this book even more as he scrutinized it for publication. But clear throughout it is his enduring affection both for the city and for the extraordinary period of which he was a part.

Through his account, Professor Petshek has performed an important service for those who wish to gain insights into the intricacies of a remarkable time in the governmental history of a great city. He is the first writer to cover in such comprehensive fashion the developmental progress of the Philadelphia reform policies and programs. He analyzes the way in which professionals such as himself were brought into municipal government and how they worked with their counterparts in civic and voluntary associations. (This linkage is important in the life of American cities, particularly in the life of Philadelphia with its Quaker traditions.)

For him, the renaissance coalesces around major themes which he believes identify it as both special and successful. In addition to the contributions of the professionals, he emphasizes the strong associations which developed between the city administration and citizens in business and civic organizations as well as the joint public-private policy deliberations which undergirded and helped shape decisions.

Both the Joseph Clark and Richardson Dilworth approaches to policy and programs, while different in style, similarly evolved as a consequence of pragmatic considerations and on-the-job learning. They were nourished by distinctive characteristics of the Philadelphia culture such as the desire for consensus. Petshek not only assesses the significance of the leadership of two strong mayors in relation to these factors but also that of supporting citizen and civic groups.

One of the notable contributions of the period was the development and utilization of nonprofit corporations to achieve objectives thought incapable of attainment through government or private means alone. Organizations which could solicit private capital through the inducements of governmental powers such as eminent domain were established to attract industry, restore older areas of the city and promote better housing. A combination of an evolving set of experiences and a holistic view of local government led to other administrative approaches: for example, many administrators of those years concluded that municipal programs needed to complement one another to be most successful. The city's six-year capital program compelled decision-makers to think not only in terms of priorities and goals but of the constraints of competing demands and available time and funds. Such considerations, in turn, stimulated the preparation of economic indicators and measurements for the city.

The continuity of such new programs was threatened by several questions, among them the lack of a professional reform organization. Associated with this deficiency was another (and somewhat curious) one. This second lack of provision for new leadership was attributed by some to the fear of the role of political influence; bright young men and women, for example, received no promises for the future.

Two of the author's contentions are of particular interest for students of politics. Petshek, while conceding that neither Clark nor Dilworth built a permanent political organization, characterizes their regimes as establishing practical social and political goals of lasting effect. He thus counters the conclusion of James Reichley, stated in *The Art of Government,* that the Philadelphia reform, like other reforms, was based primarily on an economic view of man and that it, with no other major motive to carry it forward, would come to an end. He also takes exception to the view that reform is concerned mostly with institutional changes; he writes, "Banfield and Wilson's judgment that reform is 'more concerned with *how* things are done rather than *what* is done' cannot . . . be applied to the Philadelphia of the 1950s." He argues that the Clark-Dilworth regime shifted the city's priorities, and so thoroughly that these now-established aims may prove irreversible regardless of the outlook of subsequent administrations.

Such conclusions may not be universally accepted. But readers should find value in the author's analysis of the differences in the mayors' personalities, in insights into party politics through commentaries on William Green, Sr., James Clark, George Leader, Francis Smith and others, in an insider's understanding of the impact and traits of administrators important to the period. They will learn about the contribution of Philadelphia programs to the development of federal urban legislation, including that for housing and depressed residential areas. They will find an account of the evolution of Philadelphia's programs for housing, transportation, industrial development and urban renewal including such projects as the Food Distribution Center, Center City and Society Hill rehabilitation, and the University City Science Center.

Kirk Petshek leaves the reader with the conviction that the intellectual and administrative capital, as well as the experience gained from the development of reform policies and programs, are undertapped resources for the city. Arguments over the lasting success (or lack of it) of that period of history may be less important than the actual shape of present and future developments. Beginning in the early 1950s Philadelphia's policies have often been imaginative, courageous, in the forefront of attempts to deal with urban complexities. Now that the temper of the times throughout the nation is to focus more on city problems than on urban potentialities, it may be helpful to view the Clark-Dilworth era as a burst of energy springing from a vision of city life still pertinent today.

The next steps, the next bursts of energy, may be much needed; they are not apparent. But whatever happens, Philadelphia no longer matches the description Lincoln Steffens provided in *The Shame of the Cities:* "Other American cities, no matter how bad their own condition may be, all point with scorn to Philadelphia as worse—'the worst-governed city in the country'." I like to think that these words and the epithet, "corrupt and contented," used by Steffens seventy years ago hold no more.

MARTIN MEYERSON

Philadelphia

# Preface

Philadelphia's reform government received national attention in the 1950s and 1960s. One article after another appeared in national magazines, mostly praising the new approach applied to the municipal problems in one large city, at a time when the "crisis of the cities" had not yet become a cliché. Yet no serious attempt has so far been made to analyze the methods and programs of the Philadelphia "renaissance." This book is such an attempt.

Why should a city so long smug, self-satisfied, and corrupt suddenly embrace new ideas, seek new approaches, and adopt an entirely new way of directing its development? What occurred in the 1940s in preparation for the reform of the 1950s was a concatenation of events for which there is no logical explanation. It started with the concern expressed by a number of civic groups and citizen organizations for the long-neglected fate of the city. The concern led first to the adoption of a new Home Rule charter, and then to avid support of the reform administration, especially its first two mayors, Clark and Dilworth. But it is unlikely that the mayors could have carried out their extensive programs without the outstanding professionals brought in from all over the country. This study explores the interrelationship of civic and political forces, leading to the unique method of joint public-private policy-making for the city's development.

The new reform government wanted to go beyond building up what had been so long delayed in public maintenance and public activities. It was concerned not only with physical rebuilding but also with programs which would change the economic and social environment of its citizens. All these aspects of development were closely interrelated, and it was the strength of the reform administration that it came to realize this interdependency and built on it. The substantive programs of the renaissance thus dealt primarily with developments embracing simultaneously physical, economic, and social aspects, and it is with these programs that I have been primarily concerned in the following pages. Any local government must, of course, deal with housekeeping issues like personnel, police, and public property; with matters affecting individuals, like welfare, health, and recreation; and with such broad social issues as race and poverty. I have excluded special treatment of these activities in order to concentrate on those issues in which the reform could claim interesting innovations— programs combining social and economic aspects with physical development.

Philadelphia saw an unprecedented degree of community involvement through a wide range of civic, professional, and business organizations. This also resulted in the public-civic collaboration upon which has been built Philadelphia's record of public-private partnership activities during the reform.

One early lesson learned by the reform administration in Philadelphia was that the sum of all the parts (the many new plans and programs) did not add up to a whole. Priorities had to be established, so that the community's depleted resources could be mobilized to insure the greatest benefit to the greatest number of citizens. Viewing the total picture rather than isolated pieces was a new approach. Top policy-makers realized that programs for housing, urban renewal, public improvements, industrial development, and their social effects were but different aspects of the indivisible development of the total community. In realizing this, Philadelphia moved ahead of other cities.

Readers should bear in mind that the federal poverty program with its emphasis on "maximum feasible participation" was not enacted until 1964: by that time Mayor Tate had been elected in his own right, and the period under discussion in this book was nearing its end. When the reformers spoke of citizen groups and their participation, they were thinking, not of grass-roots organizations or representation of the poor, or of ethnic minorities and public bodies, but of the wide variety of civic groups who brought about the charter changes, the reform, and its developmental programs. These were essentially of middle-class bias. To have attempted to discuss events of the 1950s and early 1960s in the light of the attitudes prevailing in the late 1960s and early 1970s would have falsified the picture. It is an error all too easily committed by the average reader. Being forewarned will prove important in what follows.

The idea for this book grew as I began to reflect, after I returned to teaching, about my years in Philadelphia between 1954 and 1962. I had been Urban Development and Economic Coordinator in the mayor's office. Joseph S. Clark had been elected in 1951, and by 1954 enthusiasm at City Hall was at its peak. Some of the badly needed administrative and civil service reforms had been carried out, clearing the way for the substantive developmental programs. By 1964, I felt that I could look back with objectivity on the events which I had observed at such close range.

My own files included, among other documents, minutes of the numerous meetings I had attended in my official capacity, memoranda written and received, and reports read and used. My relationship with City Hall colleagues and many other figures in the Philadelphia renaissance was such that I had ready access to the voluminous material from that period reposing in archives and in public and private files. It was also easy to conduct long interviews with well over one hundred of these people, often more than once. I perused reports on various phases of reform activities and newspapers covering the entire period.

A research leave for the academic year 1964–65 granted by the University of Wisconsin Graduate School, combined with some assistance from the American Philosophical Society, enabled me to spend an uninterrupted period in Philadelphia to do the research.

My intent in writing this book was to set down—as objectively as I could—the way in which Philadelphia's development programs came to be adopted, especially those starting during the renaissance. Although my viewpoint is inevitably influenced by my years at City Hall, I have tried to be impartial about those approaches which varied from the positions taken by the two reform administrations in which I served, and I have tried to evaluate both viewpoints. Any attempt to transplant these experiences must take into account the special circumstances surrounding a particular development, or the kinds of individuals responsible. No one who has watched at close range all the interactions involved in Philadelphia would presume to draw a blue-print that would serve equally well in all cities.

During Philadelphia's reform, the tools of diverse social science disciplines, including economic analysis, were applied to the city's problems. Although written by an economist, this book is addressed to all those concerned with cities—academics specializing in urban affairs, politicians both professional and amateur, and civic-minded laymen who want to see the cities of America flourish and to find out how this can be made to happen.

As a cutoff point for a story like this must be decided on, the mid-1960s seem appropriate. In 1965 I could observe the Philadelphia situation myself and felt clearly that the reform was still alive. Although that was still true for the next year or two, clearly the picture appears to have changed by the 1967 election. A number of events that have occurred since then have been touched on, but only incidentally.

The first four chapters (part I) deal with the historical roots, the civic groups and their accomplishments, the backgrounds, personalities, and characteristics of the three mayors presiding during the reform period, and the policy-making methods of the reform. Chapters 5 through 9 (part II) provide case studies of specific developmental programs. The last four chapters (part III) discuss some general characteristics of the reform government and review what has happened in recent years to civic groups and to Philadelphia's reform spirit. In the epilogue, freed from the constraints of a time cutoff, I have also attempted to evaluate the Philadelphia reform in terms of recent trends in the country as a whole.

KIRK R. PETSHEK

Jacksonport, Wisconsin

# *Acknowledgments*

Research into contemporary events leaves me with a debt of gratitude to many people. There are, first, the many—mostly colleagues—who were willing to spend time with me in detailed and often prolonged interviews on a number of occasions. Second, there are those who opened their official and personal files beyond reasonable expectations, making possible extensive documentation. I was gratified by the virtually unanimous willingness to help that I encountered. In the third place, drafts of some chapters were shown to individuals familiar with the events of the reform. Their opinions were sought regarding factual accuracy and the merit of my analysis. Finally, scholars elsewhere were asked for their judgment of the analysis in one or more specific chapters. Some of them spent much time and effort to give me the benefit of their criticism. At that, these groups are not mutually exclusive; a number of persons were good enough to help in more than one of these respects. It is impossible to thank all of them individually. However, the names of those in the first group, who were interviewed, are enumerated in appendix 2.

But there are some among those referred to above who spent so much of their time on my behalf that I would like to thank them individually for help way beyond anything I could have hoped for. They are Charles Adrian, University of California, Riverside; John A. Bailey, deputy managing director, under Dilworth, and executive director of two quasi-public transportation corporations; Harry Bredemeier, Rutgers University; Cushing Dolbeare, managing director, Housing Association of the Delaware Valley; Graham Finney, assistant executive director, City Planning Commission, and director, Community Renewal Program; Charles Frazier, chairman, Urban Traffic and Transportation Board; Charles Gilbert, Swarthmore College; William Grigsby, University of Pennsylvania; Richard McConnell, finance director, city of Philadelphia, and executive vice-president, Philadelphia Industrial Development Corporation; Lennox Moak, director, Pennsylvania Economy League–Bureau of Municipal Research; Dorothy Montgomery, executive director, Philadelphia Housing Association, and member of the Redevelopment Authority; Oscar Ornati, New York University; Walter M. Phillips, civic leader and director of commerce under Clark; William L. Rafsky, development coordinator; Henry Sawyer, councilman during Dilworth's term; Donald Wagner, managing director under Dilworth; William Wilcox, executive director, Greater Philadelphia Movement. The titles mentioned refer to the positions held either at the time I worked in Philadelphia or when these people helped me.

I would also like to express my gratitude to the American Philosophical Society for a grant which made possible an extended stay in Philadelphia while I carried out my research there, and the Graduate School of the University of Wisconsin-Madison for a research leave. Finally, I want to thank the University of Wisconsin Press for granting permission to reprint portions of an article previously published in *Land Economics.*

I have been helped in documentation, research, and editing by several persons, to all of whom I am grateful. Chronologically they are: Margaret Halsey, Linda Niebank, Daniel Schmelzinger, Gerald Peters, Susan Ruff, Susan Beetle, and Margaret Flack of the University of Chicago Press.

Usually an author also thanks his wife for her help. In this case, however, her encouragement, patience, and assistance go way beyond what is usual. She was willing to put up with me while I tried to present, analyze, and reevaluate the events of the Philadelphia renaissance, for what seemed to be a period without end. She shared with me her own insight and understanding of these events and was able to express some of my thoughts much better than I could. She was forever ready with advice when I needed it and encouragement when my patience failed. In comparison the fact pales that she also typed the many drafts of each chapter—though that activity strained her own patience more than anything else. It is difficult to express adequately the extent to which her instinct for the right approach and expression, and the importance of her consideration and help, are responsible for whatever merits this book may possess.

# I

# The Making of
the Reform

# 1      *Background for Reform*

Like a reluctant dragon after a long, sound sleep, Philadelphia in the late 1940s opened first one eye and then the other, stretched, groaned, and slowly awakened to face life as a large northern industrial city beset by the effects of needs long ignored. Chained to the dragon's neck was a City Hall controlled by an entrenched Republican party which had outlasted the New Deal, the Fair Deal, and the events which gave them birth.

What happened between 1776 and the eventual emergence in Philadelphia of the American two-party system, which seemed for many years to have bypassed that city? Why did reform come about in the mid-twentieth century to a city which Lincoln Steffens described in his famous statement as "corrupt and contented"? What had prevented serious reform movements in Philadelphia in the past, while other cities experienced them, and why was Philadelphia now more deeply affected by its own reform?

## English Tradition and the Quaker Influence

To find an explanation for the events of post-Depression Philadelphia, one must go back to some unique features of the city's history. There seems little doubt that here the English tradition took hold stronger than elsewhere and lasted longer. Also, the influence of the Quakers was not only present in Philadelphia at the time of its founding, but lingers on in spirit to this day, though members of the Society of Friends are now far fewer in proportion to the population of the area.

The Puritan tradition with its "Protestant ethic" is part of this heritage. Most of the inheritors of wealth or family tradition were Protestants, and Anglicanism was also part of the English tradition. "In many ways Philadelphia . . . in its flatness, its monotony of row houses, its grim industrialism is as English as can be. . . . It is very like an antique Toryish England; the England perhaps of Galsworthy," says Nathaniel Burt.[1] Englishmen like Philadelphia "better than any other American city . . . because Philadelphia men are so quietly self-assured that, like the English, they are given to amused understatements and to enjoying jokes about themselves." [2]

An American democratic community dominated by an aristocracy of relatively few "well-born," as Philadelphia is, creates an inescapable impression for the contemporary observer.[3] "It is true that you cannot describe Philadelphia at all unless you emphasize the fact that, in contra-distinction to most other American cities, these same families . . . exercise a power far in excess of their numbers." [4]

The traditional prominence of these families is based on the fact that they are important to themselves and to each other, and that they are tied to one another by intermarriage. They are, like Galsworthy's Forsyte family, the prototype of the upper-middle class—which can be called Philadelphia's ruling class— and very consciously the accent is on "upper." Taste, breeding, education, certain professions, and, of course, a certain amount of wealth are the hallmarks. An individual will be admitted to the circle if he is related, even by marriage, to some of the "old Philadelphia" families who already belong. Philadelphia society includes a long list of families going back to the seventeenth century, and their scions are distinguished even today from those whose antecedents are of more recent vintage. Mayor Joseph S. Clark, the first reform mayor (1952–56), used to emphasize that he was not an "old Philadelphian" because his family roots in Philadelphia did not date back to the Revolutionary era.

Dixon Wecter describes the kind of society that dominated Philadelphia thus: "A group of families with a common background and racial origin becomes cohesive, and fortifies itself

1. Nathaniel Burt, *The Perennial Philadelphians* (Little, Brown & Co., 1963), pp. 31–32.
2. Struthers Burt, *Philadelphia, Holy Experiment* (Doubleday, Doran & Co., 1945), pp. 346–47.
3. E. Digby Baltzell, *Philadelphia Gentlemen: The Making of a National Upper Class* (Free Press, 1958), based much of his analysis on an exploration of the 1940 Philadelphia Social Register.
4. Struthers Burt, *Philadelphia,* p. 348.

. . . by friendship and intermarriage. . . . The second and third generation, relieved from the counting house and shop, now begin to travel . . . and cultivate the art of charm." [5] In the Philadelphia of the 1940s, however, some members of such families realized that the time had come for them to stay home and cultivate the art of politics.

The early Quaker influence seems to permeate Philadelphia's social structure to this day. From 1683, when William Penn founded the city, until about the middle of the eighteenth century, the Quakers dominated Philadelphia. For the first quarter of the eighteenth century most of the mayors were members of the Society of Friends.

Among Quaker traits still observable in Philadelphia is a certain unself-conscious openness and frankness. Civic groups still speak about "concerned" money, that is, funds sought for a cause, and a "sense of the meeting" is widely sought in discussions among public officials and civic boards. General acceptance of this attitude toward consensus leads to a balanced approach to problems. A preference for consensus rather than for mere majority approval is shown by some civic groups and public boards.

While the Quakers quickly acquired wealth and social prestige, they felt that social inequities, of which they were keenly aware, should be corrected through charity rather than by changing the system.[6] As they acquired power, they lost their position of exclusiveness. By the 1770s they embraced only one-seventh of the citizens.[7] Furthermore, the convictions of the members of the Society of Friends often conflicted with the patriotic instinct and loyalty demanded of those living in the newly emerging nation. Some, barred by their religious convictions from bearing arms, concentrated their energies in the struggle for social betterment within the existing political framework. Others withdrew increasingly from public life. Their ambivalence about politics made them ineffectual even when fighting corruption, which they tried to do toward the end of the nineteenth century when they

5. Dixon Wecter, *The Saga of American Society* (Charles Scribner's Sons, 1937), p. 6.

6. Frederick B. Tolles, *Meeting House and Counting House* (University of North Carolina Press, 1948), p. 119.

7. Carl Bridenbaugh and Jessica Bridenbaugh, *Rebels and Gentlemen* (Reynel and Hitchcock, 1942), pp. 16–17.

became involved in the mugwump movement.[8] However, Quakers started the Civil Service Reform Association of Philadelphia; one became a founder of the National Municipal League and another of the Philadelphia Committee of Seventy, which is still a watchdog group for clean elections.[9] The modern Quaker, Rufus Jones, has said: "Had the active public-spirited Friends, who went off with the Revolutionary movement, remained to mould their generation, a type more outward, more progressive, more intellectual would have resulted." [10] The much later attitudes of "Proper Philadelphians" toward governmental service, and their relatively small contribution to the ranks of distinguished public servants, may have had roots in this Quaker heritage.[11]

Philadelphia's concern with civic problems, which reawakened in the mid-twentieth century, may well be due in part to the influence of the Quaker spirit on Quakers and non-Quakers alike. The schools that Quakers conduct have exerted a continuing influence on the leaders of Philadelphia society. The planning committees of these schools have included many non-Quakers, whose own children were often educated in, and in turn influenced by, Quaker schools.

## Politics, Professions, and Economic Activities

In contrast to most Quaker families, Philadelphia's socially prominent families were vitally concerned with politics during the second half of the eighteenth and the early nineteenth centuries. Philadelphia was the capital of the new federation and then the seat of the new federal government. But Philadelphia's develop-

8. In trying to present a picture of Philadelphia in the nineteenth and early twentieth centuries, I became aware of the fact that, while a fair amount has been published about colonial and eighteenth-century Philadelphia, relatively little is available for the later periods. Sam B. Warner's book, *The Private City* (University of Pennsylvania Press, 1968), has proved useful, especially as he deals with the transition from the nineteenth to the twentieth century.

9. Much of this information was graciously given me by Professor Philip S. Benjamin, of Temple University, from his Ph.D. dissertation, "The Philadelphia Quakers in the Industrial Age, 1865–1920" (Columbia University, 1967), pp. 186, 226, and an article, "Gentlemen Reformers in the Quaker City, 1870–1912," *Political Science Quarterly*, March 1970.

10. Rufus Jones, *The Quakers in the American Colonies* (Macmillan, 1911), p. 579.

11. Baltzell, *Philadelphia Gentlemen*, p. 245.

ment was more directly affected by its economic activities. A prominent port had made it a mercantile center, which served a rich hinterland in Pennsylvania and southern New Jersey. Philadelphia also provided other services, not only to its own growing manufacturing activities. Commercial banking and insurance were prominent. In 1752, Benjamin Franklin started the "Philadelphia Contributionship" with a board consisting mostly of Quakers, which started one of the country's largest concentrations of insurance.

One of the features of Philadelphia's economy in the eighteenth and nineteenth centuries was that many of its firms had long been in the family, especially smaller service firms, such as those engaged in investment banking. However, after the First and Second banks of the United States were allowed to expire, New York gradually took over as the financial capital of the country. Its commercial and port activities also began to surpass Philadelphia's.

When Washington became the nation's capital—depriving Philadelphia of political power as New York had deprived it of financial power—Philadelphia's leading families became increasingly concerned with their growing industries, especially textiles, chemicals, coal and iron, and machinery, as well as steel ships and railroads. Gradually the economy became more diversified, and as family dominance of many manufacturing firms gave way to the corporate business structure, members of prominent families increasingly chose medicine or law as their calling. A law degree was often a way station to a career in banking or in some other corporate business. And important legal business in Philadelphia was concentrated—more than in other cities—in a limited number of law firms. Membership in one of these firms often led to civic or public service.

Prominent families, however, continued to play an important social role during the nineteenth century and into the twentieth, especially when their interest began to focus on the city itself— although many much families themselves lived "on the Main Line," as the western suburbs on the Pennsylvania Railroad were customarily called. The social position of this elite, however, did not imply political influence. To the contrary, "ancient family associations counted for virtually nothing in leading political parties and selection of higher public officials." [12] Thus rejected, the socially prominent leaders showed their community concern through nonpolitical activities. Unlike the Quakers, who often fulfilled what they saw as their responsibilities through the improvement of social conditions, but did so within the political and social framework, members of these business families fulfilled theirs through concern with the culture and beauty of the city. Many an architectural masterpiece was built in or near Philadelphia as a quasi-public contribution, and cultural and civic institutions continue to be supported financially by the social elite. Until the mid-1940s, this nineteenth-century concept of service continued to satisfy those who should, through social position, education, and financial self-interest, have exercised some personal commitment to the better government of the city.

The immediate reason for not wanting to get involved in politics was a seemingly invincible series of machines in both Philadelphia and Pennsylvania. Simon Cameron, Matthew Quay, Boies Penrose, the Vare brothers—men whose names became better known for misdeeds than for their civic virtue—characterized the period between the Civil War and the world wars. Members of Philadelphia's prominent families rarely ran for public office, as they realized that the influence they could exert would be small. They went along with the system, in return for whatever favors they needed for their businesses. An exception was George Wharton Pepper, one of their legal patricians, who was appointed to the U.S. Senate to succeed Boies Penrose and was then beaten by Vare. But even he said: "Never in my life have I felt the itch for public office." Those who should have been exercising intellectual and political leadership preferred not to dirty their hands with politics—and the politicians were careful not to antagonize them.

## Progressivism and Civic Consciousness

At the end of the nineteenth century and the beginning of the twentieth, when mugwumps directed local government in many places and the Progressive movement held sway, the city of Phila-

12. Herman Le Roy Collins and Wilfred Jordan, *Philadelphia, a Story of Progress*, 3 vols. (Lewis Historical Publishing Co., 1941), 1:406.

dephia was only slowly adjusting to national economic forces and to the possibilities of modern economic development. Given its conservative bent, Philadelphia was slow to respond to potential growth developments. The policy-making role in many leading industrial enterprises had been relinquished by the sons of the founding families to professional managers of corporations, whose primary loyalties were to their own careers rather than to Philadelphia's needs. It was not until the middle of the twentieth century that these managers saw that their positions—and the reputations of their companies—were tied to the role they were to play in the civic and public life of the area.

The mugwump movement, intending to restore integrity to City Hall, was effective in Philadelphia only in the 1870s, when Quakers participated in starting the "Committee of One Hundred," which exposed the corruption connected with a public utility—the "gas ring scandals." The committee helped elect Mayor Samuel King in 1881, a weak reform mayor, who temporarily abolished the spoils system and introduced a civil service. But the machine returned to office after one term, and the problem of the gas utility lease continued. The National Civil Reform League was the only remnant of the Philadelphia mugwump movement.[13]

After the turn of the century, another reform party succeeded in getting a uniform primary law passed, which cleaned elections of prevailing fraud and eliminated the stuffing of ballot boxes. A watchdog committee to assure clean elections was started, the "Committee of Seventy." Again it had strong Quaker support. This organization, still in existence today, was a forerunner of many later civic organizations watching government activities or furthering specific voluntary programs.

The demand for reform in the cities emanated from the Progressive movement. One reason for local reform in the cities lies, I believe, in what Richard Hofstadter has referred to as the "status revolution." The middle classes "were Progressives not because of economic deprivations but because they were victims of an upheaval in status—they were being overshadowed and edged aside in the making of basic political and economic de-

13. Philip Benjamin (see n. 9 above).

cisions." [14] Nevertheless, little response to Progressive thinking could be detected in Philadelphia at the time. The reason for this unresponsiveness may help us to understand later developments.

In 1910, another reform party was started, taking most of its planks from Progressive thinking. It too has been seen as a status protest by middle- and upper-class businessmen against corporations and corrupt politicians, rather than a broad popular revolt.[15] In the following year, Rudolph Blankenburg was elected mayor—thirty years after the previous, meek attempt at reform. Another forty years were to elapse before Joseph Clark took over.

Blankenburg was a nonpartisan reform mayor, principled, bold, and inflexible. His lack of political acumen made him a single-term mayor. He was a humanitarian who had spent his own time and money to help those who had been wronged or who needed food and shelter. He was deeply committed to the principles of good government and civil service. An earlier charter reform (the Bullitt bill in 1885) had given the mayor control over the departments of City Hall—an advantage missed by Samuel King (1881), who had presided over a chaotic, decentralized establishment. Blankenburg had a wide business following, who approved of his running the city on an efficient, businesslike basis. Morris Cooke, a disciple of Frederick Taylor (the "father of scientific management") was his public works director. In his successful effort to prove that Philadelphia's consumers were overcharged by various utilities, Cooke brought in a number of experts from technical schools elsewhere. Consequently he found his appropriations held up by the council in order to stop him from hiring "foreign advisers." [16] Drawing up standard specifications for contracts, insisting on open bidding, and streamlining the administration departments, Cooke saved the taxpayer millions of dollars.

14. Richard Hofstadter, *The Age of Reform* (Alfred A. Knopf, 1955), pp. 135–40.

15. Donald Disbrow, "The Progressive Movement in Philadelphia, 1910–16" (Ph.D. dissertation, University of Rochester, 1956), p. 35. See also his article "Reform in Philadelphia under Mayor Blankenburg, 1912–1916," *Pennsylvania History*, October 1960.

16. Philadelphia *Inquirer*, May 14, 1912, as quoted by Disbrow in his dissertation, p. 79.

But Blankenburg went beyond these reforms, which were quickly undone by the returning machine: he also initiated long-term developmental improvements. In his inaugural address he called for transportation expansion, and he started a new Transportation Department. The extension of the existing subway to the north and the west was proposed, and the blueprints were drawn up, but only a small portion of the money asked for was appropriated, so that it was kept back from Blankenburg's non-partisan regime pending the return of the Republican machine four years later. Not until 1928 was the transit system, proposed under Blankenburg, finally built. He worked for the expansion of port facilities, and he increased municipal wharves; but he only laid the foundations for the vastly expanded shipping and ship-building facilities that were to be built during the First World War. Blankenburg also strove to lower the cost of living for the consumer by improving food distribution and markets and stimulating cooperatives. But again he was hampered by the council's refusal to appropriate funds.

The political machine that persistently blocked any emerging reform spirit in Philadelphia's city government was further strengthened by the ever increasing number of immigrants, mostly from Ireland, Italy, and Poland, who debarked at Philadelphia's port. Unaccustomed (and often unable because of language barriers) to assume the role of active citizens, these new arrivals quickly developed loyalty to the city bosses. Almost totally preoccupied with earning a living and raising families in alien surroundings, they found the existing system responsive to their immediate needs. Hofstadter puts it this way: "The typical Progressive and the typical immigrant were immensely different. . . . The loyalty of immigrant voters to the bosses was one of the signal reasons why the local reform victories were so short-lived. . . . [To the Yankee] politics was the business, the responsibility, the duty of all men. . . . The gulf between them was not usually bridged with much success in the Progressive era." [17] The mood of European immigrants discouraged reform in other eastern ports too.[18]

---

17. Hofstadter, *Age of Reform*, pp. 180–81.
18. Warner, *Private City*, pp. 201–2, 223, sees slightly differently and in a more far-reaching way the reasons that the prevailing progressive mood of

New approaches were slow to emerge in Philadelphia. While no discernible effort at government reform was made, the Progressive spirit of the time did result in some deep-rooted, long-range improvement in the social fabric of the city. Lawyers, academicians, writers, and other professionals joined to form new citizens' organizations, as the ethnic and occupational associations and neighborhood clubs, first started after the Industrial Revolution, lost importance. These new organizations laid the foundation for the reform movement of the mid-twentieth century, which cut much deeper than earlier Progressive era reforms in some cities, especially those in Philadelphia. Some of these organizations exist to this day and are the main channel for the involvement of thoughtful, respected citizens. Many of the civic groups discussed in the next chapter, led by citizens who thought they could help to improve their community, started after the turn of the century as a direct response to the problems of the times—specifically the problems raised by industrialism. Active citizen participation through civic initiative was never again to leave Philadelphia.

Civic involvement in Philadelphia was generated in part by a spirit of noblesse oblige filtering down from the city's earlier history, in part from enlightened self-interest, and in part, as de Tocqueville might have suggested, from the newly discovered sense of democracy and the pluralism that goes with it.

As early as 1909, sixty social and philanthropic organizations created the Philadelphia Housing Association to improve housing throughout the city. The association aimed for a decent home and a decent living environment within the income of every family, and promoted research on the relationship of housing to problems of transportation, city planning, health, tax reform, and so

the country failed to affect Philadelphia. He believes that Philadelphia's productivity and durable social order were due to "private institutions and individual adjustments" depending on "successes and failures of thousands of individual enterprises, not upon community action. . . . It was a private city and the public dimensions of urban life suffered accordingly. . . . It could not deal effectively with the economic, physical and social events that determine the quality of life." And: "The unwillingness and inability of Philadelphia's citizens to conceive of democratic regulation of their private economic affairs prevented . . . defining the problems of the city in a way suitable for public action."

forth.[19] It pressed for passage and enforcement of housing, zoning, and health codes. It drafted and helped pass the first City Housing Code in 1915. In the 1930s, it helped locally with the Zoning Ordinance and nationally with the passage of the Public Housing Act. In the 1940s, it supported city planning, the Citizens' Council on City Planning, and the planning exhibit (see chapter 2). In the 1950s, the association helped to establish a Housing Authority, drew up a new housing code for the new administration, and contributed to setting up the new Department of Licenses and Inspections.

Other groups focused on one specific area of concern on a city-wide basis. In 1908, business leaders and wealthy individuals with social prestige started the Bureau of Municipal Research to exert their influence on governmental affairs. They conducted a series of studies objectively, without fear of consequences. The bureau became part of a nationwide movement in the big cities, and most big city administrations came to recognize that research studies such as those the bureau carried out were reliable. "No other agency was as productive of ideas," said a former staff member. Low-pressure salesmanship was practiced, letting ideas follow their own course in civic and political channels. Some of the proposals actually were accepted by the entrenched City Hall machine in Philadelphia long before the reform.

By the 1940s, the bureau had fallen on bad times, but some of the best-known members were able to build up the board and its finances by convincing bankers and top businessmen that Philadelphia needed the bureau's objective research and creative thinking. After a young man, Robert K. ("Buck") Sawyer, had impressed the business community in 1946 (see next chapter) and was persuaded to take over as director of the bureau, new studies of all aspects of governmental reform started to flow from its staff. Eventually the bureau became instrumental in the fight for Philadelphia's home rule.

A similar organization was the Pennsylvania Economy League, with which the Bureau of Municipal Research merged in the 1950s. The league, started during the Depression, was a state-

19. Philadelphia Housing Association, second and fifth Annual Report, 1912 and 1915.

wide organization with two other offices in addition to the one in Philadelphia. It was especially concerned with economy for the taxpayer. Like the bureau, the league concentrated on studies of government, but was inclined to undertake them for the use of individual government officials or government committees which had asked for them, rather than for publication and general use. It undertook studies for the "Committee of Fifteen" (see chapter 2), which investigated city finances in 1948 prior to the reform and ended by exposing graft and corruption.

These civic groups were an important element in stirring up interest in the issues that led to a new reform movement. But they could not have done it on their own. Another ingredient was needed. And the New Deal provided it.

## The Influence of the New Deal on the Reform

The end of the First World War, with its unparalleled prosperity, did not provide the soil in which reform would take root and thrive. The technological and financial revolution of the twenties lent new status to the middle class—businessmen and members of the professions alike—and both lost interest in reform. Indifference and complacency—nothing new for Philadelphia—prevailed.

Then came the Depression and the New Deal. Whether the New Deal was a successor to the Progressive movement or a new departure has not been determined.[20] But the New Deal was the first reform movement whose basic problem was to cure the ills of an economy which had broken down. Older protest movements had tried to share prosperity fairly within the entire community, and to preserve and support the market economy—a market which occasionally had to be policed and brought into line with the competitive spirit and the particular desired ends. But the New Deal had to find ways of dealing with an economy of mas-

20. Otis Graham, *An Encore for Reform: The Old Progressives and the New Deal* (Oxford University Press, 1967), pp. 5, 186–87, asked: "Was Progressivism in temper, in method, in social base an early version of FDR's welfare state? Or did the New Deal improvise out of new social and intellectual materials a governmental framework for American life which owed little to, in places even affronted, the progressive vision? . . . It demanded more openness to experiment with political institutions . . . than most progressives could produce."

sive unemployment, lack of purchasing power, and collapsing businesses. Experimentation, improvisation, flexibility, and pragmatism became Roosevelt's watchwords as he tried to find new ways to repair the machine which had ceased to function.

Philadelphia was not as hard hit by the Depression as were some other cities, for its industries and financial activities were diversified. Still, the fact that corruption, generally accepted by Philadelphia's population, had led to the neglect not only of the city's public improvements but also of its social and economic problems made the effects of the Depression particularly shocking. The disruption caused by the outbreak of World War II failed to conceal the need for new measures to get the city back on its feet. Although nobody knew what should or could be done (any more than the New Deal had known) it was the national example of pragmatism and experimentation that showed Philadelphia the method of approaching the many newly recognized problems.

The tradition of previous reforms would have pointed only to changing the governmental structure. But Philadelphia reform came after the New Deal had changed the basic principles of the nation's social and economic system. Though Philadelphia's reformers had not planned to get as deeply involved in developmental changes, they were caught up in the necessity of finding long-term remedies to the problems they faced. So they tried by trail and error to tinker with the system itself and make substantive changes in the developmental programs. This probably would not have been attempted if Philadelphia's reform government had not learned from the pragmatic approach of the New Deal.

The last charter reform for Philadelphia had been passed by the Pennsylvania legislature in 1919. It had abolished a cumbersome bicameral council and instituted a manageable unicameral one. It had strengthened somewhat the position of the mayor, though the proliferation of city and county offices with unclear authority of the executive, and interference of the council in his activities, led to some equivocality in mayoral duties. It had provided for a limited civil service system, which was in effect only a facade for continued patronage under council supervision.

An ambitious attempt to change the charter was made in 1939.

A bipartisan commission proposed a plan with major changes including a modernized merit system and a major reorganization of departments and agencies. Although the movement to adopt it relied widely on citizen support, the plan failed to pass the state legislature. But the need for citizen participation was recognized, and the names of many of the young people who worked on that City Charter Committee appear repeatedly in the annals of the later Philadelphia reform.

The real impetus for reform came finally with the end of the Second World War. Again this movement began with a large number of civic groups, long before any reform candidates were elected. But while widespread civic involvement was a prerequisite, it could not have succeeded without dynamic overall leadership. The quality of this leadership and the kind of following it engendered, in the executive departments as well as in the city at large, determined the kind of reform administration witnessed in the next decade.

With the election of Joseph S. Clark to the mayor's office, the groundwork was laid for a unique relationship between City Hall and the civic groups. Most of those elected with him, and most of his appointees to the top administrative posts, were from these civic organizations. Partnership with the civic groups became one of the mainstays of the reform administration. Clark and his colleagues soon began to deal with substantive aspects of development—which previous reform administrations had failed to do —and to make long-term substantive changes by the pragmatic, trial-and-error method of the New Deal.

Philadelphia is an old city based largely on eastern tradition, its British heritage, and its Quaker history. It is also a city which over time has found a way to bring together civic organizations and the concern of public agencies to use experimentation to come to grips with new challenges of urban changes. It has been led by outstanding leaders who have commanded respect. It is hard to tell which of these elements was primarily the one responsible for the events in the Philadelphia of the 1950s.

# 2    *The Civic Groups*

*A massive citizen effort such as we have had
in the last twenty-five years in Philadelphia
has two distinct stages, only the second of
which brings into play the power elite. . . .
The people who are active in the first stage
are not members of the power elite. . . .
They are the indispensable one-hundredth
of one percent. . . . They are the public-
spirited non-prestigious workers in the civic
vineyard, who have the time and patience
to study through these vexing questions, to
sort out the alternatives to make the solutions they arrive at respectable and even
commonplace, and thus to prepare the way
to usher in the second stage when the
power elite can take over.*
John W. Bodine, *Planning 1963.*

*When you think about it, our reform
movement really was sparkplugged by the
planners and not the politicians! The first
impetus to move the city out of the rut
came from those concerned about corruption, and the push for a city seen in terms
of organized planning brought about the
demand for orderly and honest government.
This is probably a unique experience.*
Richardson Dilworth, Address to
American Institute of Planners, 1957.

## A Different Beginning

Younger citizens, emerging with enthusiasm and social science
interests from colleges and law schools, had become convinced

by their futile fight in 1939 for a new city charter that political battles were then hopeless. But they had learned from the Depression that lack of planning could wreak social and economic devastation. Planning seemed exemplified by New Deal agencies, which had proven capable of cushioning the effect of economic crises. The halt in Philadelphia's public improvements because of the Depression, war, and corruption made it imperative to plan future public efforts. The young liberals found that the business community shared their concern. Because city planning could unite different citizen groups behind it and public officials could be persuaded to support it, it appeared to some as the first step in a broad change in the city's affairs.

City planning goes a long way back in Philadelphia's history. In fact, William Penn designed his "greene Countrie Towne" by dividing Center City into four main quadrants, with City Hall where they meet. Today's Philadelphia still shows much of Penn's influence.

Walter M. Phillips was the man primarily responsible for starting this movement. In an early 1941 memorandum to the Bureau of Municipal Research, Phillips said that "the general spread of civic enterprise and extension of democratic participation in municipal affairs would stimulate, support and supplement a civic movement for planning which might be a major contributing factor in a wave for civic rejuvenation." [1] And he has said since that this "confirms my clear recollection that the motive of some of us who served to launch city planning was the idea that improvements . . . involving many civic groups could be the *raison d'être* for good government," and "a necessary prelude to a reform of quality and depth." [2] Others disagree with this interpretation.

### The City Policy Committee

The civic story should probably begin with the City Policy Committee (started as early as 1940) in order to throw some light on the ferment then existing. The committee consisted of many of

1. Walter M. Phillips, "Philadelphia, Unprepared, Faces a Vast City Planning Problem," April 18, 1941.
2. Letter from Walter M. Phillips to the author, March 24, 1965.

those professionals (bankers, businessmen, architects, lawyers, planners) who had fought (and lost) the fight for a new home rule charter in 1939.[3] They were still full of enthusiasm. There was an accent on youth, designed to bring in "young leaders from untapped sources," provided they had "gained unusual recognition for their age" in their professions and had "intellectual capacity and integrity." [4] Given their age and their penchant for introducing new approaches without their elders' stamp of approval, they were called the "Young Turks."

A large part of the group's first roster consisted of men still prominent on the Philadelphia scene in the late 1950s and early 1960s. They studied local issues in small subcommittees, using professional help and advice, and suggested policy positions which the groups as a whole should take. It should be stressed that the "citizens' group" idea was by no means a front for the professionals; rather, the citizens were using professionals to undergird their endeavors. The restricted membership of the City Policy Committee made an invitation to join it a coveted honor. The soundness of its position earned it respect from the community. In the various subjects it studied and debated—debates in which eventually many city officials participated—it was able to exert an influence on the formulation of public policy, in part because it became a recruiting ground for men to fill public positions and leadership lists of civic organizations.

Looking for a topic on which this newly formed group could concentrate and agree, Phillips presented a report on planning to it early in its deliberations. In cooperation with two other similarly concerned groups, the Policy Committee formed the Joint Committee on City Planning. It decided to try to convince the city administration of the need for planning. Mayor Lamberton —an unusual mayor and former judge—requested a detailed report on city planning possibilities, after the committee had convinced him that its case had some merit. The committee ap-

3. Roger Scattergood, "The City Policy Committee: A Philadelphia Story of a Civic Organization which 'Made Good,' " 1956 (mimeo). The City Policy Committee was merged in 1952 with the Committee on Public Affairs, whose organizational principles it had followed.
4. Chairman's report, 1940–41, November 12, 1941 (mimeo).

pended to its report a proposed city ordinance establishing a planning commission.

But Lamberton died the very day he received the report of the Joint Committee.[5] His successor failed to see any need for city planning and refused to take any action. A councilman was finally persuaded to introduce the ordinance, but he was reluctant to fight for its enactment.

A wide range of citizens' organizations were rallied around this ordinance by the active Joint Committee and members of its constituent groups. An amazing number (certainly amazing at this stage of civic development in Philadelphia) of civic and neighborhood groups was lined up to testify at the public hearing, for it was clear that only such an outpouring would move the city council. (In November 1942, there were eighty such organizations.) These groups gathered before the hearing, where they received a regular scenario prepared for the public hearings by the men who had worked assiduously for the planning ordinance. Parts were assigned to different groups. A cross-section of the population appeared and urged this ordinance on the amazed councilmen: there were businessmen and housewives, labor leaders and local Chamber of Commerce representatives, people of different interests and localities from all across the city. Not in years had such a representative group appeared at a public hearing.

Later, Edward Hopkinson, senior partner of the investment firm of Drexel and Company, appeared before the council and impressed its members by the fact that a man of his standing in the community was in favor of such an ordinance. As chairman of the executive committee of the Chamber of Commerce, as an "old Philadelphian," and as a patrician-looking descendant of a signer of the Declaration of Independence, his influence was considerable, at a time when the support of the Young Turks' organization was much less impressive to the council than that of such a prominent member of the Establishment. Hopkinson himself had been impressed with the arguments in favor of planning, including the impact it would have on Philadelphia's public

5. The report, prepared for Mayor Lamberton, was dated August 15, 1941, and entitled "Suggested Organization of the Philadelphia City Planning Commission."

image. Carefully planned public improvements would make postwar pressure for a number of long-neglected capital projects less onerous, and municipal bonds would be easier to sell, he realized. The ordinance passed in December 1942. The Young Turks had started the movement, but Edward Hopkinson's concern about the city, its credit, and its public improvements speeded up the process.[6] Some contemporaries feel that his help was decisive.

The important task of appointing a good commission met fewer difficulties from the mayor than had been expected. This assured the commission of appropriations and a good staff. Councilmen failed to obtain for their political workers a share of staff appointments with the commission—Hopkinson stopped such demands by his mere appearance at council meetings, if necessary. Eventually the city administration began to regard city planning as the "clean shirt-front of its long-term programs"—possibly very long-term, if the politicians could have their way.

Hopkinson continued as commission chairman through Joseph Clark's term as reform mayor.

## The Planning Commission and Its Staff

The Planning Commission consisted of nine members. The appointments of the six citizens were carefully made, and usually included a banker, a lawyer, a builder, a representative of labor, and a representative of one of the universities. The other three were members of the mayor's cabinet, which gave the administration's wishes an important voice, but it was exerted only in joint deliberation with the commission's citizen members. At the commission's executive meetings, only the top planning staff and very few other top city professionals were admitted. These meetings made possible a true dialogue with an open exchange of opinions dealing with broad, long-term planning problems—a full opportunity for frank discussions among city and civic members, which the mayor's representatives did not attempt to dominate. It was possible on these occasions jointly to think through new policy problems or questions of the impact of existing policies, and to arrive at mutual understanding, even consensus. (As

6. John McCullough, in the Philadelphia *Bulletin*, June 10, 1965, and letter from Walter Phillips to the author, July 27, 1965.

will be seen later, this kind of policy-making became typical for Philadelphia's reform activities.)

As first chairman, Edward Hopkinson helped the newborn commission to steer clear of political interference and to get the city council's approval. He was largely responsible for the commission's early accomplishments and could get good cooperation under either party. Mayor Clark, on coming into office, had first been inclined to make a clean sweep but was soon persuaded otherwise. Letters to Clark mentioning that Hopkinson had never used his position for partisan political advantage and had always deferred to the majority of the commission, whatever his own position, persuaded the new mayor.

When Richardson Dilworth became mayor, he appointed Albert M. Greenfield chairman. Greenfield was a well-known realtor and Democratic "fat cat" who had very much wanted to occupy a position of this much prestige. The feeling among Dilworth's official family ran high that appointing Greenfield to such a sensitive position was a mistake. His clear bias in favor of profit-making over governmental action created some conflicts between him and Dilworth. Occasionally conferences between them were necessary, and Greenfield usually went along with the mayor who had appointed him. (Greenfield's relations to the reform government are discussed in chapter 7.)

After less than two years, Greenfield resigned and was succeeded by G. Holmes Perkins, dean of the School of Fine Arts of the University of Pennsylvania, in whose school the Department of City Planning was located. With a trained architect in the chair, expert advice in the planning field now seemed assured, as was a good relationship between chairman and executive director, for Perkins gave more discretion to the commission's staff. He stayed on into Mayor Tate's second term.

Robert Mitchell was appointed the commission's first executive director in 1943. He came from Washington, where he had been with the Urban Planning Division of the National Resources Planning Board. His first task, as he saw it, was to sell the community on "planning as a way of life, a way of doing business," and then to involve the people at large as much as he could in planning activities. Mitchell's aim was to have the decision-makers see the possibilities, the kinds of choices they had to make, rather than to convince them of the "right" decision. He would have preferred to present the public with alternative methods of meeting such problems and to ask for their reaction. He would have liked to have the commission decide on long-term goals and discuss the best strategy to reach them, but the commission was not ready for such a course. Mitchell realized the importance of collecting the kind of data on which decisions could be made. When he left to teach at Columbia University in 1948, before any of the political reformers had obtained a toehold at City Hall, his only visible accomplishment was the installation of properly designed utilities, but he had laid the groundwork for future thinking.

One of Mitchell's achievements, as early as 1947, was the "Better Philadelphia Exhibition." It offered a stage on which to show planning as the environment for cooperation by civic organizations, public officials, and business, and emphasized the importance of planning communication between volunteer organizations and official commissions. Mitchell, Walter Phillips, and Edmund Bacon conceived the idea of a visual and three-dimensional presentation of Philadelphia's past and future. The head of Gimbel's department store was persuaded to donate space for it. A quasi-public nonprofit corporation was started, sponsored jointly by the Chamber of Commerce and the Citizens' Council on City Planning. It was the first of a long series of such corporations for achieving a governmental objective—a successful model to be used over and over again during Philadelphia's reform period. It was a "demonstration of what a coalition of brass and grassroots can accomplish if it wants to." [7] Standing in front of the exhibition, many a businessman began to think more concretely about what his city could become. Dioramas of different parts of the city at various historical periods showed what Philadelphia had been like. A scale model of some central parts of the city showed what a variety of proposed projects would make the city look like in the future. To their surprise, Philadelphians realized that their city could be exciting.

7. William H. Whyte, Jr. (editor of *Fortune* magazine), "Philadelphia Story," unpublished.

Edmund Bacon followed Mitchell as executive director. His main concern—and the strength of his staff—lay in the area of design, which still can be seen in magnificent buildings and good juxtaposition of land use in Philadelphia. His weakness, which proved of growing importance as the ideas of the reform developed, was the fact that he was not particularly concerned with social or economic aspects of new development; he clearly perceived "design totality," while overlooking the need for "program totality."

In fulfilling the mandate of the charter, the Planning Commission had to devise a comprehensive plan. Walter Blucher, a Chicago consultant who was asked early in the reform to review organization and achievements of planning in Philadelphia, said: "The City cannot limit itself to physical planning, as narrowly defined, but must inevitably concern itself with . . . the economic potential of the area . . . discover its competitive position and face the facts realistically. . . . The development of a comprehensive plan requires a high degree of economic and social planning at its base." [8] In 1954, a group of eleven prominent citizens asked the mayor to push for such a plan,[9] and in 1955, Mayor Clark urged the Planning Commission to assure that it be undertaken.[10] After frequent reports to the mayor by Bacon,[11] however, the Comprehensive Plan was not finally completed until 1958. Only then was there a solid framework for setting priorities.

8. Walter H. Blucher, "The Philadelphia City Planning Commission: An Appraisal" (in City Archives), p. 11. There were actually two Blucher reports. The first was very critical of the actual workings of the Planning Commission and its staff and made a series of suggestions how they could be improved. At the time, many top city officials read the report, but today it is impossible to locate a copy or to find a source indicating how one could be obtained. The version in the archives is a much milder version of his general findings.

9. *A Statement on Housing and Urban Renewal Policy for Philadelphia* (published by eleven citizens through the Philadelphia Housing Association, October 1955), p. 2.

10. Correspondence between Mayor Joseph S. Clark and Edward Hopkinson, July 22, August 10 and 22, 1955 (in City Archives).

11. Weekly reports to the mayor, February 18, April 7, 1955 (in managing director's files).

## The Citizens' Council on City Planning

Having mobilized civic groups to obtain the ordinance, the Joint Committee decided to keep them together. They had learned their lesson about the importance of the mass response, and this device would be used time and again in Philadelphia. A citizens' watchdog committee was organized less than a year later (1943)— the Citizens' Council on City Planning, which eventually had over 150 member organizations. It tried to provide a bridge between official planning activities and citizen groups, as well as to act as watchdog and critic of all actions of the Planning Commission. The citizen activity was carried out through meetings with city officials in small neighborhoods, as well as "town meetings" for larger areas. This enabled the Citizens' Council to defend the viewpoint of these groups "at court," having learned about neighborhood feelings through freely expressed opinions rather than formal votes.

With the help of a small staff, the Citizens' Council kept track of planning activities in the city. Carefully selected committees of lawyers, architects, businessmen, and other professionals, as well as the council's own board members and representatives of the citizen groups, did yeoman's work of evaluating and criticizing.[12]

One of the most interesting of its activities dealt with the capital program. In May 1944, the Committee on Public Improvements was set up. Its subgroups, each consisting of at least half a dozen professionals, were each assigned to a different kind of public improvement. They met frequently at lunch for two-hour evaluation periods. Some of the members inspected some of the proposed projects on site. For three months these different groups discussed and evaluated. Out of their judgments emerged an evaluation of the whole capital program, in terms of comparative urgency of projects, to which the city council paid the most serious attention. In fact, the council refused to take any action on the capital program until it had carefully studied the recommendations of the Citizens' Council.

William H. Whyte, Jr., calls it "The Story of a Citizens' Move-

12. Aaron Levine, "Citizen Participation," *Journal of the American Institute of Planners*, August 1960, pp. 195 ff.

ment Which Has Worked." In 1947, he wrote: "Five years ago it was only a tearoom cabal—a group who wanted . . . to do good but who weren't quite sure how to go about it. They had no funds, few friends, and hardly any enemies. But from that start . . . they went on to scare the daylights out of City Hall, get the city a Planning Commission, and generally agitate the town to the point where people are talking seriously of 'the Renaissance' " [13]—an interesting statement, as it was written years before the renaissance became reality. And in an October 1947 editorial, the Philadelphia *Bulletin* claimed that "discussion has been stirring in a way that Philadelphia has not experienced previously. . . . A new awareness of the need for doing something about some of the City's civic ailments has been created."

## The Basis for Civic Reform Is Laid

The mayoralty campaign of 1947 was the beginning of the end for the old administration. Richardson Dilworth named names, unveiled scandals, and shocked Philadelphians about what City Hall had done—and had failed to do—over the years. Philadelphians, not quite believing all they had been told, defeated Dilworth, but their confidence in the integrity of City Hall had been shaken. Businessmen, taunted by their friends across the country, began to feel that some unusual civic action would soon be necessary, and that time was running out if they were ever to assume any civic responsibility.

### The Committee of Fifteen

About this time an employee pay demand caused the mayor to appoint the blue ribbon Committee of Fifteen, including five councilmen, to find out how the money could be raised. The mayor hoped that they would recommend tax increases, thus lessening the pressure on the politicians. To the surprise of the politicians, committee members were not satisfied with looking into the pay demand of city employees and decided to look into departmental efficiency as well as the whole budget. Eventually they asked a young professional to direct the committee's work. Civic organizations as well as private industry furnished the committee with research help.

13. See n. 7 above.

A year before (1946), an able young engineer on the staff of the Bureau of Municipal Research, Robert K. ("Buck") Sawyer, had been asked to investigate the proposals of the Water Commission and its engineering consultants. These firms had recommended that Philadelphia develop upland water sources and bring the water down from the mountains. The capital costs for the various alternative projects would have ranged up to $450 million for the Upper Delaware project, given the great expense of bringing the water down. Consulting the literature on water purification, Sawyer showed that, if treated at the intake, the purity of the water after filtering could compare favorably with that brought down from the mountains and would require only a 13 percent increase in water rent income compared to a 150 percent increase for the Upper Delaware project. The businessmen's reaction to his presentation was ecstatic and led to requests for repeat performances at a series of businessmen's luncheons. Capitalizing on the impression Sawyer had made on the business world, the bureau persuaded him not only to reject competing offers and to take over the bureau, but also temporarily to direct the work of the Committee of Fifteen.

The committee eventually suggested in 1948 that, if less money were wasted or allowed to drift into private pockets, there would be enough for pay raises. No tax increases would be necessary if city housekeeping were reformed. Digging further, the committee uncovered illegal and unethical practices which wasted public funds. When their final report appeared, it was brutally frank and pushed Buck Sawyer further into prominence. It was also clear that the committee had only been able to scratch the surface.[14] The Bureau of Municipal Research and the Pennsylvania Economy League were asked to make further exhaustive studies of efficiency and economy in different city agencies.

Shortly after a report of the Pennsylvania Economy League on one of the city departments had been published in May 1948, one official committed suicide, leaving a note indicating that men in the tax office had conspired to embezzle city funds for years. Impeachments, grand juries, city, state, and federal investigations

14. Richardson Dilworth in his testimony before the Philadelphia Charter Commission, January 6, 1950, stated: "It is imperative that a complete study be made immediately" (in file of the Charter Commission, GPM office).

followed. The different public investigations, especially one by a Grand Jury, verified not only the committee's findings, but also many of the accusations Dilworth had made in the campaign. The dike had burst.

## An Important Group Organizes

Some top businessmen returned to Philadelphia from business trips and reported what they had been told, in no uncertain terms, by firms which *might* have moved to Philadelphia. As a result, some key executives in important companies felt impelled to do something to improve their city's image. The slogan of the group was: "The trouble with Philadelphia is *us.*" This is a slogan not easily forgotten. It eschewed self-satisfaction, and its self-criticism continues to be an interesting feature of the civic groups of Philadelphia.

It was not clear how such a group might organize. Should it be representative of the diverse economic and professional activities in town? [15] Was it advisable to imitate Pittsburgh's Allegheny Conference, concerned with public improvements, including smoke abatement? The elimination of the smog had turned the tide in Pittsburgh, so imitation was worth consideration.[16] Should controversial issues be tackled? What staffing would be necessary?

While the existing groups like the Philadelphia Housing Association or the Committee of Seventy had citywide concerns, they each concentrated in a special field: this was, in fact, their strength. The new group, on the other hand, saw itself dealing with broad problems concerning the city as a whole and the relationship between issues. Its members meant to represent the apex of the Establishment, and, given the otherwise pluralistic and fragmented power structure, they thought they could manage it.

15. Joseph S. Clark in an early letter suggested it would be preferable not to try to reach for democratic representation.

16. In a letter dated November 26, 1948, to Arthur Kaufmann, then president of the Chamber of Commerce, from Walter Phillips, Lewis Stevens (later councilman), Earl Harrison (later dean of the University of Pennsylvania Law School), and Walter Miller, a manufacturer, the writers said that there was no time for an experiment like the Allegheny Conference. The important concern should be to lay the foundations for bipartisanship before opinions crystallized, and work on government reform and education of the public on it should start immediately.

In December 1948, about one hundred business leaders met in the Midday Club to hear about the need for positive actions to improve government, the industrial climate, and working and housing conditions in the metropolitan area. A public improvement program of $70 million was outlined. A policy statement emphasizing the need to improve the living conditions and expand industry, business, and employment was presented. An executive committee was designated, which became the guiding arm of the group. After refusing an earlier invitation, Buck Sawyer was persuaded to leave the Bureau of Municipal Research to become the first executive director of the Greater Philadelphia Movement (GPM). Early in 1949, the GPM began to operate. Sawyer moved in 1952 into Clark's cabinet as managing director, but barely two years later he succumbed to a heart attack.

## The Principles Governing the GPM

Several decisions were soon made: First, the work was going to be done by the members themselves. Although most of them lived outside the city, they were willing to come into town on Saturdays or even Sundays. They did not delegate the work to staff or to employees in their own companies.

Second, there would only be a small staff—usually an outstanding professional as executive director with secretarial help. A staff was necessary to assure continuity and communication with its board and with other civic groups, and to provide the board with information on the background and ramifications of the issues, although GPM members felt it advisable that they personally grapple with problems before advocating action. They assumed that the executive committee should give the board all the needed policy guidance. This was an excellent educational device, and the directors of the GPM came to feel that theirs was "the best educated civic board in the country."

The sequence of executive directors indicates the close tie between the GMP and the city administration. Buck Sawyer, the first executive director, became the first managing director of the Clark administration. Donald Wagner, who took over at the GPM, eventually moved into the managing director's position in 1956, under Dilworth. William Wilcox, GPM's executive director for about seventeen years, was appointed in 1971 by the governor as state secretary of community affairs. He was followed at the GPM by William L. Rafsky, Clark's first executive secretary, then housing and later development coordinator, and executive vice-president of the Old Philadelphia Development Corporation.

Third, nobody would become a board member unless he was fully independent and did not have to seek anybody's agreement before taking a stand on a public issue. Once committed to a position, a member seldom backtracked, as this would adversely affect the morale of the group as a whole. Nor could the firms of board members be beholden to a larger chain or concern. The moment members of the group could be overruled within their own organization, or were subject to indirect pressure with regard to the group's decisions, the principle of the GPM's structure was threatened. While GPM members could make decisions within their organizations, they did not bind those organizations by their actions as individual members of the GPM board.

Fourth, the board was small in number. It was not intended to be representative of all the interests within the community. In fact, each member understood that he represented the entire community rather than the organization to which he happened to belong. Two union officials and a Negro professional were asked to become members at the start, but they were asked as individuals because of the respect they engendered as persons and as leaders. While their knowledge of special conditions, their viewpoints, and their community contacts would be useful, they understood that they were to act on the board only as individuals and with total community interest as their concern. Since board members felt they had to keep informed about new issues arising, they invited outsiders, particularly public officials, from the mayor down, to their lunches.

### The GPM's Concern with Civic Issues

Most other civic groups were oriented toward specific issues, such as housing. The GPM, on the other hand, applied its interests citywide and concentrated on one broad issue at a time. Board members judged issues in terms of what appeared to be the community's immediate needs rather than long-term community benefits. The problems they tackled were clearly of great importance, but they seemed afraid of getting too deeply involved in any area, committed for too long a time. Part of the reason may have been the members' realization of the magnitude of the total civic agenda, while their small staff only permitted tackling major projects one at a time; they seemed afraid of too comprehensive a view. They may also have feared the need to collect too much detailed material, which might prevent their organization from paying attention to currently pressing problems.

This author tried to find out what prominent members of the GPM felt about the issues their organization should tackle, and in what order of priority, at least in terms of general categories. But either the answers obtained were vague, or members fell back on naming a large number of issues deserving attention, with no priorities expressed.

From time to time Mayor Clark appeared before the GPM board or its executive committee, urging them to take up an issue that would involve them in a continuous series of related actions. Early in his administration, he urged upon them the field of intergovernmental relations and city-suburb cooperation. Since many directors lived outside the city, and some even had part of their economic establishments there, they could have taken up many topics, from the flight of industry and residents, to transportation and housing for city dwellers. Though the GPM was never afraid to take a stand, it seemed afraid to get deeply involved in projects of long duration.

The significant point is that in a period when the reform administration was considering the revival of the city systematically and, as far as possible, in a logical, priority-conscious way, an organization like the GPM, dedicated to the same ends, and working closely with the administration, went about contributing to this revitalization on a strictly project basis. It approved of the city's striving for coordinated goals but refused to get involved in broad issues and priorities among them. The reason may well be that the GPM felt that it was more effective in supporting specific projects which the reform administration proposed, rather than trying to carry the burden of a broad overall program which it would have to defend not only to outsiders but possibly to some of its own members.

## Intercivic Relations

Two features set the GPM apart from other civic agencies: First, it was concerned with the city or area as a whole, so that few issues were outside its concern. Second, it desired to pass on to other organizations the task of carrying on the responsibility for issues it had raised and for which it had laid the groundwork. If none of the existing organizations was ready to take it on, a new specialized one was likely to be started by the GPM. Examples, some of which will be discussed in subsequent chapters, are the Food Distribution Center Corporation, the Citizens' Budget Committee, the Capital Program activities of the Citizens' Council, and the Skid Row Diagnostic and Treatment Center.

It was important from the start for the GPM to coexist with other civic organizations which might have felt threatened. To be sure, the power position of the GPM's board members gave it an edge, but there were other civic groups which wanted to exert influence on specific issues and persons. The Bureau of Municipal Research and the Pennsylvania Economy League, for example, clearly felt their positions threatened, perhaps from fear of being eclipsed by the new organization's ability to get civic and public decisions changed through the sheer weight of its influence, especially through advice to individuals in and out of public office.

Staff relations were sometimes cemented by the GPM director's making all information he had assembled freely available to the staffs of other organizations; he might give other civic groups arguments on both sides of an issue, thus making it more likely that the other group would take over any needed activity in that particular area. The GPM was also able occasionally to finance specific research by other civic organizations in areas in which these groups were interested and competent.

One touchy problem the GPM had to solve was its relationship to the Chamber of Commerce. Although both groups were business-oriented, their emphasis and purpose could not have been more different. While members of the GPM readily admitted the Chamber's usefulness for protection of individual business firms, they did not see that their activities regarding general civic issues were very effective. This was partly because the Chamber required consensus among the many members of its board and its various councils, which made it difficult to enter into any potentially controversial activity. On a personal level, it did not help relations that the Chamber had for a time been considered the instrument of Albert M. Greenfield, the city's largest realtor. Relations between him and the board members of the GPM were strained: the GPM felt that it was difficult for Greenfield to differentiate between public and private interests, at least where his personal recognition was involved. Also, they suspected that his opposition to public action might have been based on knowledge that private transactions were more easily negotiated if removed from public scrutiny.

After a few years an attempt was made to change the Chamber's image. In 1955, Robert Sessions, partner of a major consulting firm who had been with the Tennessee Valley Authority, became the unlikely president of the Chamber. Shortly after he took over, the Chamber became a full partner with the city in the nonprofit corporation founded to bring about Philadelphia's industrial development (to be discussed in chapter 7). His new executive director, however, believed that the Chamber should only operate in its members' interest ("Action for profit" should be its motto). In contrast, the succeeding executive director, Thacher Longstreth, appointed in 1964, viewed the Chamber clearly as a civic association. (He ran for mayor against Dilworth in 1955 on the Republican ticket against the wishes of the Republican organization; in 1967, he was slated by the Republicans for councilman-at-large and was elected.) He has remarked wryly that many areas which elsewhere fall in the Chamber's bailiwick are preempted in Philadelphia by specialized civic organizations and nonprofit corporations. Board and committee structure of the Chamber was strengthened in 1962, spurred on by the GPM. The last two Chamber presidents were members of the GPM board.

The new executive director was apt to follow tactics somewhat similar to those of the GPM, and the Chamber has taken its place among civic groups concerned about the city as a whole. For instance, it helped start a new nonprofit corporation in the mid-sixties, dealing with improvements of port facilities.

Civic groups sometimes managed to get their policies implemented in unorthodox ways. For example, the Citizens' Council on City Planning did not merely pass resolutions; its members and staff often sat down and worked in detail with the planning staff, and usually found that their efforts were welcomed. The staff of the Philadelphia Housing Association worked with division chiefs of the Department of Licenses and Inspections to improve the effectiveness of code enforcement. And the executive director of the GPM perhaps accomplished more in changing the city's policy on transportation by making his point at lunch with the commissioner of streets than he would have done by taking a public stand. The director of the Pennsylvania Economy League–Bureau of Municipal Research would advise public officials how best to encourage the start of a new quasi-public corporation; in turn, they would be more willing to take his suggestions about the substantive content of their proposal.

On the other hand, public officials often used civic organizations to further their own areas of concern. While Mayor Clark was more inclined to work through individual members he knew personally, Richardson Dilworth operated through direct requests to either board or staff. He could work with them on one issue while publicly opposing them on another. But once a private discussion about an issue had taken place between the mayor and a civic group, the latter would abstain from taking a public stand on that particular problem. On the other hand, if they felt an issue was important, civic groups did not have that choice under Tate's administration: lacking the personal relationship that they enjoyed under Clark and Dilworth, members of the GPM and other groups often were forced to take a public stand on such issues.

## The Charter Passes

The Committee of Fifteen had disclosed a good deal of mismanagement; it soon became evident that an investigation of all departments of city government was necessary. The investigation indicated that a new governmental structure was needed to set things right. Five civic agencies (the Bureau of Municipal Research, the Pennsylvania Economy League, the Chamber of Commerce, the Committee of Seventy, and the Citizens' Council on City Planning) cooperated in 1948 to develop a program for the legislature to benefit Philadelphia. Their proposals included both the Home Rule Charter bill and a city-county consolidation bill. The program was presented to the Joint State Legislative Committee by Arthur Kaufmann, head of Gimbel's and president of the Chamber, followed by the testimony of other reform leaders of both parties, even before the GPM was started. James Finnegan, later Democratic city chairman, Joseph S. Clark, Richardson Dilworth, Americans for Democratic Action, many other civic bodies, and both Philadelphia newspapers supported Home Rule. The only question was whether the legislature should enact such a charter or give the Philadelphia city council the right to appoint a commission which would propose it. The Home Rule bill, which gave Philadelphia permission to write a Home Rule Charter (provided it was approved by its voters), passed the legislature in April 1949.

## The Charter Commission

Appointment of members to the commission that would write the charter became the first issue on which the GPM could exert an important influence. The appointments were made by Mayor Samuel and Council President Frederick Garman; the latter wielded a great deal more power. Though indirectly, GPM members succeeded (in spite of paramount political considerations) in having most commissioners appointed from a list the GPM submitted. Six of the fifteen were GPM members.[17] The important members were Garman, Lewis Stevens (later reform councilman), Abraham Freedman (later Clark's city solicitor), and former Attorney General Schnader, who dominated the commission and the writing of the charter.

After some debate the commission decided to hold public hearings. The testimony, taken over many weeks, fills several volumes. Among those appearing were Clark, Dilworth, and Lennox Moak, director of the Bureau of Municipal Research, who presented four different schemes for departmental organization. His ideas appealed so much to the commission that, after his allotted two hours were gone, he shrewdly prepared to leave and was begged to stay—in fact for several days. Drafting of the charter was done in the face of opposing politicians of both parties who

17. This story is told differently by Roger Butterfield ("Revolt in Philadelphia," *Saturday Evening Post,* November 1952) and Joseph Crumlish (*A City Finds Itself* [Wayne State University Press, 1959]). Interviews by this author did not fully bear out either story.

kept hoping that they would not have to live by it. (One important exception was the Democratic chairman, James Finnegan, who realized that he had to support the charter if he wanted to elect a mayor in 1951. His contention that good government is good politics was vigorously fought by his ward leaders.)

*The Charter Committee*

While the Charter Commission was still deliberating, some citizens were giving thought to the need to get public support and acceptance of the document upon its completion. It was felt that the 1939 effort had failed because of a lack of community understanding and support, even though a Citizens' Charter Committee had agitated for its adoption. Walter M. Phillips recalled his experience with the city Planning Commission ordinance and with the Citizens' Council on City Planning; he felt that mobilization of groups within the community would be imperative for success. Although a member of the GPM at that time, he found it difficult to persuade the board of the need for such broadly based support, but eventually, with the aid of Buck Sawyer, he succeeded in doing so. The result was the formation of the Citizens' Charter Committee, organized out of the office of the GPM late in 1949. Again an impressive number of civic and neighborhood groups joined forces—there were at least five hundred organizational members. The director of the Charter Commission urged all those organizations to set up committees which would keep in touch with the progress of the charter, study the various proposals, make suggestions if they had any, and keep the membership informed of their positive or negative opinions.

While the members of the Citizens' Council on City Planning were civic organizations, the Charter Committee was structured differently because speedy communication was essential. All members designated by these numerous civic organizations throughout the city (on the basis of their expressed interest) acted as individuals, but the memberships of all the groups involved were kept continuously informed as the charter took shape. Providing immediate liaison between the committee and the civic groups through interested members permitted them to move quickly to take positions on issues. Later on this model was followed by other civic groups, such as the Water Research Association of the Delaware River Basin. Members were asked to contribute their ideas, to make suggestions, and to testify. They felt that the final product—whether or not any individual suggestion was taken— was *their* document, for which they could take credit. In September 1950, a draft was released. The commission sponsored a day-long conference and held several public hearings, again to get citizens' suggestions. They received ample criticism, sound and unsound. After making decisions on all the suggestions received, they submitted the final draft in February 1951, to be voted on in the primary election.

The new charter established a strong-mayor type of government. The mayor has more administrative and appointive powers than before and has more control over expenditures. His power corresponds to his responsibilities, so that he can be held accountable for his administration's actions. His cabinet of four members, while responsible for supervising the fourteen city departments —whose commissioners are appointed with their concurrence— can concentrate jointly with the mayor on determining the administration's policy. The managing director, in charge of the ten service departments, is a new institution, rarely found in other cities: though the charter framers made the deliberate decision not to make him a city manager, his span of control puts him next to the mayor in power. He, the director of finance, and the city representative–director of commerce are appointed by the mayor without council concurrence; that approval is needed only for the fourth cabinet member, the city solicitor. The director of finance is the chief financial, accounting, and budget officer, whom the mayor appoints from names submitted by a nominating panel consisting of three incumbents of significant positions (for example, the dean of the Wharton School of the University of Pennsylvania). The city representative was conceived as taking public functions over for the mayor, but the substantive assignment of supervising port, airport, and economic development was given him as director of commerce, almost as an afterthought.

The Civil Service Commission, newly reestablished, is responsible for policy-making of the all-permeating merit system. It has made certain that patronage among city employees is abolished. Its staff is under the direction of the personnel director, whom the commission appoints. The mayor appoints the commission from names submitted by the civil service panel, consisting of heads of institutions of higher learning and specified civic, business, and labor organizations.[18] Among the departments a newly created one was that of Licenses and Inspection, which not only supervises the granting of licenses, but has become in its inspection function increasingly important for problems of shelter. Eventually one of the deputy managing directors became directly responsible for all questions of housing. Aside from boards attached to specific departments, like the Board of Health, the Fairmount Park Commission, or the Art Commission, there are independent boards and commissions appointed by the mayor. The most important one for the purposes of this story is the City Planning Commission, which has already been discussed. Another independent one newly created by the charter was the Human Relations Commission, concerned with all kinds of discrimination. The office of development coordinator—or, earlier, housing coordinator—was surprisingly not provided for in the charter, although the need for some such coordinating device soon became evident; this oversight had to be corrected by the mayor's action when the administration's concern with development became clear, and its incumbent was made a de facto member of the cabinet. Two independent authorities, established not by the charter but by separate state legislation, were the Redevelopment Authority and the Housing Authority.

The charter also changed the legislative body. The city council consists of ten district councilmen from the different geographic areas, and seven at-large councilmen, of which at least two must be from the minority party. The idea behind this division was that some councilmen should feel that they represent the city as a whole, not only their own districts.

The charter improved city administration immeasurably. But its shortcoming was that it contained so many safeguards against corruption and other abuses that it ran the danger of creating inflexibility and inability of permitting discretion.

18. I.e., the presidents of the University of Pennsylvania, of Temple University, and of the Philadelphia Fellowship Commission; the chairman of the Board of Trustees of the Bureau of Municipal Research; the presidents of the Chamber of Commerce and of the Local Congress of Industrial Organizations; and the business manager of the Central Labor Union of Philadelphia, AFL.

*City-County Consolidation*

Although city and county had been coterminous since the 1854 consolidation act, some smaller county offices were still independent of the city structure, as a result of either legislative oversight or judicial interpretation. A constitutional amendment to complete the merger had been urged on the legislature by several civic groups, including the GPM. The Charter Committee seemed ready-made for it—and the issue remained with it for a while. Much persuasion was needed to get support for a measure which would not really affect those living outside Philadelphia. Again excitement ran high. The same organizations which had pushed for charter adoption worked for this amendment. A judge who earlier had been active in the adoption of the City Planning ordinance resigned from the bench and toured the state in support of the measure. In November 1951, the amendment passed. But the meaning was not clear. Was it up to the legislature or the city council to accomplish a merger of city and county offices, or had the constitutional amendment plus the Home Rule Charter accomplished it? As it was interpreted, the merger of each of the offices involved had to be separately approved. It thus took many years to accomplish, and one office still remains separate. The main offices involved were the Election Commission, the Registration Commission, and the Board of Revision of Taxes and their merger with the city government. City-county consolidation really meant that the merged county offices would be subject to the same budgeting, accounting, and purchasing controls as the city offices. Of greater political impact was the fact that the employees of these offices would fall under all the strictures of civil service and hence were not subject to patronage, which both political parties tried to safeguard. An attempt by the council to exempt some of these jobs from civil service was vetoed by Mayor Clark. Several lawsuits dealing with different offices were then tried, which took their tedious course through the courts, before the merger was declared legal.

The Charter Committee, having worked for consolidation, stood behind the measure when it was periodically attacked. The passing of the charter and the completion of city-county consolidation convinced all the civic groups that had been involved, especially the GPM, that they should not argue with success. This conviction became very important later, when the reform weakened and the confidence of civic groups in their strength was vital.

## The Educational Charter Commission

The method by which the Philadelphia Home Rule Charter passed—the extensive input of ideas by citizen groups, the careful studies of legal implications, the mobilization of the citizenry for passage, and their continued watchfulness over the charter's implementation—became the paradigm for other measures.

Throughout a large part of the reform period it weighed heavily on the incumbents in City Hall that one important activity, education, continued beyond their influence, in fact so much so that even the city jobs incidentally concerned with education were outside civil service. Before citizens' groups could begin to exert an influence on education, however, they had to change the pertinent charter, and they did this by the same means as the reform had used before.

"The wave of municipal reform brought local government functions to a crest of excellence, never before achieved. Philadelphia was an outstanding national example of this movement. Yet the wave of improvement swept around the school system. Public education remained isolated in an eddy of public unconcern," said John Patterson, one of those close to the architects of reform, who was also deeply concerned about education. Of course, the lack of concern for public education might be partially explained by the comparative importance of private schools for Philadelphia families. More than one-third of the intellectuals and civically concerned who lived within the city sent their children to parochial schools or to private schools, including the several Friends' schools in the area.

Politics continued to rule unabashedly in matters of education, though they were right next door to the changed system of having city employees dealt with by the merit system. More importantly, the schools' capital program, including recreation, could have benefited the entire city, if it were dovetailed with the city's developmental programs, if the schools were used for neighborhood activities after school hours, and if other benefits were derived for citizens at large from funds earmarked for schools.

Add Anderson had been the schools' business manager for many years. He reported directly to the Board of Education, as did the superintendent—an unusual situation for large cities— and the board membership was in effect determined by the political leaders of both parties (although it was done via the Board of Judges). Add Anderson had come up through the ranks of business administration and learned how to rule with an iron fist—even the velvet glove had worn thin over the years. He engaged effectively in lobbying with the state legislature about taxes. (He agreed, given the coal interests in Pennsylvania, to let coal heat continue in school buildings irrespective of dirt or inefficiency.) Throughout the school system nonteaching jobs were subject to patronage. But gradually Anderson also dominated educational positions, maintaining his power for over twenty years. "Add just took charge of the system. . . . It was Add who decided who would be principals and Add who decided which departments would get money." [19]

In time the forces surrounding the reform became increasingly interested in finishing the job in the one field where they had been unable to be effective. Civic concern gradually gathered momentum. The first lance was broken by the Greater Philadelphia Movement in May 1962 by the first part of a report on education, in which a panel method of board appointments was suggested.[20] A few months later Add Anderson died unexpectedly.

In November, the second part of the report appeared. "Public apathy is disappearing," it stated. "Public education is now in the center of community attention in Philadelphia." [21]

In the late 1950s, a new Citizens' Committee on Public Education had been started, taking over the charter of a moribund association going back to the 1880s. As one of their first actions they asked for an independent survey of the entire school system, which was eventually undertaken. Sixty civic groups gathered in the early sixties to support the Citizens' Committee's demand for a change in appointments to the School Board. The Philadelphia

19. "See Mark Shedd Run," *Philadelphia Magazine,* June 1969, p. 76.
20. Greater Philadelphia Movement, *A Citizens' Study of Public Education in Philadelphia, Part A,* May 1962.
21. Greater Philadelphia Movement, *A Citizens' Study of Public Education in Philadelphia, Part B,* November 1962, pp. 2–3.

Home Rule Assembly was set up in 1962 to provide a forum for discussion about the system of education. In an address to the Community Leadership Seminar, its chairman made the point that the public schools, which should be the cornerstone of democracy, were actually rejecting the workings of democratc institutions through the decision-making of their board.[22]

In 1963, the General State Assembly passed a law permitting the establishment by the city council of an Educational Home Rule Charter Commission of nine men, three each appointed by the governor, the mayor, and the Board of Judges. The new commission was charged with deciding on the method of selection of the Board of Education and of raising taxes for the operation of the system. Testimony was taken from many different civic groups. Consensus was reached to constitute a board of nine members, serving six-year terms and eligible for not more than one reappointment. The candidates were to be nominated by a panel of elected representatives of citizens' organizations, assuring wide public interest.

The composition of the nominating panel caused the greatest difficulty. Which method would most clearly eliminate the intrusion of politics? Should the citizen organizations from which panel members would be taken be enumerated in the charter or only described by category? Finally, a nominating panel of thirteen was agreed upon, nine of whom would be the highest-ranking officers of citywide organizations and four of whom would be appointed at large by the mayor.

The most controversial questions thus appeared to be settled and only waiting for the commission's final ratification.[23] In July

22. Gustave Amsterdam, "The Legislative Program of the Educational Home Rule Assembly Should Be Adopted" (address to the Community Leadership Seminar, March 5, 1963, Fels Institute of Local and State Government, University of Pennsylvania). In the address he quotes extensively from a Carnegie Corporation series, *The Economics and Politics of Public Education.*

23. David H. Kurtzman, *A Home Rule Charter for Philadelphia Schools* (Fels Institute of Local and State Government, University of Pennsylvania, 1963). William Wilcox, "Who Should Set Tax Rates for Philadelphia Schools?" December 4, 1963 (mimeo). Preliminary report of the Educational Home Rule Commission on Selection of the Home Rule School Board and Placement of Local School Tax Power, December 28, 1964 and February 19, 1965.

1964, however, two weeks after most witnesses had favored the mayor's appointive power, a regular commission session was suddenly declared an executive one. Two members were out of town, the commission's counsel was excluded, and a "preliminary" vote was taken to hand the appointment back to the judges. It was to be ratified a week later. This author has searched in vain for a plausible explanation.

This action was reversed, and after more public hearings the earlier consensus was ratified. But it is important to appreciate the effectiveness of immediate civic pressure. The Philadelphia *Bulletin* said that the action "flies in the face of virtually unanimous community opinion." [24] The chairman of the Citizens' Committee wired the commission on its behalf. "Your tentative proposal . . . is unbelievable. It is as harmful to the Judiciary as it is to the schools of Philadelphia. . . . You will face an organized campaign to defeat such a proposal when it comes to the polls." [25] And he corralled the 4,200 members affiliated with the Citizens' Committee. The power of the community made itself felt. At the commission's meeting a week later, its chairman explained the "preliminary vote" in a nine-page statement and suggested postponing the final vote and holding more public hearings. Two hundred angry opponents were present. The GPM's Wilcox said that the proposal was "dead." And he turned out to be correct.

In the early spring of 1965, a Citizens' Education Campaign Committee was founded, similar to the Citizens' Charter Committee of an earlier period. It consisted of many of those who had fought fourteen years earlier for adoption of the Home Rule Charter. Richardson Dilworth and Thacher Longstreth, who had opposed each other in the 1955 mayoralty race, served as co-chairmen. The Educational Home Rule Charter was passed in May 1965, to become effective in December. Nine members were appointed to the Board of Education by the fall, and Richardson Dilworth was elected board president. On October 1, 1965, he appointed three task forces to make recommendations on many policy questions to the new board.

24. Philadelphia *Bulletin,* July 30, 1964.
25. Philadelphia *Inquirer,* July 29, 1964.

It is worth reviewing what happened in the cases of both the Home Rule Charter and the Educational Charter.

Three major elements are usually needed to move a community or a large bureaucracy: (1) there must be widespread recognition of the need for a change. (2) A convincing prescription for what the patient needs (a clear program of action) is required. (3) A leader must be present who can coalesce these elements toward action.

In the Philadelphia political reform, starting in 1947, all these elements were present: a sizable group of civic agencies recognizing the necessity for reform and, once they saw the need, beating the drums energetically to convince the citizens that a change was imperative; carefully prepared proposals for a new Home Rule Charter (the program-prescription); and the clear leadership of Clark and Dilworth.

These three elements were also present in the educational reform: a coalescence of civic groups, from both the power structure and the grass roots, urgently demanding school reform that was long overdue; a survey and then a citizens' group working out the prescription; and a strong mayor acting as hammer.

## Civic Leadership

Philadelphia's pluralistic power structure never looked to one major family like the Mellons (of Pittsburgh) or the Wolfs (of Cincinnati) or to those running a particular industry such as oil or automobiles. While thus the leadership of Philadelphia may be directed for each specific issue under consideration (for example, industry, or housing, or Center City institutions) by a small group, it is apt to be a slightly different group each time, depending on the issues.

During the reform period, many interested persons as well as newspapers referred to the "movers and shakers" [26] when speaking about the men who exerted some influence. While many of the civic leaders were businessmen or lawyers or bankers or professionals active on the civic scene, their followers came from a variety of groups. They were geographically assorted, or occupa-

26. See, for instance, the Philadelphia *Bulletin* series by John G. McCullough in June 1965.

tionally grouped, or had a common interest in planning or zoning or housing. In other words, the citizen groups were pluralistically organized.

Pluralism may well mean that there is "a variety of resources that may be used to influence public policy," as well as "critical differences in the settings and significance of business decisions and official decisions," says Charles E. Gilbert. Referring to Robert Dahl's study of New Haven, he emphasizes—what would hold in most respects also true of Philadelphia during the reform —that resources "are not concentrated in a few hands, official positions are not typically held by members of social or economic elites, and the participation of such notables is usually confined to specific fields of policy." [27]

The interests of different segments of the community in New Haven were best reflected by a coalition of public officials and private forces, Dahl observed, particularly if this coalition was coordinated by vigorous executive leadership—a pattern Dahl calls "executive-centered coalition." This picture clearly fits Philadelphia as well as New Haven—public agencies and leading civic groups forming a coalition under a strong mayor's leadership.[28] Robert Salisbury calls this kind of recently apparent urban power "new convergence." [29] In addition to Dahl's elected leader and local economic interests, it consists also of professionals, technicians, and experts who initiate public and private programs and have taken over the innovative element of the reform. Salisbury describes the mayor as having "enough awareness of the complexity of urban problems to rely heavily on a professional staff for advice and counsel, and the ability to negotiate successfully . . . to mobilize public and private resources in efforts to solve core city economic and social problems." [30] Salisbury also describes the economic interests participating in city policy-making as those recognizing that their future depends on

27. Charles E. Gilbert, *Governing the Suburbs* (Indiana University Press, 1967), pp. 6, 327.

28. Robert A. Dahl, *Who Governs?* (Yale University Press, 1961), p. 186 and chapter 17.

29. Robert H. Salisbury, "The New Convergence of Power," *Journal of Politics*, November 1964, pp. 775–97. Reprinted in Leonard Ruchelman (ed.), *Big City Mayors* (Indiana University Press, 1969), pp. 349–68.

30. Ibid., p. 357.

the growth of the community, so that they are willing to "help to trigger a variety of problem-solving programs." [31]

It is submitted that Salisbury's model fits the Philadelphia experience and helps to explain it. Unlike Salisbury, Dahl feels that the mayor's continuous thought of reelection determines in what issues he is willing to get involved. This was not true of Philadelphia with its four-year mayoralty term and the continuation of issues throughout at least fourteen years and more than two mayors. Nor, for that matter, was it probably true of other "new mayors" like John F. Collins of Boston or Raymond Tucker of Saint Louis. [32]

It must be added that, for most of the reform period in Philadelphia, the civic groups were dominated by members of the upper-middle class and followed a middle-class ethos. Their tradition went back to both Progressivism and the New Deal, and while the leaders of the reform and of the civic groups supporting it belonged to the upper class (names like Clark, Dilworth, Walter Phillips, John Patterson, Edward Hopkinson, Francis Biddle), their followers were widely diversified, belonged to a variety of groups, and followed different interests. It was only toward the end of the 1960s that new groups of lower-income classes arose and exerted some influence through different leaders. The pluralism of the reform leaders was perhaps an even stronger influence on the period than their common ethos.

"Philadelphia enjoyed a decade of superb leadership from City Hall and spun off a dizzying number of quasi-public corporations in which citizen leaders engage in the unprecedented intervention that is so necessary to the city's plans. . . . Many sources of power and interest can be marshalled in a big, multi-centered city to help meet the new challenges." [33]

There is a growing literature on the question of power structure in the community. [34] Studies of pluralism and how it should

31. Ibid.
32. Ibid., p. 365.
33. Jeanne Lowe, *Cities in a Race with Time* (Random House, 1967), pp. 316–17.
34. The literature is discussed extensively by Nelson Polsby, *Community Power and Political Theory* (Yale University Press, 1963), and Robert Pres-

be defined usually try to identify those leaders in their community who influenced important civic decisions. Where this has been done, in communities such as "Middletown," "Jonesville," "Cibola," New Haven, Syracuse, Bennington, and others,[35] investigators either have inquired of those who have the position or reputation as leaders what they consider important decisions in their communities, or have relied on their own observation of contested decisions to judge who the community leaders are and whether they are diversified in different strata of the community or form a single elite group.[36]

Neither method of research has been followed in this book, partly because its purpose is not to examine community leaders and their actions. Rather, we observed in the broad areas of developmental interests that different leaders concentrated their civic concern in specific fields rather than in specific decisions. Having singled out developmental areas as the main contribution of the reform, we proceed in subsequent chapters to identify those individuals primarily responsible for leading citizen groups toward particular developments—for example, Walter Phillips in industry, Harry Batten and Stewart Rauch in the Food Distribution Center, Judge Lewis and Mayor Dilworth in Society Hill renewal, Gaylord Harnwell in starting the Science Center. Other individuals, not discussed here, would include, among others, Morris Duane in health planning, Charles Frazier in transportation, John Marshall and Jane Freedman in education, and Herman Niebuhr in the Skid Row alcoholics rehabilitation clinic. This kind of pluralistic community leadership during the period

thus, *Men at the Top: A Study in Community Power* (Oxford University Press, 1964).

35. Robert S. Lynd and Helen M. Lynd, *Middletown* (Harcourt, Brace, 1929); W. Lloyd Warner, et al., *Democracy in Jonesville* (Harper & Bros., 1949); Arthur Vidich and Joseph Bensman, *Small Town in Mass Society* (Princeton University Press, 1958); Robert Schulze, "The Bifurcation of Power in a Satellite City," and Harry Scoble, "Leadership Hierarchy and Political Issues in a New England Town," both in Morris Janowitz (ed.), *Community Political Systems* (Free Press, 1961).

36. It should be emphasized that our concern here is the fact of the manner of pluralistic civic impact on decisions, rather than that of power and influence, or the indirect power exercised on nondecisions. Hence, the criticism of Peter Bachrach and Morton Baratz (*Power and Poverty* [Oxford University Press, 1970]) of Dahl's analysis does not affect directly the aspects used in applying Dahl's (or Salisbury's) analysis to Philadelphia.

of Philadelphia's reform was reflected in the policy decisions which were made in important developmental issues.[37]

## Interlocking Directorates

Let us now look at the relationship among civic leaders, the questions of how much duplication there was among them, and how many individuals appeared simultaneously on the boards of different civic groups.

In Philadelphia, as elsewhere, most civic boards are self-perpetuating bodies, constantly on the lookout for new members with leadership potential. Only after World War II was new blood brought into Philadelphia business life in contrast to the prior dominance of old Philadelphia families. Mayor Clark defended his hiring of professionals from across the country (see chapter 3) as being in line with current business practices, though not with the philosophy of the politicians. It is interesting to note how many top business executives were also involved in Philadelphia civic organizations and in nonprofit corporations founded by business for public purposes.

In 1955, a number of leading organizations were asked to each name the 10 persons who had provided leadership in the city since World War II.[38] Of the 240 named, 182 were named only once, 37 twice, 13 three times, 2 four times, and 4 six times. It is not surprising to find that among the 19 mentioned more than twice are Joseph S. Clark, Harry Batten, Albert M. Greenfield, and Edward Hopkinson; but it is surprising to see how many persons *fail* to appear among these groups: Walter Phillips, Robert Mitchell, and Dorothy Montgomery appear only twice, and Dilworth, Bacon, and Rafsky only once. This would indicate less of a concentration in leadership than might have been as-

37. Cf. Anthony Downs, *An Economic Theory of Democracy* (Harper & Bros., 1957); Wallace Sayre and Herbert Kaufman, *Governing New York City* (Russell Sage, 1960); Nelson Polsby, *Community Power and Political Theory* (Yale University Press, 1963); Norton Long, *The Polity* (Rand McNally, 1963); Raymond Wolfinger, *The Politics of Progress* (Yale University Press, 1963); Aaron Wildavsky, *Leadership in a Small Town* (Bedminster Press, 1964); Robert Dahl, *Who Governs?* (Yale University Press, 1961).

38. "Survey of the Men of the Renaissance," *Greater Philadelphia Magazine,* February 1955.

sumed. Another survey of about two hundred Philadelphia organizations and their leaders pointed in the same direction.[39]

To find out how many leaders of civic organizations, nonprofit corporations, and business concerns overlapped, this author sent a questionnaire in 1965–66 to about four hundred men in top civic and business positions, asking them on which of the boards of the important organizations they served. As was to be expected, the relatively small number of directors of the GPM served also in many other capacities, but even here decision-making seemed generally well shared among them. Of the thirty directors of the GPM, ten also served on more than one board of nonprofit (quasi-public) corporations, and one on four of them. Eleven GPM directors served on more than one other civic organization board. Altogether, three GPM directors served on five other civic or quasi-public boards, and nine served on two or three boards.

The leadership of civic boards other than that of the GPM is much more widely distributed. Of the eighty-eight board members counted, only twelve were members of *both* quasi-public and civic boards. Eleven and six, respectively, held office in two quasi-public *or* civic groups. Only two were directors of five or more groups.

Thus, there were altogether about 120 men and women who participated in important civic and quasi-public decisions. Their distribution seems such that none was overburdened with too many boards and policy decisions. While thus the GPM can be called the inner circle of the power structure (thirty members), the decision-making activities of Philadelphia's civic leadership appear to have been comparatively widely distributed.[40]

39. Henry L. Klein, "Community Organization Leadership in Philadelphia" (Ph.D. dissertation, Temple University, 1964). It has been written up in the *Greater Philadelphia Magazine*, October and November 1965, under the title "Anatomy of Power: The Closed Circle." As Dr. Klein included all social, cultural, and welfare institutions, his results are different from those in the survey mentioned in n. 24 above as well as from the one conducted by this author.

40. For further comments on Philadelphia's civic leadership during the reform period, see John W. Bodine, "The Indispensible One-Hundredth of One Percent," *Planning 1963* (American Society of Planning Officials), pp. 198–212.

# 3 *The Reform Leaders*

Citizen groups had campaigned enthusiastically for the charter, and it had been adopted. By 1951, the city seemed ready to elect a new "strong mayor" to carry out the charter's mandate.

The people of Philadelphia had first noticed Richardson Dilworth, as mentioned earlier, when he ran for mayor in 1947. It had been an exciting, hard-hitting campaign. A noteworthy occasion was Dilworth's projected debate with Sheriff William Meehan, the unquestioned "boss" of the entrenched Republican regime. Despite the overflow crowd, it was a "debate with an empty chair," as Sheriff Meehan did not show up, and, although Dilworth's accusations were specific and shocking, Meehan failed even to comment.[1] Though the voters rejected Dilworth, his campaign began to change the attitude toward the city government. Shortly thereafter similar revelations were made by the Committee of Fifteen, and a grand jury investigation bore out the various accusations.

In 1949, Joseph Clark ran for city controller and Dilworth for city treasurer. This time the Republicans took the Democratic reformers seriously, and Sheriff Meehan appeared to debate Dilworth in the Academy of Music before a packed house. All news media covered the event in detail. The Democratic ticket was elected.

This gave Clark two years before running for mayor to investigate other official scandals and report his detailed findings to the citizens of Philadelphia. Hence, in 1951 the stage was set, both in terms of established facts of official corruption, and of extensive involvement of civic groups in renewed hope for the city. The fall campaign—Clark for mayor and Dilworth for district attorney—followed the charter adoption in the spring. Clark was able to campaign on what his investigations as controller had re-

1. Philadelphia *Bulletin*, October 15 and 24, 1947.

vealed, and he won on the idea of "throwing the rascals out." Not much was learned about his ideas beyond the promise of honesty in office and carrying out the mandates of the charter. Plans for Clark's term as mayor were developed only after his victory, and even then only gradually.

This victory of the reform government inaugurated a period widely referred to as Philadelphia's renaissance. Actually it was not a rebirth of a previous era in the city's history, but a time so full of new ideas and innovations that this rather presumptuous term was applied by those taking part in it. Philadelphians have continued to use it with reference to the period.

Joseph Clark's first political job after the war had been as manager of Richardson Dilworth's unsuccessful campaign for mayor in 1947. In 1949 they had run together for the "row offices" of controller and treasurer. In the crucial year of 1951 it was Joseph Clark who announced for mayor—or rather who announced to an astonished party caucus that he had released news of his candidacy to the press an hour before. Dilworth had by then been defeated twice (in 1947 and, for governor, in 1950) and he told all comers that he and Clark had agreed that it was Clark's turn, and he, Dilworth, would run again in another round. (Later, in 1955 and in 1959, Dilworth was elected mayor by an overwhelming majority. But he never lost his ambition for the governorship: he decided to let it pass in 1954, a decision he often regretted, especially when the Democrats won with George Leader, and was maneuvered out of the nomination in 1958. In 1962 he decided to run and had to resign as mayor to do so. On Dilworth's resignation, city council president James H. J. Tate automatically took over as mayor.)

## The Urban Challenge

Speaking of reform movements in the metropolitan context, Scott Greer emphasizes that they are based both on existing rules and those of "what ought to be" in society, and thus on a moral framework crucial for social action. Because of the common political culture and morality on which reform is based, Greer calls it a "morality play" and its various actions "rituals." [2] The play's most obvious first action is that of removing the misbehaving in-

2. Scott Greer, *Metropolitics: A Study of Political Culture* (Wiley, 1963), chap. 1.

cumbents—an action reinforced by the new civic movement in Philadelphia. Greer's second ritual of making municipal government more efficient and improving its form and structure was strengthened, in Philadelphia, by the new charter. The new government then went on to the third ritual—that of giving a specific direction to the city's growth, rather than viewing urban growth as a desirable end in itself, regardless of what it might be growing into. What seemed to move the Philadelphia reform was the question of how, given the importance of growth as such, both growth and specific developmental direction could be turned into social change—change, in fact, in the *quality* of life. Not satisfied with the first two kinds of actions, as were other reform movements, Philadelphia decided gradually that it should tackle those problems which would in the long run affect the quality of life and the environment of urban living.

Historically, municipal reform has been short-lived. Its legacy has been a minimum of programmatic innovations, while reform governments have again yielded to the politically dominated groups they had for a time replaced. Theodore Lowi describes New York's reform governments as temporary sparks.[3] Edward Banfield and James Wilson [4] make a crucial distinction between structural changes in the government and substantive changes in the program of the reform. They (and, for that matter, Reichley) [5] depict Philadelphia's newest reform as another flash in the pan, much like the brief reform administration under Blankenburg in 1912. Is there any reason to assume that this time it should be considered differently?

*Substantive Programs*

Every new government needs an administrative framework which will support its innovative programs. In Philadelphia during the first year of the new regime a great deal of attention had to be given to the mechanics of "good government," that is, the setting up of workable administrative machinery, including a valid per-

3. Theodore Lowi, *At the Pleasure of the Mayor* (Free Press, 1963).

4. Edward Banfield and James Q. Wilson, *City Politics* (Harvard-MIT Press, 1963), chap. 11.

5. James Reichley, *The Art of Government* (The Fund for the Republic, 1959), pp. 114–16. This pamphlet's thesis is discussed in more detail in chapter 12.

sonnel merit system. Unlike some reform governments in which "meritocracy" becomes an end in itself, the new Philadelphia regime directed its efforts—as soon as the mechanics of government had been straightened out—to the *substantive* changes to be wrought. During the 1950s, *Fortune* magazine, in evaluating municipal governments, differentiated between those which did an excellent job in routine housekeeping functions and those which carried out new ideas and innovations in the areas of city planning, urban renewal, industrial revitalization, or transportation. Philadelphia topped those excelling in the latter group, but got a poor mark in the former.

Thus, the most distinctive contribution of Philadelphia's reform administration was to embark on programs which would affect the development of the city—physically, economically, and socially—and leave a permanent imprint. This was of much more concern to the reform leaders than procedural improvements, which might be easily changed back by a subsequent mayor. Backtracking would be much harder where substantive innovations had achieved new developments in the city. Banfield and Wilson's judgment that reform is "more concerned with *how* things are done than with *what* is done" [6] cannot, I submit, be applied to the Philadelphia of the 1950s.

## Philadelphia and Washington

The reformers' concern with long-term development programs, which would require extensive lead time, made it important that these programs be properly evaluated and continued to their completion, rather than buried by a later "politics-as-usual" government. Where the substantive and financial help of the federal government is needed, foresight is particularly important. In the late forties and early fifties, when Washington began to sense the urgent need for solutions to urban problems, it was still struggling to define those problems. While ameliorative measures such as depressed-areas legislation, training for the disadvantaged, and transportation aid were being discussed, even though they were not yet on the books, Philadelphia's reform leaders and professionals were among the first to grasp the significance of the help that the federal government might provide.

6. Banfield and Wilson, p. 331.

Today we are familiar with the sequence of federal initiative leading to legislation and with local governments determining whether the remedies can successfully be applied to their local situation. But in the early 1950s, when this sequence was not as clear, ideas often originated with the professionals in Philadelphia. Some experiments tried there influenced subsequent national legislation, and federal officials often accepted advice and suggestions from Philadelphia.

Philadelphia's influence on Washington seemed obvious at the time, though difficult to prove. It was exerted in part through the testimony of Clark or Dilworth before congressional committees, discussions between Philadelphia officials and Washington administrators, resolutions suggested at meetings of the American Municipal Association (now the National League of Cities), and informal relations between federal officials and outstanding Philadelphia urban thinkers, many of them faculty members at universities in the Philadelphia area. Many new legislative devices in the fields of housing and urban renewal originated or received new emphasis and application in Philadelphia (for example, conservation as a practical approach to urban renewal; the "used house" program; industrial and commercial development through local development corporations; housing rehabilitation toward achieving "balanced" communities; and urban use of depressed area legislation).[7] These Washington-Philadelphia relationships existed among professionals rather than elected officials, which made service in Philadelphia particularly rewarding for many professionals.

In such areas as welfare, specialized social improvements, and the planning of interurban highways, ideas were more likely to originate elsewhere and were brought to Philadelphia by suggestions of the federal government or other city administrations.

## Clark and Dilworth: Was Either the Knight in Shining Armor?

Even though the time seemed ripe for reform, it could have passed Philadelphia by if its leaders had been honest but dull; things happened only because the kinds of leaders who could in-

7. These and many other new substantive ideas are discussed in chapter 5 and subsequent chapters.

spire citizens to change their environment were there at the opportune time. Why was it that Clark and Dilworth were able to get the city and its people moving again? (Later in this chapter we shall try to determine the extent to which Tate, who followed, could also be considered a reform mayor.)

## Background and Personalities

Joseph Sill Clark was a partner in one of the city's best-known law firms, having graduated from Harvard and the University of Pennsylvania law school. A specialist in corporation law, he was a man of logical and orderly mind. During the war he served in the Air Force under General Stratemeyer, known as an excellent administrator. Clark, not himself a flier, learned all about administrative relationships and delegation of authority—an experience he could put to good use as mayor.

Clark belonged to one of the well-known old Philadelphia families, and his great self-reliance partly stemmed from being accepted as a member of the Philadelphia elite. But he did not always make use of his natural charm, which served him well if he chose to apply it. He was a hard taskmaster, abrupt and aggressive if opposed or if his staff let him down. This unusual combination in a "Philadelphia gentleman" made him, on balance, successful, but he was not universally liked. Those reporting to him or suggesting new ideas had better know the answers if they wanted to keep his respect! He did not suffer fools gladly, and bitterly resented an evening wasted at a poorly attended political meeting. His impatience sometimes caused him problems even among his admirers.

His elite background served Clark well, as he maintained his personal associations and knew most of them by their first names. These personal relations were based on his social and economic heritage, his growing up in an exclusive neighborhood where civic leaders and businessmen were his neighbors, and the contacts acquired in practicing law in a prominent firm. His close ties with the Establishment did not endanger his relations with labor or university groups: to act on the basis of the traditional heritage was a strong and widely accepted way of doing things in Philadelphia, whatever a person's philosophy. And over time his philosophy had changed from his family's—and his own—Republicanism to a growing belief in the New Deal philosophy, from which he drew increasingly. His reform government has, in fact, been compared to the early New Deal period, and Schlesinger's description of the New Deal regime might be applied to Clark's: while "they represented all classes . . . they were predominantly middle-class. . . . The common bond that held them together was that they were . . . prepared to use intelligence as an instrument of government." [8] Clark was thus able to bridge the gap between his background and the philosophy of reformers and labor leaders, and he established a new relationship with the business community.

While both he and Dilworth had dabbled in politics before the war, their period overseas convinced both that they had to do something about their city. Personal ambition (to become senator or governor) may have played a part, but their conviction of the need for an honest and progressive city government was paramount, as was their desire to improve the lot of the little man, sponsor economic legislation, and create new jobs and better housing.

It is well to recall that Philadelphia, up to the early 1960s, was dominated by the upper-middle classes. Their noblesse oblige attitude made them and the reform government concerned about improving the "quality of life" not only for their own class but also for the poor, who could not themselves improve their situation. Not until the middle sixties did participation of the poor in determining their lot become an acceptable idea. The social elite in mid-century Philadelphia was well aware of the need for the lot of the poor and the black to be improved.

Richardson Dilworth originally came from Pittsburgh but had lived for many years in Philadelphia. Although he too came from a similar upper-middle-class background, the tradition of the Philadelphia elite was not likely to let him forget that his family was not one of theirs. He told this author in his usual self-deprecating manner: "I was never really part of the social structure. To many of the elite, a man from Pittsburgh is a semi-savage." He served in the Marines, and was wounded in both world wars. He never forgot that he was a Marine, and this may

8. Arthur M. Schlesinger, Jr., *The Coming of the New Deal* (Houghton Mifflin Company, 1958), p. 18.

have accounted in part for his natural readiness to fight. While lying in a military hospital, he met some lawyers from Philadelphia with whom he formed close friendships as they discussed how they would change their home town once they got back. A graduate of Yale and Yale law school, he became a trial lawyer, specializing in libel suits.

## Presenting a Case or Fighting a Cause?

While Clark concentrated on the more detailed and logical aspects of corporation law, Dilworth was involved in courtroom trials, where he could expect—and often enjoyed—a real fight, especially if he felt it was for a good cause. When asked to champion a cause, he agreed to appear on behalf of it, no matter how hostile the group before which he was to speak. Both he and Clark made numerous appearances before congressional committees, sometimes making a case for more money for Philadelphia or for legislation which would clearly benefit the city. Both also were glad to testify where a matter of general principle was involved. While Dilworth's staff tried to keep him with the "bread-and-butter" issues, he also testified for minimum-wage legislation, broader "depressed area" support, natural gas legislation in favor of the consumer, and similar issues. He loved to strike fire in those who heard him and was best in what lawyers call "adversary proceedings."

Clark, on the other hand, preferred to present an airtight, logical case in court—and he prepared for a meeting on city matters in the same way. Quickly grasping complicated subject matter, he expected its mastery from all others present. He also testified willingly before congressional committees, but he enjoyed the logic of his case more than the fight it entailed. If, however, the issue demanded a stiff fight, Clark too was willing to give battle.

Both men were frank in public and obviously meant what they said. But Dilworth was less cautious and at times made statements which returned to haunt him; he then usually made light of his own lack of foresight. He clearly was the warmer personality, communicating easily with his audience. Both men knew how to arouse loyalty in their followers, although they did it in different ways. Clark was a perfectionist who expected brilliant performance from his aides and knew how to spur them on to their best efforts. His seriousness, however, did not encourage any humor—certainly not humor about himself. Dilworth was able to inspire a much larger group if he set out to do so, but he preferred to make people feel at ease in smaller gatherings. His sense of humor was often directed at himself.

Even before the war Clark and Dilworth had managed each other's (unsuccessful) minor campaigns. But their approaches to others and to their own ambitions in life were so different that misunderstandings could happen easily, and there were times when their relationship suffered. Still, they always knew that their basic purposes regarding Philadelphia were the same.

The contrast between their personalities was reflected in their behavior—though not in their performance—as mayors. Both were good mayors. Their sequence in office helped determine their respective achievements: the first reform mayor was necessarily engaged in setting up a civil service system and making new appointments, while his heir took over a going concern and could propel the ship of state further along. But it is also possible that their different temperaments and gifts well fitted them for this sequence. The question was frequently asked by this author of many participants in both administrations whether the two mayors' preoccupations with different subject matter (for example, health and welfare legislation in Clark's case as compared with economic renewal and improvement of the central business district in Dilworth's) indicated a difference in their inclinations. There seemed virtual consensus that it was the sequence of events which was decisive, rather than any personal predilections of the two mayors.

Dilworth's underlying concern was what his administration would be able to "build for the future in developing the city." Much that Clark had sown Dilworth could reap. The Urban Traffic and Transportation Board had completed its overall plan before he became mayor, and it was his task to carry it out. The Food Distribution Center battle had been fought, and he could observe and help its execution. Industrial development devices had been thought out, and he could watch the inception of the Philadelphia Industrial Development Corporation. Center City renewal had long been talked about but was only realized under Dilworth.

## *Top Staff and Cabinet*

Each man found discussions with individual top members of his administration or with outside advisers preferable to group meetings. Dilworth relied on a small number of trusted individuals for his information, but he plied them with searching questions about the consequences of any action he wanted to take—especially the political consequences—so that he would be well informed before making up his mind.

Clark preferred to use personal friends for informal advice, many of whom had some connection with civic groups, either through other members of these groups, or often through their professional staffs, which many civic groups in Philadelphia had hired. His own professional staff was permitted also to use these personal connections, so that they too could benefit from these associations. This then led indirectly to a tie-in between the professionals in both the government and the civic groups, which helped in bridging whatever public-private gap might have existed. Clark felt that his own learning process would be furthered if he had good enough people close to him who would think out problems on their own, with whom he could share his thinking, and to whom he could delegate responsibilities. He collected widely differing opinions before he made a final decision. He encouraged young people to follow careers in government and politics, and he tried to foster professionalism in the public service. As recipient of the $10,000 civic "Philadelphia Award," for example, he contributed the proceeds toward the education of aspiring young public servants. To Clark, the true government professional—the man who feels strongly the integrity of his calling—is at the apex of government service. In his inaugural address he stated: "I want to make it fashionable to serve the City of Philadelphia. . . . I hope that public-spirited citizens will feel that every man and woman owes something of himself or herself to the service of the community which gives them the opportunity for civilized living." [9]

Cabinet meetings under the two mayors were quite different. To begin with, Clark had minutes kept of the proceedings, until

9. Joseph S. Clark's unpublished speeches (in private collection; perused by courtesy of its owner).

the city solicitor felt that the keeping and distributing of minutes might inhibit free discussion, since they might fall into the wrong hands, and he persuaded Clark to discontinue them. Dilworth refused from the beginning to permit minutes to be kept.

Clark's cabinet meetings were structured carefully and—aside from daily operational problems—he tried to concentrate on broad, long-term solutions. He sought cabinet advice on issues of priorities, though he liked to first consult his excellent personal staff. Dilworth preferred small groups of personal friends, and the operational details discussed in cabinet held his attention only for a limited period. Clark's concern for properly structuring his administration led him to ask a specialist in public administration from a nearby college to sit in on cabinet meetings for some weeks and give him a critique of whether the cabinet was performing its administrative role as it should.[10]

Both mayors were thoroughly bored by details, but Clark was basically a much better administrator. Dilworth, unhappy with day-to-day chores, was much less willing to spend time on administrative problems. He made almost no use of the Administrative Board created by the charter as a tool for better handling of these problems. Letters to answer or specific issues to be disposed of were handed to his cabinet members without regard to the fields for which they were responsible—and they had to exchange these assignments among themselves later. Dilworth was apt to undercut and go around his administrators, but he was so personable that they forgave him. Clark, on the other hand, knew how to use proper channels and support people all down the line—but made little use of personal charm. One of his executive secretaries wrote to him in a confidential memo, August 3, 1954: "The mayor can delegate paper work; he cannot delegate relationships with people."

Finally, in line with their different attitudes to staff advice as against personal friendships, it is not surprising that some difference in the immediate staffs of Clark and Dilworth could be observed. Where Clark had had outstanding executive secretaries

10. The professor was Herman M. Somers, then of Haverford College, now of Princeton University. While this author has seen some of his notes, which are instructive, the main impact on Mayor Clark was in comments given him personally at the time.

throughout, with experience and training in political science and public administration,[11] Dilworth had a staff of much more modest academic and professional backgrounds, excelling primarily in a mastery of personal political strategy—in addition to rather uncritical admiration of Dilworth.

Though Dilworth did not start with Clark's connections with the business community, he was able to get along well with top business and civic leaders and was at ease when dealing with them. He preferred to deal with individuals with whom he could establish personal relationships and whom he could therefore trust. He was close to some of them and admired them for their "sense" of what was realistic. In his bid for reelection in 1959, thirty top leaders of business and civic groups—reading like a *Who's Who* of the business elite—supported him in a full-page advertisement in the newspapers, though it was a partisan election and most of them considered themselves Republicans. Nor did their endorsement encroach on his continued support by labor.

## Appointments

Clark had to make two different types of appointments immediately on taking office: (1) cabinet members and commissioners of the various departments, and (2) members of the wide variety of boards and commissions. For the latter, Clark wanted a broad spectrum of talent from the community. Right after being sworn in—although his victory was not based primarily on their votes—he told a hundred businessmen: "We need the business community on our side. We need intelligent, hard-headed, common-sense businessmen to serve on the many boards and commissions that I will appoint. One of the most apparent weaknesses in the new administration is a lack of good businessmen." [12] And he warned that he was going to "twist arms" to make businessmen perform civic duties. In consequence, Philadelphia's renaissance was widely applauded by the business community, though Clark's broader goals were foreign to some of its members.

11. William L. Rafsky, Clark's first executive secretary, is still deeply involved in Philadelphia's affairs. The three others all have Ph.D.'s and have spent their entire careers in higher education or public service, e.g. Paul Ylvisaker and Harold Enarson.

12. Philadelphia *Bulletin,* January 9, 1952.

## The Principles

Clark wanted to corral into his administration the "best brains" in both full-time and volunteer positions, and to have his boards represent a variety of viewpoints and different groups. This attitude toward appointments, while engendering respect in the long run, also made enemies for the mayor.

For example, labor, having helped the reformers in the campaign, wanted badly to have a representative on the Civil Service Commission. But Clark felt that the State, County and Municipal Workers Union was too closely affected by civil service decisions, and he turned a deaf ear to their demand, while accepting labor's membership on the City Planning Commission and on other boards and commissions of the city. Dilworth stuck to this same principle, and Tate did so also, although only for his first term.

The Pennsylvania Truckers' Association complained about having been bypassed when a board of particular interest to them had been appointed. Clark told them: "The problem of selecting individuals for various boards and commissions . . . is a very difficult one. I have felt that, on the whole, it was wiser to pursue a policy of informal consultation with individuals in particular fields for the purpose of obtaining adequate representation in each case rather than to consult formally and officially with trade associations and other groups. Implementing this policy during the last two years, it has never been my practice, for example, to request the Chamber of Commerce to name a business representative for a commission, but rather to consult with individuals in the general business field to obtain appropriate representation." [13]

A different use of special interest groups is illustrated by the composition of the Urban Traffic and Transportation Board. Clark saw that it was representative of every group interested in transportation (railroads, truckers, Transportation Company, Automobile Club, and so forth). He pressured an outstanding businessman (Clifford Frishmuth) to take the chairmanship, and the former executive director of the City Planning Commission, Robert Mitchell, to become its executive. The interesting result was that, after considerable research, the conclusions of the board were adopted almost unanimously.[14]

13. Letter from Joseph S. Clark, January 29, 1954 (in City Archives).
14. Frishmuth's letter of transmittal to the mayor, April 16, 1956.

The charter required the mayor to nominate the finance director and the personnel director from panels. Clark carried the concept further and set up citizen panels for selection of appointees for a number of other jobs as well—for example, for commissioners of welfare, of recreation, and of health.

Cabinet members had been chosen early, before the campaign had started. Of outstanding quality, most of them came from the civic groups involved. Commissioners and their deputies heading the fifteen city departments were primarily appointed for competence in the fields in which they were to work and came from all across the country. True, some political appointments also had to be made, but they proved more competent than could have been hoped if the primary criterion for their selection had indeed been politics.

## The Fight about Residence

In the civil service ranks no compromises were permissible. But the many new jobs would have been hard to fill even if the past reputation of City Hall had not led to a dearth of local talent. So the requirement of prior residence in Philadelphia had to be waived. Before long, planners, personnel administrators, public health and sanitation experts, and other professional technicians were attracted, particularly as the new political climate prevailing in Philadelphia's City Hall became known.

This was one of the important features of Clark's administration. For policy-making positions he tried to attract these outside experts. For lower-echelon jobs he wanted to see promotion from within. One is inclined to applaud this policy. But in retrospect one also wonders whether some deviation from this strict principle might not have enabled the city to acquire new faces and talents in the lower echelons by bringing in bright recent college graduates. Without such a reservoir of talent, a vacuum in professional leadership became apparent after a time. Dealing only with the top stratum, Clark failed to perceive this important need early enough.

Soon the disappointment of the politicians became obvious. They had expected plums and had been given "foreigners." They had been stunned when so few top jobs went to their ranks. Now the feeling of estrangement between the city council and the mayor made itself felt. In April 1953, after many but not all top appointments had been made, the council passed a bill requiring a year of *prior* residence before appointment to city jobs. A year earlier, a similar ordinance had been passed, requiring six months' residence, which could be fulfilled *after* the appointment had been passed; this possibility (and the fact that this requirement could be waived upon request of the personnel director) made the ordinance tolerable. But Clark felt differently about the new one. Before it passed, Clark pointed out publicly that "in all those cases where nonresidents were appointed, efforts were first made to find qualified Philadelphians willing to accept the jobs at the prescribed salaries." [15]

In his veto message (backed publicly by the GPM), the mayor made clear that it was folly to expect first-class government if the city was not able to recruit the best men in every field of activity regardless of residence. He pointed out that business did not limit itself in this way; nor for that matter did baseball teams. "We cannot expect to find the best qualified people in any one place," he said. This bill would show "that we are unwilling to welcome to Philadelphia government our fair share of that free flow of brains and ability whose uninterrupted opportunities for employment across the whole wide spread of this continent have done so much to make our country great; and, in short, that we are not fit to be accepted in the company of liberal and educated men." [16] The message did not help Clark's relations with the council. The ordinance passed over Clark's veto. The waiver provision now had to take care of all cases of important appointments.

The talent search for top staff was over by the time Dilworth became mayor. Dilworth agreed that the team was good—so why change, even if he had not assembled it? The director of finance and William Rafsky stayed, but otherwise Dilworth's cabinet did not measure up to Clark's. For instance, his managing director had been a very competent city manager of several cities, executive director of the GPM, and Philadelphia's personnel director, but for various reasons he did not play as large a role in the Dilworth administration as a managing director would be expected to. Dilworth retained most of Clark's department heads, however,

15. Philadelphia *Bulletin,* February 5, 1953.
16. Veto message, March 27, 1953 (in City Archives).

and virtually the entire professional staffs near the top of the departments. And in his own office he managed to assemble a number of top professionals as advisers.

## Political Constraints

Clark and Dilworth had been elected on the basis of their own actions, and with the support of civic groups firmly convinced of the need to have the new charter administered by an honest reform government. But it was not a nonpartisan election: the reformers ran on the Democratic ticket, for they were opposing the Republican machine which had ruled the Philadelphia municipality for over two-thirds of a century. But the very fact that they beat a party machine made them fearful lest a revived Democratic party develop over time a similar influence in the city. This ambivalence ruled their every movement, as the reform ticket had to run consistently both on the reformers' own merits and under the party label.

### The Party Organization

The Democratic party was only a minor force before the reform movement made itself felt, and it acted in effect like a group "kept" by the dominant Republican party, receiving the crumbs that the Republicans threw from their heavily laden patronage table. It was not until Dilworth's 1947 campaign for mayor that the Democratic party again began to wake up, after the ground for reform action had been laid by civic groups. The party had nothing to lose and a great deal to gain by backing a candidate who did not come from the party's ranks; in fact, he was able to stir up for the first time a large number of concerned citizens.

Before the reform government came to power, the newly awakened Democratic party named, upon Dilworth's urging, an alert young man as city chairman. James Finnegan had testified at length in favor of the new charter during the hearings on its merit, because he fervently believed that "good government is good politics." Finnegan, though reared in party politics, did not agree with the kind of "reward politics" which had been so customary. He was honest about abiding by the rules of the new city charter, and in his dual role as Democratic city chairman and president of the city council he had little time (or opportunity) to worry about patronage. Thus, for Joseph Clark's first two years in office, he had the weight of party support behind him under Finnegan. Clark was not inclined to risk this arrangement for the sake of starting his own organization.

Finnegan's health did not stand up to his two concurrent jobs, accompanied by the constant assault on him by Congressman William Green and his forces. He fell out with party treasurer James Clark and with Green, over the question of who should get credit for the Pennsylvania delegation's support for Adlai Stevenson in 1952—or at least that was the official reason for the rift. Finnegan resigned first from one of his positions, then from the other. Congressman Green became the new city chairman. Thereafter relations between the reform administration and the Democratic party were quite different. The professional politicians continued to feel that, since Clark had run under their banner, they deserved the credit for his election.

Green was less inclined than Finnegan had been to see reform as good politics. So he kept trying to bargain with the reform mayors to gain concessions for the party from each program the mayors wanted to enact. Green was really not much interested in the developmental programs, of such concern to both reform mayors. His stance emphasized the difference in approach between administration and political party. "Green's rise to power in the party organization in Philadelphia had little effect on the content of public policy," one commentator has said.[17] Still, a political party is rarely program-oriented; thus, the reform government, oriented as it was toward the substance of programs which had become its hallmark, constantly feared lest the desire of party stalwarts for personal advantages and patronage might endanger the unencumbered implementation of these programs.

## The Dichotomy between Party and Reform

In 1949 and 1951 the victory of the reform owed much to the existence of the local chapter of Americans for Democratic Action; the Philadelphia chapter—founded in opposition to

17. Robert M. Salisbury, "The New Convergence of Power," *Journal of Politics*, November 1964, pp. 775–97. Reprinted in Leonard Ruchelman (ed.), *Big City Mayors* (Indiana University Press, 1969), pp. 349–68.

Communist infiltration of local liberal organizations—predated the founding of the national organization. It was the meeting place of idealists, eggheads, and hard-nosed reform politicians. Dilworth called it later the "conscience of the Democratic party in Philadelphia." At the beginning there was no question but that the reform had carried the Democratic party into power, and the reformers in general and Mayor Clark in particular enjoyed the public's confidence. But in later elections, with both party and reform movement working for the same candidates, it was difficult to prove which of the votes came from the party and which from the reform. No matter how hard a reform group worked to be recognized as a major force *within* the party, the party organization was apt to be credited for victory in the minds of most citizens. Had the reform group been able to run candidates on its own "line" on the ballot, as the Liberal party in New York is able to do, it would have had a visible impact. It was even hard for some of those benefiting clearly from the reform (like Negroes or labor; see chapter 12) to be clear about the distinction between the two groups supporting the same ticket. Yet the recognition of the difference was the essence of the reform's independence and its ability to carry out its programs without interference.

The dichotomy between the political party and the reform groups persisted even beyond the administrations of Clark and Dilworth.

## State Patronage

The possibility of receiving patronage from the state could have become a very important influence in the disagreements between the Philadelphia party organization and the reform, at least after the election of Governor Leader in 1954. Leader had, at least in theory, the choice of funneling patronage jobs through the party or through the reform city government—or possibly of dividing them between the two forces. While Clark was opposed to patronage in principle (he made the unequivocal declaration as mayor that he would never run for governor as long as the state administration was wholly under the influence of patronage) and would not tolerate its interfering with the administration of the city, his task might have been eased considerably if he could have repaid some reform-oriented helpers—who were not on the city payroll—through state patronage jobs.

Had the newly elected Democratic governor George Leader thrown in his lot with the reformers, letting them dispense a major share of Philadelphia's state jobs, he might have laid a sound basis for a long-lasting reform organization. Governor Leader seemed to start in just that direction and even fired from his cabinet some party members who had abused the public trust. But he was not strong enough to stand up to William Green, and he was too much in need of votes in the generally hostile legislature to risk the organization's ire. Possibly he also failed fully to understand the kinds of problems the reform government faced and his own potential role in solving them. An opportunity for undergirding the reform at the expense of the regular party was lost.

### Clark and Dilworth Compared

Clark's most important shortcoming was his failure to appreciate politicians and his tendency to act as if they were beneath him. Too often he made it clear that he thought ward leaders unimportant. He never invited local politicians to his home, and failed to establish informal relationships with them. It was not until he ran for and served in the U.S. Senate and had to deal with politicians across the state as well as in the Senate itself that Clark learned to work through politics. Then, and only gradually, he learned that accomplishments could only be achieved by the art of compromise. He found that a necessary compromise need not conflict with his principles, that "a Senator's conscience need not be impaired by these concessions." Nonetheless, his attitude to politicians caught up with him when he was defeated for a third term in the U.S. Senate in 1968.

Clark's lack of innate political acumen took its toll during his term as mayor. A close political associate said: "Substantial elements of the Democratic party are angrily, determinedly, energetically against Joe Clark. They are held in check only by one thing: a disturbing fear that the people might be with him." Fortunately for Clark, he had been swept into office with a city council which afforded him a majority vote when he really needed it. Respect for his integrity and leadership carried him—but the politicians were not going to accept his ideas any longer than they had to. How many times did Clark lose battles when he could not call on loyalty to a principle? His personal friends in civic groups and his political allies such as labor could exert pressure only on a small number of councilmen in a geographically limited area, and many of the councilmen-at-large who might be influenced more easily were already in Clark's camp.

Clark was able, however, to use to advantage the fear prevailing in Pennsylvania of a party primary. His nominations for mayor in 1951 and for U.S. senator in 1956 had been secured on the basis of this fear.

But when Dilworth's turn came to run for governor, he so badly wanted the party nomination that he lacked the courage to take a similar stand. Nor did Dilworth jump into Democratic city politics when the party treasurer, James Clark, died, or when a real vacuum was created by City Chairman William Green's sudden death. Neither, for that matter, did Tate.

After Green had become party chairman, he tried to whittle down some of the charter provisions, though the charter seemed to have become a sacred cow to many Philadelphians. In 1954, Clark won over to his viewpoint two nonreform councilmen to help him narrowly defeat an attack on the charter. In 1956, however, he was not able to secure the same kind of council for Dilworth.[18] He lost the six certain votes he had to have to override a veto or to place a charter-changing amendment on the ballot by a two-thirds majority. Hence, Dilworth had to exercise moderation in dealing with the council. An example of Dilworth's efforts to establish his own relationship with councilmen, different from Clark's, was his early attempt to pacify the party with some minor patronage jobs through a change in a charter provision. He also attempted to reverse the charter provision that compels any officeholder to resign his current office if running for another. If passed, this change would have given Dilworth the

18. A reform-minded Republican councilman was not reslated, another Democratic reform councilman was defeated, and two others who had supported Clark gave in to party organization pressure after Clark was gone. Shortly after the election an independent organization councilman who had often supported the reform died suddenly.

right to stay on as mayor while running for governor. The voters defeated all such "charter-ripping" amendments overwhelmingly. Dilworth failed to assess the potency of the reform he had helped to build.

Dilworth's defeat in this measure marked a turning-point in the balance of power. He had to fight a rearguard action thereafter and was forced to make compromises, since William Green and James Clark were able to influence the council to a much greater degree. Even those councilmen who had all along been willing to accommodate the party's policies became more subservient to it after the changes in the council of 1956. (Shortly thereafter Tate began to consolidate his position as council president.)

Dilworth was interested in political strategy and felt at ease with politicians at any level. He appeared willing to make small concessions, especially in terms of a few political jobs, and felt it would pay off in the long run. He was known to be emotional, with a low boiling point, a personality trait which his political enemies exploited systematically. (He himself stated that he lost the 1962 campaign for governor because the backers of his opponent—William Scranton—succeeded in their systematic effort to get him to lose his temper.) In order to get his programs through, he had to find a modus vivendi with the council. He found the party treasurer, James Clark, to be a more powerful politician—and a greater help to him—than Green. At least once a month he met with the members of the council's Democratic caucus to discuss the administration's program, which brought him relative peace in council meetings. He was often able to charm councilmen into accepting programs by convincing them, through informal bantering, that the programs would do no political harm (a feat Clark would never have managed or even attempted). The feeling was that Dilworth would not hesitate to make a deal to achieve a large enough objective. Yet, "I trusted him to make the right compromise and to hold the line," said the chairman of one of his more important boards.

The real touchstone, however, was the making of appointments to those boards and commissions where really important contracts or substantial amounts of money were involved. Given the changed situation in the council, Dilworth's concern was centered on preventing the party faithful from securing positions which would give the party economic or program leverage. He successfully kept politicians off the City Planning Commission, the Redevelopment Authority, the Housing Authority, and the Procurement or Public Property departments. In spite of all his efforts, individual officials were caught receiving benefits from their position, and the resulting scandals, especially in the Department of Public Property, were most embarrassing to Dilworth in his second term. In 1961 former Councilman Henry Sawyer said about Dilworth's performance: "It is fair to say that the mayor has fought a rearguard action in recent years, at best, but it has been a skillful rearguard action and I should say it has resulted in few major concessions." "To get some of his programs adopted," said one of his close associates, "Dilworth had to compromise through a patchwork of alliances with councilmen, bankers, developers—and Albert Greenfield."

## The Question of Priorities

In spite of the long gestation period of the new charter and the new government, no clear-cut plan of action had emerged. Nor had the policy direction for the city among possible alternatives been decided. Many local problems had been studied by research organizations and civic groups, and many individuals had thought about goals for the city, but there is no evidence in any available documents that Joseph Clark had studied the reports and recommendations of these groups and decided on priorities on the basis of the advice of knowledgeable individuals. Nor, apparently, did Dilworth, while sitting on the sidelines in the district attorney's office for four years, sort out his own ideas of what a mayor's priorities should be. The many capital projects proposed in the Public Improvement Programs issued earlier by the City Planning Commission—from individual transportation improvements to expansion of the universities to redevelopment projects—represented no consistent plan. It must be realized that, in terms of urban thought and action, January 1952 was an extremely early period. Nobody had yet thought seriously about a federal urban department. The Housing and Urban Renewal Act had been on the books only for a couple of years, and hardly any city had any experience with it. Area redevelopment legislation with its possible use for depressed central cities was a long way from being enacted, and so was the Urban Mass Transportation Act. Cities which tried to face urban problems early were groping for solutions jointly with the federal government. Indeed, had the new Philadelphia government approached its task with a blueprint, it would have missed the dynamic experience of trying new solutions.

One of Clark's first concerns was for better shelter, especially for renewal of slum areas and improved housing for the poor. He mentioned it incidentally during the campaign; [19] and a year later he emphasized the importance of redevelopment,[20] and a few months after that he singled it out as one of the city's most urgent problems.[21] Clearly, growing blight was related to poor health, crime, and other social problems. Clark started isolated projects as soon as his administrative house was in order. When he realized that he had to charge one person with taking care of this entire area, he created the post of housing coordinator for both housing and urban renewal (see chapter 6).

Clark soon saw that the next important task was to relieve the unemployed—especially the disadvantaged unemployed—by halting industry's flight from the city, attracting new firms, and training the poorly skilled. In the second half of his term, when the end of the Korean War brought in its wake much higher rates of unemployment, Clark was made even more forcefully aware of the problem. As early as his inaugural address, Clark had spoken of the need to "stimulate the growth of commerce and industry . . . [and] the creation of more and better jobs." [22] He fought hard to help the GPM against odds to start the Food Distribution Center (a nonprofit corporation)—one of the first such organizations. Walter Phillips, Clark's director of commerce, suggested to Clark new ways to attract industry and to stimulate the expansion of existing industry by the creation of an industrial park within the city. Since Clark could not afford another fight, the

19. Speech to the Greater Philadelphia Movement, October 8, 1951, in Philadelphia *Bulletin*, October 9, 1951.
20. Speech to City Business Club, January 9, 1953 (in private collection).
21. Speech at Public Housing Authority luncheon, April 17, 1953.
22. Inaugural address.

plan was left to Dilworth to carry out (see chapter 7). Clark also tried to obtain federal funds for training the disadvantaged. But neither he nor Dilworth was successful in this attempt, partly because of national policy, specifically President Eisenhower's opposition to such legislation (see chapter 11). For other attempts to stimulate economic revival and employment, the reader is referred to chapters 8 and 9.

Clark gradually realized that his various programs must complement one another in order to be successful. Interrelations between programs must include the social as well as economic and physical aspects. The Community Renewal Program most fully exemplified such interrelations toward the end of the period, but they were realized in part as each program was undertaken. A home and an environment accessible to places of work, a sufficient income, an education adequate for useful work and constructive leisure—the attainment of these goals had to be effected jointly, or none could be attained. Housing, income, education, and mobility are inseparably linked in expressing the social and economic structure of the city. "Of all the big cities," writes Jeanne Lowe, "Philadelphia has come closest to a comprehensive approach to the complex of challenges, confronting our urban centers. . . . It recognized relationships between basic elements, and these perceptions underlie its planning and revitalization strategy."[23]

### The First Budgets

The first set of choices the administration was called upon to make concerned operating and capital budgets. Before the year was out, the administration had to make the tough decisions which would determine priorities. It was the first time that careful deliberation led to long-range budget choices, because the new Home Rule Charter had regularized the method of dovetailing financial policy and operational as well as capital program decisions.

Brown and Gilbert say of the system prevailing in Philadelphia: "A number of significant capital budget and program decisions are made in the cabinet. . . . Decisions of the cabinet on

23. Jeanne Lowe, *Cities in a Race with Time* (Random House, 1967), pp. 313 ff.

such points are not reached by votes, but by a process of discussion and progress of consensus, often extending over several meetings. . . . Such review necessarily requires scanning the entire capital program to determine where room can be found for the larger items relating to administration policy. . . . Such large projects have usually been matters for decision by the Mayor and the cabinet and have often originated at the top of the City Administration." [24]

The capital program in particular had an automatic priority system built into the process of time scheduling for a particular program or set of projects within the six-year program. The higher the assigned priority, the earlier the program was to become a reality; the later its timing, the greater the possibility that other projects would supersede it before the time for its execution arrived. This important administrative tool forced cabinet members to think in terms of goals and directions they wanted the city to take. And it forced them periodically to make decisions which at least implied priority considerations (see chapter 5).

## The Cabinet Gropes for Guidelines

As decisions were made in the cabinet, it was easy to lose awareness of the fact that some headway was being made in the developmental program as a whole. Careful study of those handwritten cabinet minutes of the first years of Mayor Clark's administration provides evidence of the progress made in these meetings: [25] "We tend to try to be too efficient, rather than to concentrate on matters of importance for the public," said Walter M. Phillips.[26] And Rafsky felt: "The administration's strategy should be sharpened. We should tighten up on the performance and point up the objectives and priorities and then carry them out." [27] In the meeting of October 26, 1953, Clark said: "We have failed to define goals"; Abraham Freedman urged that cabinet members

24. William H. Brown and Charles E. Gilbert, *Planning Municipal Investment: A Case Study of Philadelphia* (University of Pennsylvania Press, 1961), pp. 72, 82.
25. In files of Pennsylvania Economy League-Bureau of Municipal Research. Made available by courtesy of Lennox Moak, with permission of Joseph S. Clark.
26. Cabinet meeting, January 17, 1953.
27. Cabinet meeting, November 9, 1953.

"set aside a time for a special meeting for creative thinking and ideas. We are too busy at cabinet to solve day to day problems"; and Lennox Moak suggested the need for "a statement of the tenets of this administration about the administration's views [to be] put out at an opportune time." A month later, Mayor Clark suggested: "I would like to see an overall look, not a piece-meal approach. . . . We should consider it on a higher plane. . . . I would like to find out about objectives. . . . We should put down our own goals in relation to total city growth." [28]

The new administration found itself faced with a number of new problems concerning developmental emphasis, and the question its officers had to keep asking themselves was how the problems related to each other and to the city as a whole. "It is vital to provide the necessary guides for better programming. This requires the formulation of long-range developmental policies and a determination of the best means to reach them." [29]

Before his term was up, Joseph Clark enumerated the following overall priorities closest to his heart: (1) a comprehensive approach to housing, (2) preemption of city surplus land for industrial uses, (3) improvement of mass transit, (4) improvement of parking, and (5) completion of the expressway network.[30] Dilworth, early in his term, when he came to one of the first meetings of the City Planning Commission, listed (1) a comprehensive master plan for the city, (2) overall development coordination, (3) development of industrial parks, (4) Center City rehabilitation, (5) a new approach to urban renewal, and (6) execution of the overall transportation plan.

It should not, however, be assumed that priorities are determined in relation to goals decided upon. In many cases pragmatic considerations are decisive. It is understandable that federal funds available in different ratios to local expenditures may lead to a misallocation of local resources. This is regrettable, yet if it is the only way to get the city council to appropriate the funds, it will be done. Priority- and goal-oriented thinking ultimately may be unable to change pragmatic decisions but will

28. Cabinet meeting, November 24, 1953.
29. Development coordinator, Annual Report for 1957. The report was written by William L. Rafsky while he was still housing coordinator, though he published it as development coordinator.
30. Informal talk at the American Municipal Association, November 1954.

make the local government aware of the distortions incurred when these influences are yielded to. For example, one may be willing to allow external forces to change the relative sequence of one's first few priorities. If, however, the new alignment completely upsets one's basic order of priority, it might be worth holding fast to the original decision. This was frequently the way Philadelphia tried to handle it.

To compare the accomplishments of Clark's four years and Dilworth's six years is a natural parlor game. There is no question that they both wanted the same things and worked together to achieve them. But the difference in their personalities made inevitable the use of diverse means and approaches. The substantive distinction between the kinds of programs they emphasized is, as we have seen, largely explained by the circumstances which necessitated "doing first things first." The contrast between their sets of priorities might be explained by the two administrations' gradual perception of the relative urgency of the issues involved. Ideas and programs stemmed from the "best brains" on Clark's team, many of whom stayed on. Would Dilworth, had he been the first reform mayor, have attracted a different set of men, to whom he would have delegated a great deal more responsibility? Many of the accomplishments of both administrations can be explained in terms of individual top men (not necessarily elected executives), the freedom they enjoyed, or the power they were able to arrogate.

Pragmatism is the strength of American politics. Priorities among different developmental plans should be clear in the minds of public officials; yet officials should also be ready to change their minds if more promising possibilities open up. Both Joseph S. Clark and Richardson Dilworth were catalysts in their ability to see which of the problems of urban society needed immediate remedies, to understand how they could be dealt with, and to shift to other programs as new needs arose. The minds of both mayors remained open. They listened to all the civic groups and professionals and then decided. Yet, in working out their administrations' priorities, they stuck firmly to their principles which guided the city's over-all development.

## James Tate: Decline of the Reform?

James H. J. Tate succeeded to the mayoralty automatically from the office of president of city council. Having held that job for years, he was naturally familiar with the programs the reform had introduced and with much of their detail. He ran on his own in 1963 and 1967 and won. There was, however, a difference in his approach between these two terms.

It is difficult to escape a feeling of ambivalence about his performance as far as the continuation of the reform is concerned. As he was an "organization" man, there was the fear that access to power might lead to the party "machine" taking over. But Tate held a firm grip on the mantle of reform in 1963. "I am a partner in the reform and renaissance started under Clark and Dilworth," he said. "The key to the campaign is my record and the record of the last two Administrations. I was their spokesman in City Council and had to get the program through." [31] One councilman said to this author: "He just had to get along with the reform ideas of Clark and Dilworth; he kept quoting those two as if they were the Bible." But Tate also held on to his party background and stayed as leader of his old ward. By 1965 it had become clear that, though he lost some of the professional talent he had inherited, he did not deliberately get rid of good professionals either. Nor had he discontinued reform programs, although he had not started any new ones.

Tate was a native Philadelphian who had climbed the ladder of party organization. He had been close to "Jim" Clark and "Bill" Green. He had attended parochial schools and St. Joseph's College and, though he lacked some credits for a law degree, he was granted one by Temple University in 1960. His background was humble, and it was inevitable, given Philadelphia's tradition, that Tate should feel at a disadvantage socially, especially by comparison with Clark and Dilworth.

After a long period of Protestant incumbency in the mayor's office, a number of Philadelphians welcomed the election of an Irish Catholic. Tate was inclined to pay special attention to demands made by a Catholic parish or a parochial school. This gave him an entirely different power base from his predecessors—

31. *Pennsylvania Guardian,* October 4, 1963.

ethnically, religiously, and even geographically within the city. His electoral support came largely from the working and lower-middle class—traditional Democrats and largely Catholic. A tight ward organization was the basis of his political strength. By the primary in 1967, he had moved away quite decidedly from the reform base, the embrace of which he had needed so urgently four years earlier.

Probably Tate's most important characteristic was his preoccupation with minute details—the exact opposite of Clark and Dilworth. He seemed to prefer to spend his energy on the "nuts and bolts" of governmental machinery. He was unwilling to delegate to others, whether dealing with major matters or small details, and seemed to endow everything with equal importance. His was a "taut ship" (a popular Tate phrase), in which scandals such as those toward the end of the Dilworth administration could not have occurred undetected. His perennial tardiness, though accounted for by his having to check on some routine matters or deliver a minor speech, did not help his image.

Tate expected his staff to be on call twenty-four hours a day and demanded absolute loyalty from those working for him; he was known to vilify them publicly if a mistake was made. His irascibility made him a hard man to work for.

### The Problem of Politics

Shortly after Tate's election in 1963, William Green died. Green's contention that he could control Tate was borne out by correspondence in which Tate sought Green's approval before making appointments.[32] As Tate was unable to get his friends aligned as fast as did Francis Smith, the latter became city chairman; the feud between Tate and Smith lasted throughout the four years. Smith's position made Tate even more anxious to continue his identification with the reform. City councilmen showed him sufficient loyalty not to oppose many of his programs. "The point is simply that he is one of ours," said one councilman to this author. "He basically got what he wanted, although he has not asked for outlandish ideas; actually, he asked for a good program."

When the office of district attorney came up for reelection in

32. E.g., Mayor Tate to William Green, Jr., February 18 and March 13, 1963 (in City Archives).

1965, there was a strong movement, which Senator Clark supported, not to slate the incumbent district attorney as he had acted too much as apologist and captive of the Democratic organization. But when Clark refused to nominate him instead for a federal judgeship, Francis Smith insisted upon the incumbent's renomination for district attorney. The Republicans, under new city leadership, thereupon nominated a reform Democrat and ADA member, Arlen Specter, who won. In 1965, Senator Clark, who had endorsed Tate two years before, stated frankly: "The last three years have shown disturbing signs of a backsliding toward the bad old days." While he felt that Tate was "attempting sincerely to carry on the tradition he inherited," he thought that "Philadelphia's reform movement is unquestionably in bad health. Unless new blood is pumped into its system, it may not be long before the patient dies . . . and, in a few short years, another political revolution takes place and the minority Republican party . . . [may] bring another reform movement to the city." [33]

Clark's warning that another reform movement might be in the offing—this time by the Republicans—seemed to be borne out in 1967. "A group of young candidates, practically all of them respectable, have managed to identify in the public mind more closely with the Clark-Dilworth style than the Democrats," said one observer.[34]

Arlen Specter ran for mayor and lost; Thacher Longstreth, who had opposed Dilworth in 1955 and was now executive vice-president of the Chamber of Commerce, ran for councilman-at-large. He was the only one of the "new breed" of Republicans to win—and many felt that he should have been slated for mayor (as he was in 1971). A number of the remainder of the ticket were known for their reform leanings. Tate won by only 10,000 votes (Dilworth in 1959 had won by 250,000); this was about as many votes as those received by the ultraconservative candidate of the Constitutional party, who, by taking votes primarily from the Republicans, appeared to be responsible for the defeat of Specter's ticket. Among the reasons evidently behind Tate's narrow victory were labor's all-out campaigning in recognition

33. Philadelphia *Bulletin*, February 19, 1965.
34. Bernard McCormick, "Billy," *Philadelphia Magazine*, February 1967, p. 53.

for Tate's relatively large number of labor appointments; job and housing promises made to Negroes; Specter's refusal to follow the charter provision that he resign as district attorney before running for mayor; and Tate's appointment of Frank Rizzo as police commissioner, which won him the Italian vote. The liberals' disapproval of this last action mattered little to Tate, since he did not count on their vote anyway. But it is important that business in general, and the GPM specifically, came out for Specter, although this did, surprisingly enough, not seem to have hurt Tate's chances. Green's son, young Congressman Bill Green, was installed as city chairman, but he broke with Tate two years later.

Tate had received a number of large campaign contributions from builders, developers, industrial firms, consultant engineers, and architects, as well as from appointees (and would-be appointees) to boards and commissions. Specter charged that this represented a "shake-down" and the selling of favors.

After the election, Tate moved quickly to reorganize many of the independent boards and commissions, to bring them in one way or another under his control. These bodies, dealing with vital city problems, had been jealously guarded against interference by the former two mayors.

"Once again," the Philadelphia *Bulletin* editorialized, "Philadelphia politics has seemed to revert to a type that weary citizens had repudiated—the old, narrow partisan view, the aroma of inside deals, back-scratching, and City Hall favoritism . . . crass political bidding for favor at taxpayer's expense . . . the familiar rumors of the cheap improprieties in city business flourishing once again." [35]

Long-time members of the mayor's staff contrasted the easy and informal communication of Dilworth with the rigidly structured and authoritarian mechanism under Tate with its clear "pecking order." That feeling was part of the reason why many of the men mentioned as being instrumental throughout the reform period, either as top staff appointees or members of boards and commissions, were no longer to be seen in City Hall.[36] Some had moved

35. Philadelphia *Bulletin*, October 29, 1967.
36. For example, Graham Finney, John Bailey, Charles Frazier, William Rafsky, Richard McConnell, Peter Schauffler, Holmes Perkins, and Howard Leary.

to civic organizations in Philadelphia and thus could continue to exert their influence on the city. Others moved to different city administrations, universities, or authorities, where they could apply the principles and ideas of the Philadelphia reform.[37]

This later period of the Philadelphia reform has been characterized as one of bifurcation between two kinds of political ethos —one "favoring the private-regarding, immigrant ethos, . . . both party machines, civil service officials, lower middle class white ethnic groups, and City Hall," the other a "coalition of the business and civic elite, reformers and moderates in both parties, upper middle and upper class . . . and professional urbanists who have a public-regarding, middle-class good government ethos."[38]

### Civic Groups and Developmental Programs

In his dealings with the civic and business groups that had formed so important a basis of reform achievements, Tate's personal approach was strained. They, in turn, were not happy. "Working with former mayors was fun, now it had become hard work." Business was leery: how long could they continue without much contact or leadership? The result of this situation "is the limited participation by business in City Hall sponsored poverty and manpower programs, matters that require much coordinated planning. Each works separately on the same problems. Business has not let its dissatisfaction with Tate curtail its participation in social programs; it has simply avoided City Hall, made end runs around it, and developed its own programs. Furthermore, the poor relationship between the mayor and business has also affected the willingness of employers to commit themselves to the hiring of specific numbers of graduates from City Hall sponsored job training programs."[39]

37. Among the institutions benefiting from the presence of these individuals outside Philadelphia are New York's Mayor Lindsay's administration, the New York City Transit Authority, the Detroit Metropolitan Fund, the Washington, D.C., Transit Authority, the Regional Science Research Institute, the Universities of California and Wisconsin, Northwestern University, and Yale University.

38. David Rogers, *The Management of Big Cities* (Sage Publications, 1971), p. 88. This analysis is partly stimulated by the writings of Edward Banfield and James Wilson, and of Richard Hofstadter, both referred to earlier.

39. Ibid., pp. 93–94.

Members of civic and business groups, who had been in and out of Clark's and Dilworth's office (board and staff) and enjoyed the goodwill and trusted the judgment of these men, felt deep disappointment with a mayor whose offhand manner made close relationships difficult. It has been suggested that Tate tried in vain to suppress his feeling that people from outside City Hall were "meddling" in matters that were not their concern, as well as his belief that they had too proprietary an attitude toward city development. His assistants have asserted, however, that he made every effort to show how much he wanted the cooperation of the business community.

Tate clearly intended to continue the developmental programs which the reform had already started, and to implement those which were only in the planning stage. He virtually had no other choice, since the commitments already made assured that the reform development plans were irreversible, certainly in the near future.

To underscore this emphasis on development, Tate created a small development council to advise him on long-range problems and to help him gain a broader view (the details he already knew from his service in the city council). He appeared to be at ease with this small group in discussing the city's future development. The members were virtually the old team of the cabinet-level members who had been involved in development.

Much as he enjoyed the advice of the development council, Tate took the position of the cabinet very seriously. "Nothing happens until it is reviewed by the cabinet. It is really an important instrument because it is so small. . . . I get a chance to get different points of view. . . . I have to make the decision, but I like to hear other people talk about it." [40]

*Priorities*

"Tate has not blocked the renaissance programs thought out by eggheads," said one councilman. "He is knowledgeable enough to know that all this must be done to maintain his image, and his image is very important to him. He has not, as might have been expected, funneled patronage into the police, nor has he ruined

40. Interview by the author with Mayor Tate, March 23, 1965.

any of the previous plans." But what would happen when Tate had to act in areas for which no blueprint had been left? As his term of office progressed, it was inevitable that Tate would express preferences. He was not inclined to make programmatic statements—even the official papers he issued in response to Specter's elaborate position papers in the 1967 campaign were full of dry facts—but one looks in vain for policy declarations. We shall have to judge from his actions what programs he thought important enough to be assigned priority status.

Tate clearly continued to feel that urban renewal was worth the effort. He also streamlined the administrative structure for redevelopment by assigning relocation to the newly appointed deputy managing director for housing (see chapter 6). Industrial and commercial renewal projects proceeded apace; Tate also encouraged the nonprofit corporation for industry to keep industrial firms in Philadelphia and to sell more industrial land so that existing jobs could at least be saved, if not new ones created. This included new developments downtown. He considered transportation an important part of his own program but failed to exert clear-cut decisions and decisive leadership in this area (see chapter 5).

The period over which Tate presided was in many ways different from that of his predecessors. Events were moving faster than Tate could move Philadelphia's programs. The participation requirement of the war on poverty had permeated all community activities, and the accommodation to it and to Negro demands called for a sophisticated strategy on the part of City Hall. (New Haven was much more successful than Philadelphia in the area of "human resource" organization in the ghetto—a precursor of the poverty program—for which both cities received Ford Foundation grants.) Other changes in the emphasis of domestic grants-in-aid legislation in the "Great Society" made it necessary for mayors of large cities to recast their policy for relating to the federal government. Thus Tate cannot be entirely faulted for having less expertise than his two predecessors would have had in this new situation.

"There are several levels of explanation for the decline of reform in Philadelphia, and it would be a gross oversimplification to suggest that the change in mayors was the prime cause," David Rogers summarizes. "Nevertheless, it was significant, and in ways that go well beyond mere differences in personality and leadership skills between Tate and his two reform predecessors." [41]

41. Rogers, *The Management of Big Cities*, p. 85.

# 4    *Policy-Making and Coordination*

Why is it so difficult to determine how policy is made in local government? To begin with, each policy is going to reflect the personalities involved, the issue that generated the need for a policy, and, above all, the structure of the government itself. Built into any policy-making model is the formal and legal mechanism by which a local government reaches decisions, and the determination of the issue itself. Included in the model must be the political repercussions which some of the policy-makers will face, including the imminence of reelection, and the degree and kind of pressures which will be exerted by groups to be affected by a new policy. The variables are infinite. Attempts have been made in case studies of localities to factor out these elements, but the validity of the resulting generalizations may well be questioned.

For the purposes of this discussion, the term "development" is used to describe the programs designed to change the physical, economic, and/or social environment of city or area, or a synthesis of any or all of them. Predominantly physical programs encompass such areas as public improvements, urban redevelopment, and historical renewal; those geared to economic improvement deal with industry, commerce, manpower, and the like; while the social development programs are addressed, for example, to minority housing, Skid Row, and issues of higher education. The extent to which these categories overlap was grossly underestimated in the 1950s, but the Philadelphia reform government realized increasingly that the three categories were dependent upon each other. Those programs which dealt primarily with social changes alone, such as poverty, race, or health and welfare, and not also with physical and economic ones are not dealt with in this book. Policy-making in these areas tends to be arrived at in a different way.

## Policy-Making by Officials

With the charter had come self-determination for Philadelphia. The mayor enjoyed the prerogative of a great deal of decision-making power, subject only to council approval where its legislative or appropriation functions were involved. The council was also a forum for citizen complaints against administrative actions by the executive, and the responsiveness of individual councilmen may sometimes have depended on whether they were elected by ward or at large. Responsiveness to the will of the dominant political party was determined more by the political security of the individual councilmen and the strength of the party chairman. Even though under the new charter Philadelphia had a "strong mayor" type of government, the will of the city council could effectively veto decisions of the executive at crucial points.

Philadelphia's reform administration had constantly to be on guard lest its decision-making in pursuit of long-range goals be preempted by day-to-day housekeeping operations. Further, it had to keep its sights fixed on its own constructive goals rather than on policies resulting from reaction to other governmental bodies such as the state or the federal government. The cabinet intended to remain free to develop its own priorities. It failed only when events beyond its control impinged on this calculated aloofness, or when it was unable to arrive at a clear priority decision. Thus, it was not statutory limitations that inhibited the mayor's decision-making powers, but rather the nature of the objective and the human element.

The official (hierarchical) chain of command within city government went from the policy-making power of the mayor and his cabinet to the fifteen department heads who were charged with implementation. They in turn delegated administration to their professional staffs. The executive branch also had a number of lateral relationships, both formal and informal. The commissioner of streets, for example, chaired a committee charged with implementing design and construction of expressways, on which at least the Public Property Department, the Planning Commission staff, the Urban Traffic and Transportation Board, and the State Highway Department had to be represented. The resulting exchange of information and coordination helped either in making policy or in implementing it. Ad hoc committees of this kind (which also existed in other cities) laid the groundwork of administrative flexibility for committees on a broader basis.

## Nonprofit Corporations

Trailblazing by the Philadelphia reform administration was manifested, perhaps most conspicuously, by the evolution and eventual proliferation of nonprofit corporations. Through this device, largely untried at the time, its developmental programs embraced both local government and private capital—a combination often expressing deep concern, commitment, and involvement. A corollary to this was a significant input from the private sector into the policy-making process. This input far transcended such predictable private-sector participation as negotiation for development of an urban renewal site or bidding on a public housing project. It meant allocating priority to long-range benefits to the greatest number of Philadelphia citizens on a citywide basis.

The sponsorship of these nonprofit corporations was often shared by a public body and a private group; commitment was to a public or quasi-public function. The first such quasi-public effort, resulting in the "Greater Philadelphia Exhibition," predated the reform administration. During the reform period the nonprofit corporations increasingly thrust upon their unpaid officers a novel degree of public responsibility. The Food Distribution Center Corporation, started by the Greater Philadelphia Movement, was created to eliminate the obsolete, unsanitary, and inefficient Dock Street facilities for wholesale trade in various food commodities and to relocate the food trade to a modern facility at a site in South Philadelphia (see chapter 7). The land was acquired through the Redevelopment Authority, the site was improved, and public services were installed. The public interest, represented by investment of public funds, fully justified its designation as a quasi-public corporation, though a single civic entity was sponsoring the enterprise. No profit was to benefit any individual connected with the corporation, and, after repayment of its obligations, all assets would be conveyed to the city of Philadelphia. By city council ordinance, nine city officials were to be appointed to its board of directors.

Throughout subsequent chapters, other such nonprofit corporations will be referred to. Purposes, articles of incorporation, by-laws, and enabling ordinances varied widely. More important, the relations between the involvement of the private incorporator and the public power which could be exercised upon the action of the private "partner" depended on the specific purpose of each corporation. The Philadelphia Industrial Development Corporation dealt with the attraction of new and the retention of old industry in Philadelphia; the Old Philadelphia Development Corporation with Center City problems; the Philadelphia Housing Development Corporation with new ways to help low-income families to obtain shelter at a reasonable price, and so forth. Thus the institution of the quasi-public corporation implied a relation of trust between the public and civic or business groups for jointly pursuing the public purpose. Civic leaders exerted an important influence on the content of programs even where programs were totally financed by a public body. Conversely, if financing was principally private, but public involvement was essential (as with the Old Philadelphia Development Corporation), the public voice was heeded. Such a reciprocal relationship could not easily have occurred in a situation where, as in Dahl's New Haven, the mayor takes central control.

The nonprofit corporations experienced little basic disagreement about what was in the public good, because the ground had been prepared by mutual understanding. Many problems were raised by the question "how?" but none by the question "what for?" In other words, Philadelphia's ability to arrive at "consensus," coupled with its inventiveness and flexibility, was exemplified by the use of this public-private institution.

## Joint Policy Determination

The representatives of the public and of these nonprofit corporations would discuss the best way to carry out their joint purpose and ensure that the specific concerns of all interested public and private parties were adequately considered. This was not, as some have insisted, a case of "bargaining" between two opposing parties and an eventual negotiated settlement.[1]

Policies for these quasi-public corporations evolved, then, from the joint meetings of executives of the corporations and representatives of public and private institutions involved. The federal government was represented when any of its installations were affected, as, for example, the National Independence Historical Park. State highway officials were present when freeways were being considered, but so also were representatives of those corporations which might be affected by the freeways, for instance in their planned expansion. The presence of other quasi-public bodies was often suggested, even if no involvement of theirs was to be discussed—they were invited naturally, so to speak, like a member of the family.

When either the mayor himself or his representative was present at nonprofit corporation meetings, the mayor's input was as a participant in the deliberations, so that while his desires may have been decisive, they only rarely had to be enunciated as such. While criticism was at times leveled at the duplication among meetings, the total program emanating was the product of gradually emerging consensus based on the concerns expressed by all those involved. This may have been one reason why the cabinet was reluctant to impose its own—or the mayor's—priorities.

The first committee established to effect coordinated decision-making reflected Mayor Clark's first priority: shelter. The "Interagency Committee on Housing" had as its regular members the Housing and the Redevelopment authorities, the city managing director, the Planning Commission, the Department of Licenses and Inspections, the Commission on Human Relations, civic groups such as the Philadelphia Housing Association and the Citizens' Council on City Planning, and pertinent nonprofit corporations as they were created over time (see chapter 6). An "Interagency Committee on Center City" was created, soon to be

1. Cyril Roseman, "Public-Private Cooperation and Negotiation in Downtown Redevelopment Decision-Process in Philadelphia" (Ph.D. dissertation, Princeton University, 1963). The detailed investigation of concrete cases is extremely useful, and the details are well carried out. It is only the conception of the relationship as a matter of collective bargaining rather than of joint policy decisions with which this author disagrees.

followed by one on "Industry and Commerce." Once the practice of discussing policy in these formal committees was established, informal ones sprang up as the need made itself felt. Along with the Center City Committee, one dealing more specifically with questions of design and buildings seemed to become necessary; the Old Philadelphia Development Corporation suggested and started it, and it stopped meeting when the particular need seemed satisfied (see chapter 8). Each interagency committee had its regular membership. Those on Industry and Commerce, for example, were always attended by the managing director, the Department of Commerce, the development coordinator, the transportation coordinator, the city economist, the City Planning Commission, the Redevelopment Authority, the Chamber of Commerce, the Philadelphia Industrial Development Corporation, the Food Distribution Center, the Old Philadelphia Development Corporation, and sometimes representatives of the regional office of the U.S. Department of Housing and Urban Development. The possibility of such committees degenerating into information exchanges, if increasingly lower-level officials attended, had been recognized by the time the other interagency committees were established. To emphasize the policy-making role, a rule was established whereby no agency could participate unless it was represented at least by its executive or his deputy. This rule, and an agenda prepared jointly by several of the departments involved (and often the executives of nonprofit corporations), helped to keep the meetings geared to policy.

On a more technical level were the facilities committees. Different departments and agencies met to discuss actions that were made necessary as a result of policy decisions, to help carry them out in the most logical sequence and as expeditiously as possible. Their deliberations sometimes showed that the policy, or at least some subsidiary policy, had to be changed. An expressway committee decided on necessary utilities and access streets; a food distribution committee laid out the necessary sequence of renewal actions as different parts of the Food Distribution Center became available; and committees on specific highways were convened.

## Coordination as an Art

Recognition of and agreement on the interrelatedness of the different issues and the sequence of steps to treat them was not enough. Someone had to make certain that full understanding of the meaning and purpose of the proposed action was shared by all concerned, and that the means chosen for achievement were those most likely to succeed. This had to be carried out at every level of execution and hence had to be directed by someone who had taken part in the policy-making process, so that basic misunderstanding or failure in communication could be avoided or at least minimized. Philadelphia attempted—with varying degrees of success—to achieve this quality of coordination in all areas of activity: development, transportation, legislation, and economic policy. The lion's share of the task of coordination had to be carried out at the level of mayor and cabinet by someone like the mayor's executive secretary, who had the mayor's full confidence, was privy to his wishes, and was aware of those actions of the various committees the mayor approved of or was at least content to see executed. As the first executive secretary to Mayor Clark, William Rafsky soon proved adept at the role of coordinator. Although he became the person most clearly identified with coordination as he operated as the mayor's direct representative, others were charged with this responsibility in areas such as transportation, administration, and economic activity. The success of many of Philadelphia's programs seemed to be increasingly attributable to the practice of charging one individual with responsibility for pulling together the various developmental programs and forging a team from the pertinent city agencies and civic organizations.

A good coordinator must have a strong sense for personal interrelationship, and, as Lennox Moak has suggested, might be compared to someone standing behind a floodlight which swings around 360 degrees: as the floodlight passes, a good observer notices many objects in the brief time. Having sufficient patience to wait for the "sense of the meeting," William Rafsky seemed to fit Philadelphia's mood. An authoritarian like New York's Robert Moses could not have been successful in Philadelphia. John Bailey, as transportation coordinator, also had the ability to wait for an emerging consensus, but was often not able to do so be-

cause, having to deal with representatives of suburban governments, he had to push harder to be sure that a clear result was
arrived at in the meeting.

A pitfall in coordination is to get overinvolved with minutiae
or with operating functions against the advice of those who are
sophisticated enough to see the dangers. Rafsky had difficulty in
delegating and thus tended to spend too much time putting out
brushfires, leaving too little time for long-term policy preparation.
Another pitfall, which Rafsky avoided, is to see each project as
important on its own and tied only superficially to the other
projects in the program. "Projectitis," a disease which Philadelphia tried to avoid at all costs, was a danger that Edmund Bacon
and his staff were apt to fall prey to. Thinking in terms of overall priorities was the suggested remedy which Philadelphia tried
to apply. Both pitfalls were apt at times to mar the performance
of Philadelphia's coordinative machinery. Any city taking Philadelphia as a model should be especially cognizant of the twin
dangers.

### Coordination Starts in Renewal

Coordination grew along with the programs of the Philadelphia
renaissance. Since housing was the first program, we shall trace
the genesis of coordination through that field of action. Mayor
Clark soon recognized that shelter, particularly for low-income
families, was basic to many of the social ills he saw permeating his
city. His inaugural address made reference to his intent in that
respect. It was not until his third year in office, however, that he
was able to announce the special action needed to ensure the
necessary coordination between housing and urban renewal. Rafsky was a natural for the position of housing coordinator, created
in mid-1953. The omission of such a function from the new city
charter illustrates the difficulty of even a new instrument's remaining responsive to rapidly developing urban needs. This coordinating job was not going to be easy. Two existing independent authorities (Housing and Redevelopment) had to be brought
in line with city policy, if possible without encroaching upon
their independent status.

The Housing Association applauded the decision in a memorandum to Mayor Clark: "Your proposal to have a Housing

Coordinator directly responsible to the Mayor appears to be the inevitable and proper next step. Again it puts Philadelphia in the lead. . . . He should be a part of the Mayor's office. . . . He would *not* have any operating functions under his direct supervision. . . . Once he engages in operations, he loses his detachment as a coordinator. . . . He would be a persuader and an expediter. This task would require very delicate handling; to be most successful it is a job for an artist in group relations." [2]

Predating the establishment of that position was a history of mutual consultation which had started in 1952 with an area planning conference. Its purpose was to bring city officials and civic groups together on a regular basis; but the participants realized that only general discussions resulted which, though very enlightening, really did not amount to policy decisions.[3] Then the Redevelopment Authority set up an official Development Committee, chaired by Dorothy Montgomery, a newly appointed member, who was managing director of the Philadelphia Housing Association. It was a small, powerful committee—Rafsky, Robert Mitchell, Holmes Perkins, and Martin Meyerson were members —which discussed seriously the question of how policy decisions should be approached. One of the first statements on the question of the consideration of policy alternatives—written by Martin Meyerson much earlier than other statements of this concept— emerged from its discussions; [4] the report of the Central Urban Renewal Area (see below) was clearly influenced by that statement. Late in 1952 the committee recommended that a system for reviewing priorities among redevelopment programs be established to review potential renewal areas and the possible solutions for the peculiar problem of each.

On that basis David Wallace, the planning director of the Redevelopment Authority, started a study of the main area where such decisions had to be made, the Central Urban Redevelop-

2. Confidential memorandum, October 5, 1953.

3. The conscientiously kept minutes of the Area Planning Conference prove this very clearly, as did its interim report in December 1952 (in files of Philadelphia Housing Association).

4. It is an excellent statement, with much theoretical value, but unfortunately was never published. Martin Meyerson was then professor of city planning at the University of Pennsylvania and is now president of that university.

ment Area (CURA). The core of the city was divided into areas of different degrees of blight, and appropriate treatment was suggested (see chapter 6). Wallace was deeply convinced of the importance of a plan as a basis for deciding priorities. He claimed that "policy explanations should be included in criteria for project priorities." [5]

Although Rafsky did not at first intend to use the CURA study in this fashion, he soon realized that its proposals gave him the necessary pegs on which to hang his coordination efforts. The study supported his desire that clear-cut priority determination be given a chance—in fact, it was the first official recognition that urban renewal, to be meaningful, must be comprehensive. In cabinet and other policy meetings Rafsky had repeatedly pushed for a clear determination of the city's goals and for a methodology which would direct the city's problems into a logical system. Though first confined to the housing area, he also saw the need for city action to support industry and other economic activities and thus to create jobs. He understood that the availability of jobs and the availability of homes could complement each other. The breadth of his approach made it natural that he should increasingly coordinate the different facets of the developmental programs.

### Different Devices Used

The various joint committees—always attended and often chaired by Rafsky—did not appear the most likely places for formulating policy, given their unusual composition. They were thought, by some, to be only the icing on the cake, with policy decisions actually made elsewhere—by the cabinet or in ad hoc meetings in smoke-filled rooms. Or it was believed that Rafsky forced the mayor's will on the reluctant participants, less openly, perhaps, than Robert Moses in New York or Ed Logue in New Haven. Did Rafsky merely make people feel as if they were participating in policy-making?

Many important policy questions were discussed and decided at the meetings. If some participants arrived "cold," the chair-

5. Joint meeting of the Philadelphia Redevelopment Authority and the City Planning Commission, May 24, 1954. Wallace had expressed similar ideas in a letter to Frank Lammer, executive director of the Philadelphia Redevelopment Authority, December 14, 1953 (in City Archives).

man certainly did not. "If I knew that somebody else had strong feelings on a particular point," Rafsky said, "I discussed it with him before, trying to straighten out any problems before it came to the open meeting." If the mayor had a strong opinion, the meeting might have to be prepared more carefully. Rafsky, or members of his staff, could achieve a great deal by discussing issues ahead of the meeting with representatives of the other agencies who would attend and who might have some doubts. "Call that structuring the meetings if you will," Rafsky admitted. A statement about New Haven's Ed Logue makes an interesting contrast: "There was some resistance to these efforts, but Logue cut through them because the Mayor was behind him and because he went to these sessions knowing precisely what he wanted. He met the opposition with logic, forcefulness . . . and, when necessary, anger. Logue also paid a personal price in these battles. His critics . . . felt that during these struggles he became increasingly insensitive to those with whom he worked." [6] The difference between Logue's personality and those of Philadelphia's coordinators—not only Rafsky—who were patient and worked with an emerging consensus, is instructive.

There was little doubt that these interagency committees fulfilled an important policy function, especially early in the reform. And most felt that they continued to do so. But there were some who later believed that they outlived their usefulness, for officials sometimes thought that policy need be discussed only once and not aired in subsequent meetings.[7] Others felt that priorities were discussed only occasionally, because the main directions had been set (as stated in a 1965 CRP report).[8]

But one point is important: the principle of joint policy-making was never side-stepped. This author knows of no case where anyone involved felt that his viewpoint was ignored or that a decision was not fully implemented: subsequent meetings of these committees would have given ample chance for such complaints.

Rafsky personally did much of the coordination, keeping his

6. Allan R. Talbot, *The Mayor's Game* (Harper and Row, 1967), p. 39.
7. Interviews with Joseph Turchi, Harold Wise, Cushing Dolbear, Mead Smith Karras, Richard Buford, William Rafsky, John A. Bailey, and William Ludlow.
8. Community Renewal Program Report, *Possible Administrative Arrangements for Renewal and Development* (April 1965), p. 83.

finger on every pulse. He attended meetings of the authority boards and the City Planning Commission, and was made a member of the boards of most nonprofit corporations and other formal and informal city committees and civic groups. He picked up his signals in cabinet and carried them out where and when he could. He did much by telephone, in the corridors, at other informal encounters, and at the "commissioners' meeting." Held quarterly for department heads, their deputies, board and commission members, and top professionals, this meeting enabled between fifty and seventy-five of the top members of the mayor's official family to meet informally. Rafsky knew who would probably be there, and he came with small cards in his pocket to remind him whom he wanted to talk to. Other professionals, too, knew how to use these meetings, especially those who had started a new program and wanted to convince others of its viability. These and other informal gatherings were prime forums for coordination.

## Relations with the Mayor

None of this top-level coordination would have worked without the full backing of the mayor. Rafsky had to speak for the mayor and be believed, and this relationship had to be taken for granted to the extent that he never had to *state* that he was speaking for the mayor. Even those who may have harbored some doubts never cared to put them to a test. If they had, the mayor would have backed Rafsky. Rafsky maintained this personal trust and confidence with Clark, Dilworth, and Tate. (Some critics of his operation charged him with eliciting the opinions of others because he "represented the mayor," but then screening them through his own preconceived notions, thus depriving the mayor of an unbiased picture.)

When Mayor Clark picked Rafsky as his executive secretary, he knew only that he had been active in the ADA during the campaign, that he was research director for the Hosiery Workers' Union, and that he had had a brilliant college career at the City College of New York. But Rafsky's computerlike mind quickly grasped the problems the city faced, and his ability and judgment gained Clark's increasing respect. When Clark was elected to the U.S. Senate in 1956, he wanted Rafsky to head his

Washington staff. Dilworth, when he ran for mayor, challenged his opponent to state whether he would keep Rafsky in his position. Both Dilworth and Tate needed Rafsky's advice and relied on his judgment.

Although Rafsky had close ties with all three mayors, he does not appear to have had a relationship based on personal friendship with any of them, even with Dilworth, who was the warmest of the three. The clearly structured relationship between Rafsky and each mayor was in line with Rafsky's personality. Discussions with Clark were somewhat in the nature of intellectual debates on issues which intrigued them both. With Dilworth, who tended to be pragmatic, Rafsky emphasized the need for taking the technical and long-range view. Though Dilworth did not always convince him, Rafsky loyally defended the mayor's approach. Under Tate, Rafsky carried on much of his old coordinating function and even continued as chairman of the CRP committee, which had become the main body for determining long-term policy. The fact that he soon took a position with a quasi-public corporation (as vice-president of the Old Philadelphia Development Corporation) may have indicated his desire to be somewhat removed from Tate personally, while in no way diminishing his willingness to do all he could for the city's needs; Rafsky's dual role benefited both the OPDC and the city.

## Expanded Coordination

Shortly after Dilworth became mayor, he expanded the scope of coordination, making Rafsky responsible for overall coordination of all developmental programs—for example, housing, slum clearance, industrial growth, and Center City development.

As development coordinator, Rafsky began sitting officially on the boards of nonprofit corporations and civic groups concerned with the areas covered by his new duties. He now had to help in working out the priorities among all these activities to put the city's resources to best use. Interestingly enough, in the cabinet meeting when Dilworth proposed a new office of development director, cabinet members objected, apparently afraid that such an office might upstage those of managing director and directors of finance and of commerce. Hence, though the mayor seemed to insist, Rafsky preferred to retain his coordinator role.

Although his area of concern was expanded, Rafsky still had no administrative or operational control over other agencies, not even the independent ones which reported to no cabinet member. He had to continue to rely on everybody's goodwill (and the mayor's backing) to have policy reached and its coordination carried out to reflect consensus. Since Rafsky was willing to undertake the task on this basis, we have no way of knowing whether it would have worked better if he had been able to "direct" public agencies; but in view of the "jointness" between private and public agencies, and the deeply ingrained feeling for consensus in Philadelphia, it is doubtful.

There was one instance where a question was put to a kind of test. His new position brought the Redevelopment Authority into a more central focus, as it was concerned with both housing and slum clearance as well as with all nonresidential redevelopment activities. There had been organizational difficulties within that agency. Frank Lammer, its executive director, had over many years established political connections, and, although he did not have Mayor Dilworth's confidence, several councilmen objected strenuously when Dilworth tried to remove him. The mayor felt, however, that it was necessary to tie the authority more closely with the coordinated developmental plans. He therefore prevailed upon Rafsky to also take on the duty of "director" of the authority; he would take care of its relations with other agencies, while the "executive director" would continue to direct the day-to-day operations. Many other top city officials as well as Rafsky's own professional staff advised strongly against this step. Not only would it strain his duties to the breaking point, it was also administratively a nonsensical appointment: he was supposed to coordinate all agencies, including the Redevelopment Authority, for which he himself would be responsible! But Rafsky complied with the mayor's entreaties and somehow managed to wear both hats. Even though his top assistant had been appointed one of the two deputy executive directors of the Redevelopment Authority, coordination was not well served, nor was Rafsky's effectiveness enhanced. As soon as Rafsky left city employment, the executive director returned to his old position.

Given this new broad approach to the whole gamut of redevelopment activities, Philadelphia soon became interested in the possibility of undertaking a "Community Renewal Program," the reappraisal which the 1959 Federal Housing Act promised to finance in part.

Philadelphia was among the first cities to embark on the program. As with many other ideas adopted by the federal government, Philadelphia was able to take the credit for this one: William Wheaton of the University of Pennsylvania, Dorothy Montgomery of the Philadelphia Housing Association, and William Rafsky seem to have convinced Richard Steiner, then commissioner for urban renewal, that such a reappraisal was a device worth trying. The idea grew out of the concern of Philadelphia civic groups for an overall approach to city development, as well as the desire of the administration to reappraise past strategy.

Philadelphia completed the study only after a number of years and untold man-hours. It turned out to be one of the most sophisticated documents of its kind (see chapter 6). "The Philadelphia program has long been marked by well thought out plans," says the letter of transmittal. "That program has geared projects and priorities to clearly enunciated goals. . . . The enclosed report, therefore, is based on a comprehensive set of goals of a variety of programs, their interrelationships, and the most effective methods to achieve these goals." [9] Among these methods, the proposed Annual Development Program was to be the most important device for tying together decent homes, good education, and adequate job opportunities.

Philadelphia's long-term concern with overall relationships, which grew to maturity during the term of the first reform mayor, was expressed in the CURA report, the Urban Traffic and Transportation Board report, the Planning Commission's Comprehensive Plan in the second reform term, and ultimately in the Community Renewal Program (CRP) study. The study is thus the capstone of the gradual recognition of the interrelationships among the various aspects of development—a realization that evolved slowly from 1952 to 1967.

## Could Planners Coordinate Development?

The way in which policies were made, priorities determined, and programs coordinated has been explored without mention of the professional planners on the staff of the City Planning Com-

9. Letter of transmittal to Mayor Tate, January 24, 1967, in the CRP Final Report, *Major Policies and Proposals*.

mission. They could have been expected to have a place in the forefront of these activities.

### Redevelopment and Transportation Planning

The staff assembled by Edmund Bacon was, in line with his own predilections, especially strong in physical design and design relationships. Much of the preceding discussion has encompassed the recognition of social and economic factors as an integral part of the planning process. Furthermore, with redevelopment and transportation removed from the planners' jurisdiction, overall policy control of developmental activities became virtually impossible.

Planning for all phases of renewal and redevelopment was carried out by the Redevelopment Authority under the direction of David Wallace, its planning director. The city administration considered him best qualified to judge the impact of renewal planning for long-range development. But Wallace's position took the most dynamic challenge away from the City Planning Commission's planners; though they took renewal planning into account when drawing their plans, the ideas and the reasons for it were not their own. Wallace reported that the earlier plans of the Planning Commission had been "a prime example of 'projectitis' "—"conceived out of context of any economic or real estate analysis." [10]

Transportation planning was at least as important for overall city development. The first Urban Traffic and Transportation Board was charged by Clark with recommending a plan, and it issued its "Plan and Program" just before he left office. Dilworth then adopted these clearly formulated transportation policies but decided to create a second board to execute them and advise him on the many problems arising in carrying them out. This action removed a second major area from the immediate control of the Planning Commission's planning staff.

10. Wallace reports in an article that all preliminary planning for redevelopment had earlier been done by the Planning Commission, though its "early program was not notable for good planning. A prime example of 'projectitis,' it was made up of a lot of different pieces tied together by some thin logic. . . . These plans contained a great deal of design detail, but were largely conceived out of context of any economic or real estate analysis" ("Renaissancemanship," *Journal of the American Institute of Planners*, August 1960, p. 160).

The Planning Commission had been established as an independent agency and as a bridge to civic representatives. A special relationship to the mayor, implicit in the coordination function, would have put the staff in the position of serving two masters. This would have violated the charter intent of combining within the commission citizens-at-large and cabinet members. The commission advised both mayor and council; and because the council took the commission's advice seriously on different land use alternatives and on a capital program, close ties to the mayor would again create a conflict. The alternative of assigning the planning staff to the mayor's office as coordinators would have kept the commission without professional help, and hence without the expertise to carry out its assigned functions.

## The Planning Staff

While the commission's staff included a number of excellent designers, it included few economists, sociologists, fiscal experts, or other social scientists, and such representatives of these disciplines as the commission employed were comparatively low in rank. The contribution to be made through a feasibility study or an indication of the social or economic effects of projects seemed to carry little weight in comparison to aesthetic considerations. The first breakthrough of the social sciences came with the appointment of Arthur Row as assistant executive director of the commission, charged with the task of working out the city's Comprehensive Plan. He never did get the social science staff support he felt he needed, however. It was only after the completion of the plan, when Row's successor, Graham Finney, assembled a staff to work on the CRP, that the social sciences began to form an integral part of the Planning Commission's staff. By this time the prime of the reform was over. Despite public lip service to the importance of the social and economic factors in development, Bacon never modified his personal priority, which was design. This is a somewhat unusual priority for a planner, though it is an important aspect for a city's physical development and the design relationship among projects. Bacon's reluctance to see the city's total development as an integrated whole, which, I believe, was the outstanding concept of the reform, was Philadelphia's loss.

On the other hand, Bacon was responsible for many outstanding architectural features of Philadelphia. He was concerned about preserving and renovating the historic area of Philadelphia. He also saw the future of the University of Pennsylvania in a renovated West Philadelphia before the university itself did. He fought and argued with many an architect to make certain that a new building would be compatible with older buildings in the environment. Even more important, his enthusiasm carried his audience and inspired them. He made his ideas and projects appear before the eyes of his listeners, and they seemed to want him to start immediately on whatever he was planning.

How well would the planners, given the high regard in which they were held, have filled the role of coordinators? In addition to the lack of socioeconomic expertise, there was an inclination to concentrate on individual projects at the expense of the way they fitted into a total program ("projectitis"). As a member of every one of the policy-making committees, Bacon used them as a forum for him to discuss many an excellent new idea, or to fight about the best location for a transportation terminal or a shopping concourse or a new park. He seemed unwilling to compromise with other participants on any idea of his. "He could have been effective [as coordinator] only if he could have carried out what he had decided was the right thing to do, without asking others," said one official. "He likes to have a great deal more freedom of movement than that position would have given him," said another.

Bacon was not accepted as a regular member of either Clark's or Dilworth's cabinet and was called in only when specific planning matters were to be discussed. Although both mayors had great respect for his competence and accomplishments, they were in the habit of asking others for advice. During Clark's term there was some criticism of the planning staff,[11] while Dilworth (as well as Bacon) had to respect Greenfield's unwillingness to let Bacon establish relations with the mayor directly rather than via the commission chairman. The absence of a close relationship deprived the planning staff of the opportunity to advise either

11. Cabinet meetings, May 8 and July 20, 1953. "When should the decision of determining priorities be made? What should be the role of the City Planning Commission?" "I am disappointed—I cannot look to the staff for real help on priorities." "The staff does not have the right approach to citizen groups—a personality problem."

Clark or Dilworth. Nor was the situation very different under Tate, who had even less personal rapport with Bacon. However, he invited him more often to attend cabinet meetings, and made him a member of his Development Council. In 1968, having tried several development coordinators after Rafsky left, Tate finally decided to let Bacon take over coordination duties in addition to his existing position.

## Administrative Devices for Development

The CRP's final administrative recommendation was the establishment of an Annual Development Program. This instrument would spell out the broad objectives of citywide development and the kind of interrelated programs which would best attain these objectives within a given time period (see chapter 6). It was an important instrument, well worth the effort—but unfortunately the first such program never saw the light of day. Again the question arises as to what kind of administrative unit should be "charged with the responsibility for preparation and administration of the Development Program" [12]—a similar question to that of policy coordination.

Let us now examine the potential coordination role of other city officials, starting with the managing director.

Vernon Northrop (who held that position under Mayor Clark) felt strongly that coordination (hence presumably the Development Program) should be the responsibility of the managing director under a strong mayor's order, giving him the power to coordinate all departments including those not regularly reporting to him. "There is room for a strong mayor who does all the broad thinking and policy determination, and a strong managing director under him who does all the operation and coordination," he said. He felt that all fiscal and personnel problems should be taken care of by the finance director and personnel department, leaving the content of the programs to the managing director. But such coordination could only be carried out successfully if the individual departments were strengthened and given clear program responsibilities on a year-round basis within the limits of actually determined policy. Each department would have to

12. CRP Report, *Possible Administrative Arrangements for Renewal and Development* (1965), pp. R-1, 2.

have a small analysis and program staff, which would serve as the commissioner's eyes and ears to keep him abreast of what could be done. For each group of departments, a technically competent deputy managing director would in turn see that programming was done properly at the department level and was coordinated among departments. Northrup was well aware of program interrelationships and long-range implications.

Donald Wagner, Dilworth's managing director, also felt that if departments were given more responsibility for their programs, they would become more imaginative in their proposals. John Bailey, his deputy, believed equally that coordination should be the managing director's function. "As he is running ninety percent of the City government, he should be responsible for pulling things together."

Richard McConnell, finance director from 1955 to 1963, saw it differently. "If you have a strong mayor form of government, you need coordination from the mayor's office. Dick Dilworth saw this need more clearly than did Joe Clark. The managing director could never function as coordinator." The CRP report on "Administrative Arrangements" seems to agree: "A programming unit should be established within the Office of the Mayor . . . as a staff arm to the cabinet. Policy planning and evaluation, because they go to the heart of defining objectives and priorities, are a vital resource of the chief executive. . . . It can be conducted only at the highest policy level." [13]

Some arguments were raised in favor of placing the function of preparing the Development Plan with the finance director. Combining development with finance could be compared with the function of the federal Bureau of the Budget. The continuing debate concerning this proposal centered on the question whether "budgeting (i.e. resource allocation) should be lumped together with policy planning, . . . as the economizing viewpoint of the budgeteer may tend to inhibit the creativeness of the planner." [14]

By the time some of these suggestions had percolated through the administrative and political process, it had been proposed that the primary responsibility be assigned to the finance director. Making full use of the planning-programming-budgeting system,

13. Ibid., pp. R-2, 34.
14. *Major Policies and Proposals*, p. 22.

he would be able to express policies in budgeting terms and hence to evaluate the results. Policies would be arrived at by carefully examining physical and socioeconomic conditions and the probable influence of city actions on them. As William Wheaton put it: "Such an evaluation must also include explicit statements on the interactions among the programs of all agencies."

The evolution of developmental programs in Philadelphia was a long process. The need to establish goals was first understood in connection with determining priorities. The time sequence of public investments in the capital program—to be discussed in the next chapter—was one method of expressing priorities. But the need also became clear to carry through on every policy decision through careful coordination with all those participating in the decision, or the plans were going to remain on paper. This was to be the fate of the carefully thought-out Development Program.

# II

# Developmental
# Programs

# 5 *Bridges Fiscal and Physical:*
## Capital Program and Transportation

Before analyzing some individual programs of the reform, we should note two specific ways in which the programs are tied to one another. The first is a fiscal relationship: if each proposed development is to get its share of resources allocated in line with the city's goals and priorities, all must be carefully aligned in a long-term capital program. Fiscal allocation is the end result of the economic evaluation of each program in comparison with all the others. Since all are in direct competition for resources, the capital program is indispensable to indicate the direction toward which city development must move.

The second is a physical relationship: in programs dealing with homes and jobs, retailing and research, shopping and education, the ability to get easily and quickly from one activity to another often determines the viability of each. Improving transportation access to the individual projects may make more operative the development of the entire area.

## A Tool for Development Decisions

Decisions on proposed development projects presuppose the understanding of which of several alternatives would best satisfy the goals which the city and the mayor want to pursue. Spelling out the consequences of different project sequences will confirm a previous decision on priorities among these projects. This can be done much more reliably with the help of economic analysis. For instance, if a politician takes a strong stand on an issue, it is much easier to challenge his position and to affect it if an analysis has been made which shows what his favored solution would do to other goals he cherishes, or how it would affect other groups of citizens than those he thought were the ones primarily involved. If citizens affected by a decision can be shown what the consequences of an alternative decision would be, in terms of advantages foregone for the city as a whole—or, for that matter, for certain neighborhoods—then they might better understand why the decision was made.

Metropolitan areas can affect their own development only to a limited extent. "Only by understanding the local growth process can local government hope to be even partially master of its own destiny," says Wilbur Thompson.[1] Political scientists ask who the immediate or long-run beneficiaries are ("Who gets what, when, how"—Lasswell) and whether the effects of different measures are compatible with each other. But although economic policy (such as in public investment—see next section) is greatly influenced by the answer, economists are only beginning to ask the question. They are only beginning to look beyond the immediate potential for a remedial policy and to consider its long-term consequences for a city or a region. "Policy-making is a matter of mastering complex relationships and of understanding the consequences of alternative courses of action." [2]

As early as 1955, the city economist had pointed out that the impact of a variety of activities on the city would "help to determine what city Philadelphia will be. Diverse considerations must enter these decisions, social, fiscal, political, and others, . . . whenever public policy is formulated." [3]

In May 1958, a group of local economists were appointed as the mayor's Economic Advisory Committee. Most of its members were second-line executives of their industries or institutions such as vice-presidents, treasurers, or controllers, and economic experts near the top of their organizations, including vice-presidents of the Federal Reserve Banks and institutions of higher learning.[4] The committee lasted through Mayor Dilworth's term but was

1. Wilbur Thompson, *Preface to Urban Economics* (Johns Hopkins Press, 1965), p. 2.

2. Lowdon Wingo, "Comment," in Werner Hirsch (ed.), *Elements of Regional Accounts* (John Hopkins Press, 1963), pp. 143–44.

3. "The City's Economic Problem" (memorandum from the city economist to Walter M. Phillips, November 22, 1955).

4. Among members of the committee were two presidents of local companies, the vice-president of the Third District Federal Reserve Bank, the economist for the Philadelphia Chamber of Commerce, the dean of the Wharton School of Finance, and the vice-president of Drexel Institute of Technology; the city economist was chairman.

allowed to lapse soon after Tate became mayor. In August 1966, a new city economist started a similar committee.

In its original charge, the economic committee was instructed "to appraise long-run trends bearing upon the future development and growth of Philadelphia as a metropolitan center, and to consider alternative courses of action available to the community, so that policy-makers, both public and private, might have the opportunity to coordinate their objectives and seek to achieve common goals." [5] The committee members were asked to watch over the effect and compatibility of the actions of different city agencies and quasi-public organizations, to assess the interrelationship of such actions, and to evaluate the desirable degree of local government involvement in economic matters, including the system of public investment priorities embodied in the capital program.

## The Capital Program

Possibly the most important use for the tools of the economist is in determining priorities for public investment. Most municipalities work out a capital program for several years in advance, in which they anticipate their needs and the impact of proposed projects on the area's development. They allocate their resources in order to maximize progress toward the (explicit or implicit) goals of the community—whether high employment, high wages, cyclical stability, modern health centers, recreation areas, or whatever. But the real question is how the allocations are made: by rule of thumb, by historical precedence, by political opportunism, or by some sophisticated variant of maximizing procedure.

When city departments or agencies propose programs, they are soon up against the city's financial ceiling, making it necessary to decide what to keep in and what to omit, and which projects to trade off for which others. More than that, city officials must first make up their minds which programs are most important in the light of the kind of development they favor for their city. The public improvement priority schedule is one of the most important tools city administrations have at their disposal. It forces them periodically to face priority decisions which at least

5. Statement on Functions and Orientation of the Mayor's Economic Advisory Committee, May 1959.

*imply* a set of goals and thus may induce public officials *actually* to decide on goals and directions. "Until very recently the development of cities in the U.S. and Canada has been accompanied by patterns of uncoordinated public expenditures for public works and uncoordinated exercise of governmental powers over privately financed developments. . . . The development of any instrument of public administration into an effective one is a slow process, necessarily characterized by a great deal of trial and error," say the authors of a 1964 manual.[6]

According to the charter, the City Planning Commission had to make the decisions on all developmental programs in Philadelphia. Decisions would be made, presumably, after the relationship of each program to the others and their expected consequences for the city's overall development had been ascertained. But these relationships were not always given sufficient consideration. Members of the Planning Commission, in listening to the testimony of one department head after another presenting their programs, gradually gained some insight into the relative urgency and importance of these programs. While these sessions provided "an invaluable learning experience," they were not priority-determining sessions. They were reminiscent of Congress making appropriations: "First the main pet projects were decided, and then you divided what was left." [7]

If the commission failed to come to a final decision on available alternatives to the projects urged by the departments on the commission, the matter would often be brought up to the cabinet. If time did not permit a detailed discussion of which programs should be cut in favor of which other specific projects, many of the decisions fell back on the three ex officio members of the Planning Commission (the managing director and the directors of finance and commerce) and the development coordinator. But even in that small circle it became clear that what was lacking was a proper basis for allocating the city's resources.

6. Lennox L. Moak and Kathryn W. Killian, *A Manual of Suggested Practice for the Preparation and Adoption of Capital Programs and Capital Budgets by Local Governments* (Chicago: Municipal Finance Officers' Association of the U.S. and Canada, 1964), pp. 4, 5, 7.

7. Confidential interview with a former member of the City Planning Commission.

*Priorities among Functions*

The costs of many projects cannot be expressed or compared in measurable terms (say, in actual dollar amounts)—and in even fewer cases can the prospective benefits be ascertained with some degree of assurance. The lack of a common denominator among alternative investments complicates the task. The relative desirability of one project over another might serve, where expression in terms of dollars and cents is impossible. On the other hand, where different "publics" would be benefited (for example, where one public improvement would benefit low-income families, while another would benefit commercial interests), comparability is virtually impossible. At best, the government may venture a subjective value judgment—a judgment made *for* those who would benefit, rather than *by* them.[8]

Criteria were needed by which to judge alternative *programs* of different agencies and their relative importance within the framework of total city development and—at least implicit—overall goals. Following that, different *projects* within the same category (for example, recreation, urban renewal, or transit) had to be evaluated against each other, to set second-level priorities. These priorities could also be expressed in terms of time sequence within the capital program, with the priority level indicating which projects would be built early in the proposed capital program and which ones in later years, or which could be squeezed into the fiscal limits of the current six years and which would have to wait for the next term. This time sequence would then permit another realistic look at the suggested results and, if necessary, a reevaluation of priorities. Occasionally such a reevaluation might not be carried out until just before the execution of a project.

After the departments concerned had made their case for particular programs and the consequences for other projects had been spelled out, further tasks might well remain. For example, if the need to install public utilities on a parcel of industrially

8. Attempts are now being made to develop social indicators as a means of evaluating in quantitative terms benefits which cannot easily be gauged in dollars and cents. One of the first publications is a volume edited by Raymond A. Bauer, *Social Indicators* (M.I.T. Press, 1966).

zoned land in order to attract new manufacturing firms had been established, the next question was whether there were better ways or means of achieving the goal of attracting industry, such as a tax freeze or an interest-free loan. The alternative method might well leave the city more funds for other projects, for instance, by affecting the city's borrowing power and thus indirectly affecting the city's ability to carry out its total capital program.

In other words, the effects of each measure on the total capital program must be explored before a total "package" of program priorities can be defended properly. "Spillover" effects on other programs, the question of economies of scale by combining programs, or the effects of project timing on the city's rate of interest for floating loans are examples of how different and unrelated programs may have an impact on the city's total development.

Any decision on long-term public investments will affect the development of the metropolitan area for many years to come. Unless it is known how projects fit into some overall plan, no intelligent decision can be made on which projects should be dropped to make room for new needs—if indeed "emergency" demands are permitted to upset the broad priority sequence set up earlier.

The long-term impact of public investment programs was recognized relatively recently. Long-term effects are, in practice, often hidden from view by the carry-over of earlier decisions. Once a project has been started, it must be continued until completion, lest the entire investment be jeopardized. As costs have risen over time, and so the period needed for completion has expanded, more allocation of funds becomes necessary; but often, in making such allocations, too little thought is given to the long-term consequences, such as the inability to consider expenditures for other projects.

For example, highways once started must be completed before they can be of use at all. Redevelopment of an area where demolition has begun must be carried to completion, so that the intended change in the character of the area can be accomplished. Assistance to an existing industrial firm for expansion may be necessary to prevent the firm's leaving the metropolis. In other words, plans made long ago may inexorably determine today's decisions and exclude possible new projects. New initiatives may require a long gestation period before their results are seen. The temptation is thus great to let past distributions between functional areas of public improvements determine future allocations.

Another influence should be considered. Federal funds on a matching basis were available at the time under discussion primarily for urban renewal and highways. But as the percentage of federal contributions varies between different programs, it exerts a powerful influence on the allocation of the city's resources, possibly at variance with what the city's decision would be without the difference in federal contributions: the city's resource allocation is thus distorted.

The city economist and other professionals working for the city during Philadelphia's reform period spent a good deal of time searching for some measure of comparability. It had been hoped that other governmental units might have hit upon a solution. Meetings with many scholars in the field and with officials from other governmental levels did not produce new insights. Interviews with professionals in the U.S. Bureau of the Budget and other federal departments showed that decisions on public investments for different functions or agencies were not rationally arrived at in the executive branch of the federal government: within any one agency, priorities were determined internally by that agency; budgetary decisions among different federal agencies were decided on the basis of political pressures at the cabinet level. Nor could discussions with well-known scholars provide any better solution.

A rational solution to the problem of priorities should, one would assume, be provided by economists, since they are forever maximizing desired ends. The economists' answer might indicate which combination of investment projects would yield the largest tax return or the most employment or the greatest productivity for the dollar spent or a more viable transportation system. This, however, would provide a common denominator with regard to only one of these goals. Any attempt to identify a measure coordinating several potential goals simultaneously appeared futile: to maximize a different end would require a different ranking of projects. The public would then have to decide how far the most important end (say, employment) should be followed, and whether, after a certain level of employment has been reached, it would be desirable to compromise now between the level reached of this goal and a certain amount of the next one, for example, taxes against employment. (This, in fact, is the same kind of problem facing the national government in relating the goals of inflation and employment.) It is difficult to avoid letting some value judgment enter the decisions on the goals to be pursued, and priorities of capital programs must follow from that decision. Some of these new insights are extremely well expressed by Brown and Gilbert.[9] In general, economic science should be able to tell us how to maximize public improvements with a given outlay, or how to minimize expenditures for particular programs.

## Cost-Benefit Analysis

The economist's domain is more precisely the evaluation of specific projects, the consequences of following a particular purpose, or the alternatives open to the public official in seeking the ends he has decided upon. The economist's evaluation is likely to be geared to the efficient allocation of resources, though "efficiency" may have a different connotation depending on whether the competitive economy is involved, or whether we are concerned, as we are here, with public projects.

The best-known tool is the "cost-benefit analysis," used most often to decide whether a specific project should be undertaken to attain a particular end or whether a different project would better attain this result. "Cost-benefit analysis can be applied to the projects individually, or to interdependent groups, to forecast the costs and benefits that would accrue to all sections of the community," says Lichfield.[10] This tool will be of comparatively little help for the social choices involved, however, since "most decisions will achieve goals in varying proportions." [11] Further-

9. William H. Brown, Jr., and Charles E. Gilbert, *Planning Municipal Investment: Philadelphia* (University of Pennsylvania Press, 1961), pp. 253–54. This is the basic work on Philadelphia's capital program. See also Kirk R. Petshek, "Economies of the Changing Urban Structure and Urban Renewal Planning," *Urban Renewal and the Changing Urban Structure* (National Association of Housing and Redevelopment Officials, 1960), pp. 12–17.

10. Nathaniel Lichfield, "Cost-Benefit Analysis in Urban Redevelopment," Research Report, no. 20, Real Estate Research Program (University of California, Berkeley, 1962), p. vii.

11. See Julius Margolis and Nathaniel Lichfield, "Benefit-Cost Analysis as a Tool in Urban Government Decision-Making," in Howard Schaller (ed.),

more, if cost-benefit analysis is used for an entire capital program, those projects which can show quantitatively a better "return" than others will probably be chosen. The bias thus will be in favor of revenues received or at least of technical efficiency, and social benefits would be likely to take second place. The quantitative exactness of economic techniques is likely to prove specious: the final decision is a value judgment. "Will the inevitable lack of comparability between projects of different departments prejudice decisions in favor of those investments most amenable to the tools of economic analysis?" ask Brown and Gilbert.[12] What is really a value preference may be hidden behind technical decisions on the rate of discount, or labor-intensive projects as against highly capitalized ones, or the anticipated length of the life of the project.

## Subjective Evaluation

One civic group in Philadelphia was deeply concerned with capital program issues: the Citizens' Council on City Planning (see chapter 2). Members evaluated all the programs of different departments and the entire gamut of the city's projects, classifying each project in one of four priority categories: essential, desirable, acceptable, and deferrable. But they did not face up to the question of priorities *across* different functions (or across departmental areas). Similarly, the city's Comprehensive Plan, finally published in 1960, did not suggest priorities *among* programs, but only goals to be reached by 1980 (for example, for highways, playgrounds, and health centers). Nor did the Comprehensive Plan give guidelines on how to arrive at such priorities.

Having failed to arrive at a method which would objectively determine preferences among areas for public investment, the city economist and other professionals working for the city turned to community leaders for their *subjective* evaluations in order to gain a fresh and independent look at the improvement programs. A carefully selected group of forty community leaders was interviewed early in 1961, and an effort to counteract biases was made by balancing the group as much as possible. They were given a

*Public Expenditure Decisions in the Urban Community* (Johns Hopkins Press, 1963), p. 122.
12. Brown and Gilbert, pp. 262–63, 271.

list of capital projects under consideration, arranged in as homogeneous categories as possible, and asked to evaluate the *relative* long-run importance of the projects. Taking into account those public improvements already built (or in progress), they were asked to judge in each category what the community as a whole still needed at the present time. While the answers of the community leaders would not be based on careful study, it was felt that their *combined subjective judgments* would provide the best available guidance for long-run development directions.

The community leaders knew that they were being asked for an evaluation of the relative importance and urgency of different program categories over the long run. They were also asked to decide the *rate* at which they would like to see each program category (not each specific project) carried out in the next six-year capital program. Judging on the basis of what still needed to be done, they knew that their priorities would have been different ten years earlier, or would be different ten years hence. They were also asked to *rank* the categories in the order of the community's needs and to attach a *weight* to each ranking to indicate how intensely they assessed the relative ranks they assigned. (Assigning weights anywhere on a scale of 0 to 100 would ensure that they correctly expressed the distance between the rankings. What emerged was simply an indication of how far the community leaders wished to deviate from the kind of capital program that had been enacted in the past by the Planning Commission and was likely to be adopted in the future.

The results were submitted to the cabinet.[13] There was a clear difference between community leaders and cabinet members in their assigned relative weights to several of the programs, though the deviations of the former's *combined* weights did not indicate a totally different direction. But there was a clear enough implication that some categories were more important to the community leaders than to the administration, while others were less important to them. Of course, no immediate changes were possible; nor had any been intended. But the results clearly influenced subsequent decisions of the cabinet members, both in their attitudes toward the programs under their own jurisdiction in

13. "Capital Program Priorities" (memorandum from the city economist, March 24, 1961).

relation to others in the program, and in their joint effect on the Planning Commission's decisions.

Another approach recommended by the economist's office (and later endorsed by the managing director and the director of finance) was to get the individual departments to engage in year-round programming of the public improvements they would submit annually. Though their pleas that departments be provided with programming officers went unanswered, an attempt was made to get department heads to fill out detailed questionnaires about their projects, which would make evaluation easier.[14]

Aside from questions on the use the departments expected to be made of the projected facility, they also were asked to state its relationship to existing or proposed projects, both within and outside their own departments. How had plans for related facilities been coordinated? How did the projects in the department's six-year program relate to each other and to the long-range plans expected to appear in subsequent capital programs? Departments which had set up specific professional standards as guides toward long-term goals were asked to indicate how the particular projects related to these standards.

The questions also sought, from an economic viewpoint, to determine the private investment which might be stimulated by the projected public facility and the likely increase in private employment because of it. Would nearby private-property values be affected, and would the economic health of the neighborhood and the income of its inhabitants improve or suffer? What persons and businesses would be dislocated by the construction undertaken, and who would indirectly benefit or suffer? Would new needs be served or would many users simply transfer from another facility? Would it be feasible to make some savings elsewhere in the city because of this new utility, or would additional expenditures become necessary before it was possible to make full use of it?

It was thought that such questions would force departments to think through their requests, if for no other reason than to maintain their competitive position with other departments. If professional standards had been set up by national professional groups in the field of activity of a particular department (as was the case in recreation), these might strengthen the arguments of

14. "Questions on Capital Program" (office of the city economist, 1959).

the particular department involved. But in spite of all the influence of professionals in the administration, it was an uphill drive to get the idea of a questionnaire adopted by the department heads, let alone to have the questions answered conscientiously.

## A Novel Approach

In the absence of an analytical system for making choices among functional groups, could these choices be made in an intelligent way? Robert Coughlin, chief of the Long-Range Programming Division of the City Planning Commission, argued (in a 1960 article) that the city's Comprehensive Plan would set forth all the projects needed from then on to meet the plan's goals in each functional area (mass transit, urban renewal, and so forth). The total cost for all projects included in the Comprehensive Plan and the percentage of the total to be incurred by each of the functional areas could be easily computed. If these percentages were followed throughout, he argued, all projects in each of the categories would be completed simultaneously at the time the Comprehensive Plan was completed, each having approached this point, year by year, at an *even rate*. But obviously programs in different categories would not march *pari passu* to their goals. It was important that programs such as those producing tax revenue or requiring land acquisition be completed early. The calculation of the cost of the programs in each functional area would be useful as a yardstick against which the *actual* rate of each group in the capital program could be measured. It should induce the public officials to ascertain precisely why one program at this particular stage should be constructed faster than the "average" rate, while another should be allowed to lag. For example, the completion of the studies of the Urban Traffic and Transportation Board (1956) made the need for additional emphasis on transportation problems clear. Hence, in the next few programs the expenditure for both highways and mass transit was pushed up. On the other hand, expensive recreation projects could be built more easily if they were deferred until the city's tax base was broadened.[15]

15. See Robert Coughlin, "The Capital Programming Problem," *Journal of the American Institute of Planners*, February 1960, p. 43. See also "Com-

The "trade-offs" necessary among the interests represented in the Planning Commission or on its staff, or for that matter in the mayor's cabinet, would now depend on how far, in any category, the city was falling behind the Comprehensive Plan, or what activities the public expenditures were favoring by implication. This might make it more difficult to ignore the consequences of capital program decisions.

Such a "profile" of public improvements necessary to lead to the goals of the Comprehensive Plan thus should provide a guide for deciding how resources should be apportioned among different functional groups. Therein lay the real advance in thinking presented by this device. While emphasis on one group in one particular period must be compensated for in another period, a development strategy for each period was now possible which would set "the rate at which each group *should* lead to a specific set of profile proportions for each program period . . . [and to a decision] on the proper allocation of funds to each functional group." [16] As this proposal is followed, priorities can be decided on by obtaining a framework through relating allocations *among* different functional areas to the total planning goal—and similarly, by relating at the next step the projects *within* each functional category to the total allocated to this group. Different six-year capital programs necessarily vary in the proportion among various groups and their speed of program completion. While the judgment of relative priority must still remain subjective, this device permitted testing that judgment against an objective framework.

## A Transportation System

Transportation shapes the development of an area in all its aspects: the location of transportation facilities influences the uses of urban land and vice versa, since accessibility makes development viable. It is necessary to fashion isolated projects into a physically workable program by making certain that people and goods are able to move freely among them. Urban development cannot become operative without freeways and buses, railroads

prehensive Plan and the 1960–65 Capital Program" (Philadelphia City Planning Commission, March 1960).

16. Coughlin, "Capital Programming Problem," pp. 44–45.

and subways, parking structures and terminals, ports and airports. The more all these can be integrated into a system, the more viable development becomes. This transportation policy became in Philadelphia the most systematically conceived aspect of the developmental program.

### Planning for Transportation

Unlike many cities, Philadelphia was determined that its various forms of transportation—highway, rail, mass transit—should complement each other and form a balanced system. This meant: (1) that the highway program had to be coordinated with the other modes so that it would contribute most to the whole system—a most unusual requirement; (2) that an economical, fast, and convenient mass transit operation was essential to provide the service necessary for preventing congestion; and (3) that the transportation operation as a *whole* had to pay for itself.[17] To bring about this last requirement, "there should be a definite point in the governmental structure where planning and programming . . . for *both* the highway and transit aspects of transportation can be brought together." [18]

Lennox Moak, even before he became Mayor Clark's finance director, called transportation "the most important single task facing the new City Administration." [19] Only if it were conceived in terms of a total system, Moak believed, could it be tied into the city's other developments. Though Clark appointed a committee within weeks, it had the wrong charge and the wrong membership, and before a year was up, it recommended to the mayor an entirely different board, dealing with broad transportation policy.[20] In a cabinet meeting the creation of an independent policy

17. Charles H. Frazier, address delivered to the Greater Philadelphia Movement Annual Dinner, October 23, 1957.

18. Charles H. Frazier, remarks at Perin Executive Dinner before the Greater Boston Study Committee, December 19, 1960.

19. Pennsylvania Economy League–Bureau of Municipal Research, "Effective Transportation," *Citizens' Business*, October 29, 1951.

20. The "Master Traffic Committee's" limited charge to traffic resulted from a disagreement between Lennox Moak and Robert K. Sawyer, the managing director. The committee's recommendations, submitted to the mayor on November 21, 1952 (reported in Philadelphia *Inquirer*, December 4, 1952) suggested a membership of top city officials and vested interests, i.e., those operationally concerned with transportation.

board was discussed, which would consider transportation as a totality in long-range terms, free of operational responsibilities. Whether its members should consist of vested transportation interests, so that recommendations would be more readily accepted by the community and "its conclusions on policy would have some finality," was fought over at length.[21] It was decided "to rely on conflicting interests and the kind of people who can rise above their own interests" in suggesting what was best for the city as a whole. The adoption of this view [22] was considered a commitment of the reform administration, foreshadowing future public-private partnerships. Policy decisions would be a cooperative venture between public and private interests, free from "normal governmental restrictions." [23]

The Urban Traffic and Transportation Board (UTTB) was created by ordinance. Robert Mitchell (then a faculty member of the University of Pennsylvania) was chosen as executive director, not only because of his planning expertise (and the fact that he had just coauthored a book on transportation), but also because he was especially gifted in getting people with different points of view together.

### The Urban Traffic and Transportation Board

In December 1955, the UTTB transmitted its recommendations to Mayor Clark just before he left office. It suggested the need for an integrated transportation system in which the parts fit together and serve each other. "Philadelphia has no coherent public policy to guide the provision of transportation services. Instead, there are many separate policies that conflict and contradict." The main burden of its recommendation was the need to arrive at the right balance between the different modes of transportation.[24] In the letter of transmittal, the chairman reported that the board had achieved a high degree of unanimity, "although the members

21. Cabinet meeting, December 1, 1952.
22. This was basically a victory for Moak, even over Rafsky's fears. On March 31, 1953, the Bureau of Municipal Research, from which Moak was formally detached, submitted a study called "A Proposed Organization to Recommend an Urban Traffic and Transportation Policy and Program for the City of Philadelphia."
23. Memorandum from Lennox Moak to Mayor Clark, February 1953.
24. Urban Traffic and Transportation Board, *Plans and Programs,* 1955 (published April 1956).

and their businesses were vitally affected by the recommendations," and that this "exhibited real statesmanship."

The board concluded that the transportation problem must be tackled on a regional basis. A regional transportation skeleton was proposed. The railroad commuter network was expected to carry the main peak-hour burden of trips to Center City. The central business district was viewed as the major focus of regional traffic flows, to be surrounded by several expressway loops at various distances to bypass Center City. Rapid transit on rails and commuter railroads were to be improved through lighter, faster, and more comfortable rolling stock, to offer an inviting alternative to the private car, where high density made this desirable. Standards for rapid transit were detailed, both to serve the central business district better and to help the region as a whole. These standards included: service to within a five-minute walking distance of all points in the inner core; practically continuous frequency (one- or two-minute headway); average speed of twelve miles per hour; convenience of service and comfort of riding (clean, attractive, and modern); and a reasonable fare. Capital improvements recommended by the report amounted to $1.6 billion over a twenty-five-year period—as compared with *annual private* expenditures in the city of about $1.3 billion for ownership and operation of automobiles and trucks. In spite of this outlay necessary for capital improvements, the report suggested that the cost of transportation *as a whole* should and could be self-supporting. One of the board's strongest recommendations was to create a regional transportation organization, vested with the necessary powers to develop and administer a comprehensive transportation system, "and a balanced reliance on rails and rubber . . . to equalize advantages over the total system. The report was thus a victory for the view that preservation of the central business district depended on regional control of transportation and restoration of rail transit to a prominent role," as Charles Gilbert put it.[25]

The blueprint was set. In it the transportation system took the needs of all other activities into account. By the time Dilworth took over as mayor he had the report to guide him on all matters

25. Charles E. Gilbert, *Governing the Suburbs* (Indiana University Press, 1967), pp. 202–3.

of transportation, and he made its recommendations a major part of his program throughout his term. In the Sunday supplement of the Philadelphia *Inquirer* which appeared on the first day of his term, he vowed to "get people out of the automobile and back into the use of mass transportation. In order to do that, our mass transportation must be speedy, more convenient, with better service, modern equipment, and at a reasonable fare." [26] Transportation, to Dilworth, was as much a public responsibility as the supply of water.

Dilworth's interest in implementing the UTTB's recommendations as a basis for his other developmental plans led him to appoint a second board for the task, now under the managing director. John Bailey, by that time deputy managing director, was made executive director of the new board, and as such became the city's transportation coordinator, while Charles Frazier became its chairman. Dilworth felt that the transportation system might be too hard a nut for the Planning Commission staff to crack. So he appointed a special five-man task force "within the administration" (Wagner, Bailey, Frazier, Harold Kohn [a member of Dilworth's former law firm], and the mass transit expert of the Department of Public Property) to coordinate all the suggestions the new board would make. (Harold Kohn claims, in a letter to the author, that many ideas originated in the task force.) Transportation became a totally integrated system, reaching out beyond the city into the region vitally affected by it. Further, the system, in danger of becoming highway-oriented,[27] was infused with a series of imaginative ideas to encourage the citizens of the Philadelphia region to use mass transit again.

## Experiments with Mass Transit

Balancing the system was not easy, since Philadelphia needed more freeways and more mass transit—for different reasons and

26. Philadelphia *Inquirer,* Sunday supplement, "Today," January 1, 1966.
27. A regional transportation study, "Penn-Jersey," was worked out by professionals who appeared to favor more highways; it used the low-density traffic pattern existing at the time it collected its data to project an essentially highway-oriented plan. Its successor agency, the Delaware Valley Regional Planning Commission, projected the same bias in 1969. See the editorial, "Regional Plan Is Found Skimpy on Mass Transit," Philadelphia *Bulletin,* April 29, 1969.

in different sections of the area. In many parts of the city—not only in its central part—there were old, narrow streets reflecting Philadelphia's early-settlement pattern. Now serving densely populated and built-up areas, some even industrialized, these narrow streets caused ever more intolerable congestion. Yet the freeways, needed to enable traffic to bypass the Center City, generated an increasing number of cars onto the narrow feeder streets. It was estimated that, if the trend continued, long before the end of the century every other building in Center City would have to be torn down to provide parking space.

Philadelphia's freeway problem was not essentially different from that of other cities. However, profitable use was made of "working committees" (see preceding chapter) to implement the decisions made by the public-private policy-making committees. All those who might have had any interest in the route or timing of a particular freeway could thus consult on each of these working committees.

One specter which had long haunted the solution to mass transit problems had been the privately owned transportation company. It raised fares, discontinued lines, and saw little reason to improve the system in order to increase ridership. From the time he took office, Mayor Dilworth was determined to have the city buy the Philadelphia Transit Company and establish policies for the more effective operation of the system. It was against this background that all attempts were made to improve mass transit during the entire period. Spokesmen for the shareholders of the PTC held out as long as they could, and even though they lost one legal battle after another, they were able to delay actions which would have improved mass transit.

Part of the problem was that Tate, while president of city council, thought that the PTC should be bought by a regional organization rather than by the city, while Dilworth was concerned about gaining policy control soon. Tate, even after he became mayor, was slow in pushing for legislation establishing the Southeastern Pennsylvania Transportation Authority (SEPTA). Labor trouble in the company convinced him of the necessity to act fast, and he then recognized the need to have a regional authority acquire and plan *all* means of transportation in the area (the city-owned subways, the PTC, the suburban bus lines, and what high-speed rail lines to New Jersey existed). Tate put all his political muscle behind it, and SEPTA was finally created. It began operation in 1964.

## The Service Standard Board

The 1957 renegotiation of the city's 1907 agreement with PTC led to a provision for the joint determination of operating policy. This was Frazier's idea; the lawyers were able to work it into the new agreement, and John Bailey made it work for as long as both the city and PTC wanted to have this arbitration procedure succeed. One member each from the city and the PTC and an impartial chairman constituted the Service Standard Board, which tried to enforce the standards outlined by the UTTB. The standards emphasized greater frequency and speed of subway trains and buses, suggested new routes, including the loop within Center City, tried to prevent the abandonment of lines, and pushed for more service in off-peak hours. The board represented a novel approach toward ensuring that a private operator would consider the public interest. Its chairman—an excellent technician—acted, in effect, as an arbitrator. But the board foundered eventually because the PTC refused to believe that better service would, for the system as a whole, increase ridership and thus revenues—and also because Tate's support for the Service Standard Board waned. Unsure that the city (rather than a regional authority) should buy the company, Tate permitted the service standard agreement to fall by the wayside. As the PTC sought to ensure stockholders' short-term earnings, it objected to many demands made by the chairman of the Service Standard Board, but the resulting compromises reached were invariably more beneficial to the riders than unilateral actions by the PTC would have been.

## Commuter Railroads

Philadelphia's commuter railroad routes were more conveniently placed than in many other areas of the country. But the railroad companies offered only slow and infrequent service, used obsolete rolling stock, charged high fares, and complained about losing money. Determined to do what he could for the transportation system, Dilworth (and Bailey) devised a method to preserve and improve commuting. The conception was that service decline and abandonment of rail lines could be halted if financial aid by the public were directly geared to improved service; the necessary fare reduction to make railroad service competitive could be recouped by more riders. Such aid would imply less of a burden to the taxpayer than the construction of otherwise necessary highway facilities. Charles Frazier put it this way: "Philadelphia believes that the mass transportation services can and must be improved and extended; that this will result in a lower overall cost to the community; and that speed and convenience can be achieved to the extent necessary to secure the requisite degree of ridership. It believes that to do this, however, it must have policy control over the services involved." [28] Because highways require low densities for efficiency, continued reliance on highways would spread uneconomic low densities and erode values in older areas. The counties, therefore, needed an overall transportation policy.

The city's desire to expand and coordinate high-speed mass transportation efforts led to the establishment of a nonprofit corporation, the Passenger Service Improvement Corporation (PSIC). Under the ordinance establishing it, the corporation could enter into agreements with the Pennsylvania and the Reading railroads for operation of certain passenger transportation services within the city. These agreements would set fixed standards, fares, schedules, and equipment and would provide a subsidy to be paid by the city, equalling the railroads' net out-of-pocket expenses up to a set maximum.[29] The city council appropriated the necessary amounts ($1.8 million in 1962, PSIC's second year of operation). As Bailey put it, if suddenly all commuter lines were discontinued, and the state had to build a highway wide enough to handle all the people who take the trains during rush hours, it would cost $77 million a year to pay for the highway. The city subsidy to keep the commuter trains running obviously compares favorably with this amount.[30]

28. Charles Frazier, address at the Greater Philadelphia Movement's Annual Dinner, October 1957.

29. Greater Philadelphia Movement memorandum, "The Passenger Service Improvement Corporation," January 1961.

30. Philadelphia *Bulletin,* Sunday magazine, January 2, 1966.

The commuting experiment started with the lines within the city proper going to the northwestern part of the city ("Operation Northwest") and then spreading to other lines ("Operation Northeast," etc.). It was agreed that new service would be added; the fares *within* the city would be cut; and modern, light, clean, air-conditioned cars would be purchased with the help of city credit. Parking facilities near railroad stations would be constructed. The railroads would thus be paid by the city to run trains more frequently, more conveniently, and a combined lower bus-rail fare would be offered (home-to-office service).[31] The first year the new arrangement was in operation, the 30-cent fare provided an increase in ridership of 41 percent on the "Operation Northwest" line, as compared to the last year prior to the experiment. "Operation Northeast," however, which served an area with relatively few expressways and highway arteries, increased ridership on the line by 430 percent, even though that line was not yet electrified. By 1964 the experiment had been extended to ten lines, and the average ridership increase had been no less than 40 percent on any line.[32] All told, the experiment "has proved its ability to increase ridership to the point that passenger income at the reduced fare is now equal to that prior to the experiment." [33]

## The Suburbs Join

This railroad subsidy was, however, only applicable within Philadelphia, as it was paid by the city. Gradually suburbanites began to complain that they paid a higher fare for poorer service than did passengers getting on the railroad at the first station within the city limits. Some even drove to that station to get on the train there. Several Pennsylvania suburban counties agreed to join in the program, and they associated themselves with the city in 1962 in a new nonprofit corporation for this purpose (the Southeastern Pennsylvania Transportation Compact—SEPACT). Delaware County was the only county of the three adjacent to Phila-

31. Pennsylvania Economy League–Bureau of Municipal Research, *Digest of Improved Transportation for Southeast Pennsylvania* (Philadelphia, 1960).
32. Philadelphia *Bulletin*, September 13, 1964.
33. Report of the (new) Urban Traffic and Transportation Board, April 1956–May 1960, p. 6.

delphia that continued to refuse to join the compact.[34] John Bailey, who had by that time (1968) left the employ of the city administration, became the executive of both PSIC and SEPACT.

The city is still unclear about what features actually provided the main attraction and to what degree—a question of importance for those public officials who want to adapt the experiment to their own cities: reduced fares, increased service, improved schedules, or new equipment? Or was it the substantial promotion through mass media? It might have been a combination of these factors, making it impossible to determine which of them was primarily responsible. It is unfortunate that the federal grant for the experiment was not structured in terms of control groups so that this question could be answered by separating experimental groups for each possible cause for the observed success.

While the nonprofit suburban railroad corporation marked the next step toward establishing a regional authority and obtaining publicly controlled, region-wide transportation, Philadelphia's improvement of mass transit had gained national attention as one of the few apparently successful local attempts to attract passengers. The program not only halted further abandonment of commuter railroad service but reactivated service which had previously been discontinued. Philadelphia followed its own area-wide comprehensive transportation plan, which provided cheaper and better access to its development programs. Both Clark and Dilworth had tried through the years to convince Congress that the federal government should support mass transit as a vital part of its aid to metropolitan areas. Dilworth got other interested groups together to support such legislation. In 1960, when he testified before Congress as president of the American Municipal Association (now the League of Cities), he could cite Philadelphia's success in subsidizing commuter railroads.

The Mass Transportation Act was passed in 1961. It provided that demonstration projects should be administered by what became the U.S. Department of Housing and Urban Development. (This portion of the department's responsibility was later transferred to the Department of Transportation.) The grant for the railroad tunnel was one such project.

34. See Gilbert, *Governing the Suburbs,* for the political reasons for Delaware County's refusal.

*The Tunnel and Regional Impact*

A run-down shopping area east of City Hall had been eyed for wholesale refurbishing for a number of years. Pedestrian walkways, shopping arcades, and underground linkages between different parts of the city were envisaged (see chapter 8), and in the winter of 1958–59 it was suggested that all this be tied into the transportation innovations planned for the area. The entire complex was to be called "Market Street East."

A tunnel several blocks long was to be built in mid-city. This would connect underground the terminals of the two railroads serving the Philadelphia area. It was an imaginative suggestion of transportation specialists to improve commuting from the entire area to Center City. It would make it possible to run trains on the tracks of both railroads, downtown on one of them, and returning on the other. The plan would not only improve service but would also reduce operating costs substantially, since the number of railroad cars and services needed for both roads would decline. Bailey estimated the cost saving at $1.7 million annually.

At the same location, a new bus terminal would be built, largely for buses commuting from New Jersey, as well as a parking facility for four hundred cars. Each would be at a different level of this large "Terminal Hall." Freeway ramps would lead into the terminal and parking garage through separate lanes, accommodating people arriving by bus as well as by car, in addition to those brought in by railroad or subway. The shopping arcades and underground walkways would make the entire area interesting and attractive.

The projected cost of the tunnel soared from an original $48 million to more than $60 million in the late sixties. But, though the imaginative idea has been widely discussed, the tunnel has so far not been built. One problem was the long delay in SEPTA's purchase of the PTC. Conflicts with labor unions of both the PTC and the suburban (Red Arrow) lines, which insisted on job guarantees first, gave the federal government pause. But Philadelphia's administration seemed uncertain about its own priorities. For a long time the grant request to the Mass Transit Administration for the tunnel had clearly held first priority. As it was now being delayed time and again, the lower priorities suffered. Finally Tate assigned equal priority to the purchase of rolling stock for the commuter railroads, and to the commercial and transportation aspects of Market Street East, as to the tunnel. Instead of speeding up the receipt of one or other grants, however, these additional requests appeared to halt progress. Washington allocated grants to other localities which had indicated clear priorities. Grave doubts were voiced whether the tunnel, far from becoming a showpiece for the Bicentennial, would ever be built.[35]

In spite of this disappointing miscalculation, the regional transportation system seems on its way, and other broad-ranging development programs are being carried with it. SEPTA, in cooperation with another regional organization—the bi-state Delaware River Port Authority—has seen to it that a high-speed railroad line into New Jersey has been built. Two more lines are planned. At least as important is the fact that civic groups are making a new effort to help Philadelphia's system reach into the region: in 1967 the Greater Philadelphia Movement added an associate executive director specifically to help organize *de novo* regional committees concerned with transportation. This is an attempt to succeed where an earlier regional nonprofit corporation ("Penjerdel") was less than successful. It is encouraging that this prominent civic group is now willing to make another attempt to have different parts of the region understand the importance of regional cooperation on all matters of development and also to perceive them as complementary parts of the total picture.

35. Philadelphia *Bulletin,* September 2 and 9, 1969.

# 6    Urban Renewal and Housing

> Mayor Richard Lee of New Haven has
> proved to many a practical politician that
> there is gold in urban renewal, and not
> just Washington gold. Mayor Daley of
> Chicago finds his planners' pictures [of
> housing developments] the best sort of
> election posters—ones that get published
> in the press—for free.
>
> Norton Long, "Planning and Politics in Urban
> Development." *Journal of the American Institute
> of Planners* (November 1959), p. 168.

In urban renewal, competition for available resources takes place within the whole capital program: there is not only residential renewal, but also industrial or commercial redevelopment, institutional renovation, rehabilitation of the waterfront, and restoration of historic areas. A renewal dollar must be stretched to cover all of these, or as many of them as policy decisions dictate. Philadelphia conceived these activities "as a balanced program providing better residential neighborhoods on the one hand, and stimulating economic and cultural development on the other." [1]

"Philadelphia is world famous for the scope and diversity of its renewal program. It has suggested many of the major innovations made in the Federal renewal program," claimed the Philadelphia Housing Association in 1965.[2] Many of its facets, innovative at the time of the reform, seem "old hat" today. Other approaches were tried in this period which, had they been given

1. Philadelphia Housing Association, *A Citizens' Guide to Housing Programs in Philadelphia* (Philadelphia, 1968), p. 37.
2. Philadelphia Housing Association, "New Housing Built through Urban Renewal," *Issues,* December 1965.

sufficient funds and allowed to work out their problems, might have proved that they were worth adoption by other cities; but the circumstances changed or the period under discussion ended before their worth could be firmly established.

There is a story about Philadelphia's renewal—really a dream. William Penn appears surrounded by a crowd of little people pulling at his coattails, crying for him to do some little favor for each. Penn's roost atop the City Hall tower is shut off from the city beyond by high walls labeled "red tape," "property rights," "financial problems," and others. Penn is huffing and puffing at a horn as Joshua did before Jericho to blow down the walls. "The striking thing is not that the road to the promised land was so long and so tortuous," says the commentator, reporting the allegorical dream, "but that the huffing and puffing was producing results. The walls shielding the city against change were beginning to crumble . . . the Revolution that renewal was designed to bring, in the face of the city and the lives of its citizens, had indeed been slow to erupt. It had crumbled and groaned and resisted. It was finally being born." [3]

Urban renewal has been described by Leo Grebler as the "deliberate effort to change the urban environment through planned, large-scale adjustment of existing city areas to present and future requirements for urban living and working—all in the framework of an overall plan for a city's development." [4]

During much of Philadelphia's reform period, the capital program allocation for urban renewal stayed at a fixed amount; this meant that the possible uses for this sum were in ever stiffer competition with each other. When Mayor Dilworth took office, the renewal of the central business district and the Center City historic areas gained ascendancy. Similarly, when federal law encouraged larger local shares to be devoted to nonresidential activities, Philadelphia's industrial areas seemed to demand a higher ratio to combat obsolescence. It was only in 1961 that in Philadelphia the relative priority of urban renewal in relation to

3. Mead Smith Karras's report to the Community Renewal Program of Philadelphia, part 6, "The Prospects," p. 392 (in Redevelopment Authority files).

4. Leo Grebler, *Urban Renewal in European Countries: Its Emergence and Potentials* (University of Pennsylvania Press, 1964), p. 13.

other capital expenditures was doubled, reaching a city cash contribution of $6 million. By the 1962–67 capital program, about 15 percent of total city funds, including loans, was expended on renewal activities.

At a professional meeting in 1960, the issue facing Philadelphia, whether the city should accede to the request of several universities for urban renewal funds, was presented as a case study.[5] If the requests were granted, the city would have to change its carefully designed priorities for rehabilitation of residential areas, industrial expansion, and renewal of downtown. If the city failed to assist these institutions, they might move out of the city.

The case study showed that a sophisticated city administration such as Philadelphia's had to face a number of questions: (1) What would be the relative effect on employment, income, and property values of the original decision on priorities and of a decision to reallocate funds to accommodate the universities? (2) How would the tax base and revenue be affected in each case as compared to the costs of services? (3) Do universities have to locate in the Center City area to facilitate attendance by area residents? (4) Is city living (given Philadelphia's cultural advantages) attractive enough to professional and scientific personnel to make their recruitment easier? (5) Would linkages with other institutions or other scientific facilities, such as hospitals and research organizations (external economies of agglomeration), be lost if the universities moved to the suburbs? (6) Would the city's prestige be impaired (for example, for the attraction of industry) by losing the universities?

On the other hand, if the question were viewed within a broader regional context—if it were assumed that the universities would stay within the region even if they moved outside the boundaries of the city—would not the *net* social product of the entire region be increased if the universities were permitted to relocate in the suburbs, leaving the city free to use its renewal

5. "Priorities in Urban Renewal Decisions," *Proceedings* (Regional Science Association, 1961), pp. 169 ff. Members of the panel were: William L. C. Wheaton, then of the University of Pennsylvania; Scott Greer of Northwestern University; Senator Joseph S. Clark; William L. Rafsky; and Morton Schussheim, then of the Committee for Economic Development. Schussheim wrote up the case.

funds as originally planned? The best interests of the city are
not necessarily consistent with the ideal solution for the entire
metropolitan area. The discussion of these alternatives was to
demonstrate the kind of priority decisions which faced the city's
policy-makers.

This prime dilemma plagued Philadelphia decision-makers
throughout. Were they to look at priorities merely from the city's
viewpoint, seeking the answer most beneficial to the economic
and social well-being of the city's residents, or even make decisions only from the narrow viewpoint of the city's fiscal advantage
—or should they, on the other hand, consider the net benefits to
the entire region? The question kept recurring. The threat to the
city's development was influenced throughout by the decisions
emphasizing the parochial as against the regional approach.

This chapter will emphasize residential redevelopment (see
table 1), leaving other chapters to subsequent discussion.

## A New Policy

As early as 1945, Pennsylvania passed a law to enable the establishment of redevelopment authorities. It was one of the first
states to do so. The law was drafted by Abraham Freedman (later
Mayor Clark's city solicitor), helped by Robert Mitchell, Dorothy
Montgomery, and Hans Blumenthal (who later became famous
as Toronto's planner). Philadelphia's Redevelopment Authority
(its five members appointed by the mayor) existed for six years
before the reform government was elected, but with only a very
small appropriation. Hence the City Planning Commission, which
has to start any renewal process by certifying an area as blighted,
declared one area after another to be ready for renewal—actions
neither necessary nor useful at the time—until the certifications
added up to a large part of the central city. These certifications
proved useful only if a developer could be found who was interested in renewing a particular area. (This was similar to the later
approach of Robert Moses in New York, which led to that city's
unplanned, project-oriented redevelopment.) The few isolated
projects started in Philadelphia at that time later haunted the
broadly planned new programs of the reform period, as the
necessity to complete these projects preempted funds needed for
the new programs.

TABLE 1    PERCENTAGES OF FUNDS EARMARKED FOR REDEVELOPMENT, 1953–67

| Period | Residential Clearance % | Residential Conservation % | Center City % | Industrial % | Institutional % | Unspecified by Program % |
|---|---|---|---|---|---|---|
| 1953–58 | 62.0 | ... | 24.0 | 8.6 | 5.1 | ... |
| 1954–59 | 66.0 | ... | 18.8 | 7.3 | 7.9 | ... |
| 1955–60 | 76.9 | ... | ... | 17.6 | 5.5 | ... |
| 1956–61 | 66.8 | 2.4 | ... | 25.8 | 4.0 | 1.0 |
| 1957–62 | 27.3 | 13.0 | 7.7 | 15.6 | 1.7 | 34.7 |
| 1958–63 | 31.9 | 17.8 | 15.4 | 21.0 | 1.6 | 12.3 |
| 1959–64 | 20.7 | 28.6 | 27.0 | 17.3 | 6.4 | ... |
| 1960–65 | 18.7 | 27.0 | 27.7 | 19.3 | 7.3 | ... |
| 1961–66 | 23.9 | 18.3 | 23.4 | 23.4 | 10.8 | ... |
| 1962–67 | 19.9 | 22.9 | 26.4 | 22.6 | 8.2 | ... |
| Total period, 1953–67 | 38.0 | 14.0 | 20.0 | 24.0 | 4.0 | ... |

SOURCE: *The Redevelopment Authority Program*, CRP Technical Report (September 1963), no. 6, Table III-I. Total monies involved: $223 million in city, state, and federal funds.

The Federal Housing Act of 1949 was the first law establishing the procedure for urban renewal—and to this day the law as amended remains the basis for renewal programs. Its purpose to renew entire blighted areas as well as individual dilapidated houses was from the start constrained by the principle that the action should not reduce the net supply of housing, especially housing for low- and middle-income families. Even before the advent of the reform government in Philadelphia, the principle was publicly expressed that redevelopment should be directed to providing adequate shelter for *all* income groups.[6] It had also been suggested earlier that housing for those who would be dislocated by public action should be built before these people were displaced from their old homes, but it was years before the need to guarantee relocation in comparable housing became an important prerequisite to any kind of redevelopment.

## The CURA Study

The Development Committee (see chapter 4), established by the Redevelopment Authority upon the urging of its newest member, Dorothy Montgomery, suggested the need for reviewing priorities among redevelopment programs. The various geographic renewal areas and their peculiar problems had first to be considered, along with possible solutions in each. Only then could the respective strategies (such as clearance, conservation, rehabilitation, and code enforcement) appropriate to each area be decided. The committee's discussions centered on the need for a broad-gauged and carefully planned approach.[7]

The Central Urban Renewal Study (CURA) was a clear outgrowth of the discussions of the Development Committee. It was carried out by the planning director of the Redevelopment Authority, David Wallace. But even before any results could be made public, an informal group of eleven citizens had urged upon the city a new "Housing and Urban Renewal Policy."[8]

6. Redevelopment Authority Annual Report for 1951.

7. Development Committee minutes, 1952 and 1953 (in files of the Philadelphia Housing Association).

8. "A Statement on Housing and Urban Renewal Policies for Philadelphia" (October 1955). The citizens included Robert Mitchell, former executive director of the City Planning Commission; William Wheaton, then director of the University of Pennsylvania Institute of Urban Studies; Martin

Carefully reasoned, it stated the need for a comprehensive plan for the city and suggested that an accelerating rise in the standard of living should be aspired to through the physical environment, so that ever widening areas should not become unfit to live in. A policy was needed "that realistically recognizes the magnitude of the problems, that sets forth goals which are explicit . . . and indicates programs necessary" for their attainment. Then followed discussion of the problems of increased private construction, including new financial devices; of clearance of existing slums (and those 5,000 dwelling units which would annually sink into the slum category) with detailed priority suggestions to be accomplished in eighteen years; of additional units of public housing, and relocation of all displaced persons; of periodic zoning and code review and their enforcement; of construction and rehabilitation of public service facilities; and of a detailed budget, increasing from $17 million to $60 million annually. While these eleven citizens did not think that their suggestions would be accepted overnight, they could justly expect that their combined prestige might exert an influence on the concerned citizenry.

The CURA study included almost all blighted or deteriorating areas of the city,[9] dividing them into three kinds of planning areas depending on the degree of blight. The worst, or oldest, areas ("A") required a large amount of clearance and strict code enforcement for houses left standing. The somewhat newer ("B") areas needed more rehabilitation and less than 50 percent clearance. The best and newest areas ("C") showed only slight deterioration and probably could be saved by eliminating "sore

Meyerson, then professor of city planning, University of Pennsylvania; Jefferson Fordham, then dean of the University of Pennsylvania Law School; Dorothy Montgomery, then member of the Redevelopment Authority and managing director of the Philadelphia Housing Association; Holmes Perkins, dean of the University of Pennsylvania School of Fine Arts; Aaron Levine, executive director, Citizens' Council on City Planning; and David Wallace, then planning director of the Redevelopment Authority.

9. There never was a "final" report, but the draft, dated March 1956, amounts to almost 200 pages. It is a companion to the shorter report prepared in February 1956 by the Comprehensive Planning Division of the City Planning Commission, containing the basic data about land uses and activities in the area, on which most of the analysis of possible and proposed renewal activities in the study of the Redevelopment Authority is based.

spots" in the neighborhood and providing more community facilities. The best areas were usually nearer the fringes of the city.

In projecting the cost of acquiring land for all necessary renewal, and then dealing only with those deteriorated areas which
already could be called slums, the study came up with the stagger-
ing figure of close to $1 billion. It would be a long time before
the city could find this much money. Moreover, the study also
made clear that, by the time the slums had been made habitable,
many other areas as yet not slums would have deteriorated into
slums.

With this information, city officials took another look. On balance, slums seemed to be growing faster at one location than they
could be eliminated at another. As redevelopment began in the
"A" areas, blight spread to the next circle. "It had been hoped
that an 'island of good' would favorably affect the 'swamp of bad'
immediatey surrounding it," Rafsky said.[10] "By clearing out the
worst spots, the area surrounding the redevelopment project
would be encouraged to undertake voluntary improvement. The
results, unfortunately, have been just the opposite." [11] The homes
that were intended for middle-income families often were not
occupied by them, thus stopping the filtering process; middle-
income potential residents may have been deterred by the bad
reputation of the neighborhood and its surroundings. Also, dislocated families wanted to stay near their old neighborhood,
thus crowding into adjacent areas and causing increasing dilapi-
dation, as homes became overcrowded and changed occupants
more often. This meant that deteriorating areas gradually extended from the center outward. (It must be kept in mind that it
has never been incontrovertibly proved what influences cause
blight to move from one area to another, although extensive ob-
servations give us a reasonably good idea of what may be responsible.) Neither creation of open spaces, nor construction of new
public facilities, nor any of the other inducements led to voluntary rehabilitation by home owners and thus to private im-

10. "A New Approach to Urban Renewal for Philadelphia" (statement
from the office of the development coordinator, March 1957).
11. William L. Rafsky, "Urban Renewal and Metropolitan Area Core—
Philadelphia" (lecture to Community Leadership Seminar, February 23, 1960,
Fels Institute of Local and State Government).

provement of these areas. It became clear that the city had to consider alternative strategies.

Philadelphia had started its renewal program comparatively early. Most of its first projects were aimed at clearing out the worst blight, and on several of the cleared sites high-rise public housing was erected to provide shelter for some of those who had been displaced.[12] Since Philadelphia appointed its housing co-ordinator and started its CURA study in 1954—the same year that the Housing Act amendments gave cities more discretion in renewal methods—it appears that Philadelphia was among the first cities to adopt federally assisted renewal programs. It was also one of the first to ask searching questions about how best to carry out such programs.

*Emphasizing Preservation*

In March 1957, following the findings of the CURA study, the housing coordinator announced a new policy for Philadelphia— a complete shift in emphasis. It was decided not to work in the worst central slum sections and to follow blight as it spread, but to start in "the outlying older neighborhoods in an effort to stop the spread and then gradually work inward through increasingly serious blight." [13] Thus the blight would be checked, and the re-development would be "anchored" to stable neighborhoods and not surrounded by areas with many substandard dwellings.

The strategy appeared to make sense. It implied the economical use of scarce public funds and the maximum encouragement of private investment by clearing only isolated blight and increasing public facilities such as parks and playgrounds, thus preserving areas that were salvageable. Philadelphia early shied away from the "bulldozer" approach and moved toward a combination of different tools in the good areas, a policy that eventually was followed by most other cities.

While public resources were being used to preserve the "C" areas on the fringes, the worst slums further in had to await their

12. These projects included East Poplar, North Allen, Southwest and Northwest Temple, and Mill Creek. It was estimated that the net reduction in dwelling units amounted to about 50 percent (Marcia Rogers, *The Re-development Authority Program*, CRP Technical Report, no. 6, September 1963).

13. "A New Approach to Urban Renewal," p. 4.

turn before any renewal was going to be applied to them, and that might well be a long time. The interim application of code enforcement proved not enough to make a real impact. The social costs of substandard housing imposed hardships which the earlier clearance policy had sought to allay.

## What Strategy?

In thrashing out alternative approaches in the 1956 meetings of the Interagency Committee on Housing,[14] it was suggested that as much of the CURA area as necessary be qualified as an area for General Neighborhood Renewal Plan (a program of the Housing Act of 1954), in order to take full advantage of all public facilities in the larger area for noncash credit. (This term, as used in the various housing acts, refers to the right of the local administration to pay its one-third of urban renewal costs not in cash, but by counting all manner of public facilities it was building for use in the renewal area.) Dorothy Montgomery and the Housing Association thought this approach advisable, as it would increase the available funds for renewal and also would take a broader view of the area to be redeveloped.[15] On the other hand, Edmund Bacon thought that if clearance provided open space in the older sections, without expanding the area for renewal, it might itself stimulate voluntary rehabilitation of housing. He spoke, in fact, in favor of a "scattered" approach to redevelopment, as compared to the more concentrated program which Rafsky advocated. A third approach was the extending of a "wedge" from Center City to areas where renewal was taking place or was scheduled—for example, from a line near the center through what might be a homogeneous area to, say, a project in West Philadelphia like the University of Pennsylvania.

The CURA report seemed penetrating. Rafsky's new policy, largely based on Wallace's recommendations, put great emphasis on conservation. He suggested that, at the rate of five conservation areas a year, all the "C" areas could be renewed in two six-

14. Interagency Committee minutes, January 17, May 3 and 17, June 17, 1956, and February 1957.

15. This is clearly explained in Dorothy Montgomery's lecture to the Leadership seminar, December 6, 1960, "Is Urban Renewal on the Right Track?" Fels Institute of Local and State Government (processed); also in a lecture by another member of the Redevelopment Authority (Goldie Hoffman) of February 19, 1958.

year capital programs, and he hoped thus to take care of the outer ring before moving on to other areas. But the competition proved too much for conservation areas; they had to compete with Center City, industry, the university area, and the old clearance areas. Most of those competing needs had vocal proponents, while the coordinator's office seemed the only "friend at court" for conservation. The 1957 policy statement allocated about a quarter of the available funds each to Center City, to industrial and institutional renewal, to completion of started clearance projects, and to conservation. *Ex post,* however, the budget looked different, for Rafsky's proposed five areas a year were whittled down to three and two and even one.

Right after the promulgation of the new policy, it was suggested that the Interagency Committee on Housing work up a timetable for conservation areas, so that every neighborhood would officially know what was being planned for it and when. But the uncertainty of costs and available funds, as well as the possible effect of such an announcement on investment in these neighborhoods, led to the abandonment of this timetable.[16] The discussion about priorities among renewal projects continued.

At its annual meeting in December 1957, the Philadelphia Housing Association presented a detailed statement, called "Let's Speed the Pace of Urban Renewal." It advocated a bolder and more imaginative approach to renewing the older parts of the city and called for pressure on Washington to ease its rules. "Compared with the need, urban renewal is still proceeding at a snail's pace. . . . The present rate of expenditures for redevelopment is six times that of the past. Even so, it will take fifty-nine years to do the job. . . . If we stop thinking in terms of projects and begin to think in terms of district-wide programs in all of the older parts of the city . . . this can mean $290 million in federal funds instead of the $64 million now expected. This would permit a redevelopment program three-and-a-half times as large as the one now planned." [17]

A larger renewal area (such as the proposed General Neighbor-

16. Mead Smith Karras's report to the CRP, part 2, "Strategy: Policy and Priorities," pp. 48–51 (see n. 3 above).
17. Mimeo outline November 22, 1957, final draft December 1957. Also published by Philadelphia Housing Association in *Issues,* January 1958, pp. 1–3.

hood Renewal Program for South Philadelphia) would not only permit federal noncash grants for all community facilities in the area, but also more imaginative renewal projects. Henry Beerits, cofounder of the Committee on City Policy (see chapter 2) and now president of the Philadelphia Housing Association, exchanged letters with Rafsky. "If Philadelphia . . . provided program activities in all parts of the CURA, [it] . . . would make the city eligible for more than $100 million in federal funds." Rafsky answered: "If the city's plans were based on hoped-for funds not in hand, we would . . . encourage residents of areas to prepare for urban renewal, then let them down if the funds did not come through, with possibly shattering consequences if we ever attempted to revive the program." [18] The Interagency Committee on Housing decided that the city was already following a practice of anticipating more renewal funds than might realistically be expected under federal regulations, and Beerits's suggestion was not adopted. (For the time it took for even a renewal project with top priority to be completed, see chapter 8, table 2.)

## The Conservation Approach

The term "conservation" is much harder to define than clearance, since it uses a variety of tools, depending on the special needs of the area to be improved. Clearance of eyesores, rehabilitation of an individual blighted house, provision of community facilities or a recreation field, availability of public funds or privately invested funds—any or all of these might result in private redevelopment of an area. Economic feasibility studies were undertaken to demonstrate that proposed government actions would bring forth enough private investment to change an area's appearance and thus to make the public activities worthwhile. Since limited public funds, in conservation projects, could primarily be used to stimulate private activities (for example, of home owners), the question was always which of the different possible devices would lead to maximum voluntary rehabilitation.

One could not always be sure, in retrospect, whether the building of a children's playground, or the removal of a junkyard, or

18. Henry Beerits to William L. Rafsky, April 9, 1957; William L. Rafsky to Henry Beerits, May 9, 1957.

the restoration of historic houses nearby were in themselves responsible for rehabilitation in an area. Experience in one neighborhood might not necessarily be applicable to the next.

A rehabilitation experiment was carried out in the East Poplar area before it was even a renewal project. In 1952, the Friends' Neighborhood Guild and the American Friends' Service Committee formed the "Self-Help Housing Program" for the purpose of building cooperative units. A block of deteriorating houses was acquired by these Quaker groups. A savings bank took the mortgage. And the previous and/or potential residents formed a cooperative. The number of dwelling units was reduced by one-third to relieve crowded conditions. The skilled work was performed by a union labor contractor; for purchasers who could not finance the down payment, the required 10 percent was advanced by the Friends' Committee but could be paid back through use of their own (unskilled) labor on the building—so-called sweat equity. In spite of this, some original tenants were unable to afford the carrying charges. Though the Quakers' interest continued to be engaged because of the fully integrated nature of the housing community, the planned rehabilitation proved to be almost as expensive as new construction. The Friends' Neighborhood Guild therefore had to underwrite a deficit for a while, not only for the construction costs but also for operating expenses. The Quakers did not repeat the experiment in the same neighborhood—in fact they were reluctant to repeat it anywhere.

## Financial Help

Financing is usually the touchstone in owner rehabilitation unless a private investor is at hand. Special FHA guarantees are provided for by law in all designated urban renewal areas so that those being dispossessed have an opportunity to relocate in a newly rehabilitated house. Unfortunately, FHA specifications are designed for new housing only. Hence, the Philadelphia administration tried to induce the Washington FHA office to issue amended standards and specifications for rehabilitation. Philadelphia also tried to get local FHA officials to modify their approach—to judge the future of any home by the way the *entire area* would look after rehabilitation had taken place—the way the law intended them to act. But who was to change the conviction of local FHA officials—often reacting as conservatively as bankers—that an area would never really change? Literal interpretation of the rules delayed any positive action, notwithstanding periodic visits by Washington teams appealed to by frustrated city officials. The city received only two minor loans after more than a year's solicitation.

Mayor Dilworth complained to a Senate committee: "FHA will simply not insure in the bulk of the neighborhoods in which rehabilitation is so badly needed. . . . The program has been mainly used for making good houses better rather than for making poor homes good. . . . FHA estimates of value are so low that the insurable mortgage is too small to cover both the acquisition or refinancing cost *and* rehabilitation costs. . . . The FHA objective should be to bring about an ample supply of good housing and not just to take the risk out of private investment and avoid losing money in the process!" [19]

Philadelphia's banks, having been dominated by the same families for generations, were rather conservative. The FHA was created to encourage banks to take risks by guaranteeing loans, but the local FHA only reinforced the bankers' unwillingness to risk capital for the rehabilitation of older areas. This double impediment proved hard to overcome and continued to be a serious obstacle through most of the period under discussion.

In 1967, the FHA attempted to set new standards for old houses to be rehabilitated. It ruled that the "belief" of a local office about the likely condition of an area after rehabilitation should not determine its actions, that what had been previously considered the "economic" life of a house should be disregarded, and that FHA programs had to be made available in older neighborhoods, to avoid the "shutting off of capital investments in these areas." [20] The change in rules did not result in an apparent change in local attitudes, however.

### Community Organization

In conservation areas it was vitally important that the residents be involved. It seemed to the city that a vigilant neighborhood

19. Statement before the Subcommittee on Housing of the U.S. Senate Banking and Currency Committee, April 5, 1961.
20. FHA letter no. 63, July 31, 1967.

group would be likely to provide a shield against decline. Philadelphia's experimental "leadership program" was instituted in the middle 1950s, long before resident involvement had become fashionable in city conservation. In 1954, Philadelphia succeeded in obtaining federal funds for a demonstration project to find out how far city-citizen cooperation could stimulate improved housing and neighborhood conditions. The project was tried by the city in four radically different areas (from heavily blighted to moderately declining), and was evaluated in the next two years by an independent special staff. The conclusion reached was that resident involvement was ineffective in seriously blighted areas, but partially accomplished its purpose where rehabilitation of homes and improvement of the environment were the basic problems. In each of these areas a neighborhood council, a settlement house, or another nongovernmental body had taken responsibility, though both city officials and citywide organizations had supported the effort. The evaluation stated that in a moderately blighted area (Morton) "citizen activity should be aimed at voluntary improvement," with the staff "a combination of City law enforcement technicians and community relations personnel." An area of beginning blight (Haddington) should push "voluntary improvement" and "organizing residents, with full-time City staff assigned." [21]

The Morton area of Germantown (which itself has suburban characteristics, though it is in the city) was a pocket of blight in a generally good residential area. The Germantown Settlement had formed the Morton Neighborhood Council, which in turn organized several "block" groups for housing rehabilitation and neighborhood improvement. The council's Planning Committee reviewed extensively the proposals of the Planning Commission staff and of a consultant, made its own recommendations, and then prepared a plan for submission to Washington. Rehabilitation of many individual blighted houses was accomplished on a voluntary basis, or through code enforcement where the owners were unresponsive. Though an active neighborhood organization

21. *Partnership for Renewal: A Working Program* (City of Philadelphia, in cooperation with the Federal Housing and Home Finance Agency, September 1960). The remainder of the present section relies heavily on this publication.

continued, and many residents devoted time and effort to it, it could not function independently of the settlement's professional assistance.[22]

Haddington is in the western part of West Philadelphia, an area which, during the "leadership" period, was attracting an increasing number of Negroes as their economic lot improved. The neighborhood had a ten-year-old neighborhood community council, which in turn organized some as yet unorganized parts of the area when the leadership program started, partly with full-time help by a staff member of the development coordinator's office. The areawide Haddington Leadership Organization was then set up, and a large number of people in the area became deeply involved. The organization established a Planning Committee, a Housing Committee, and an Environmental Committee. The Housing Committee decided which structures should be rehabilitated and which demolished on the basis of "housing goals" they had decided upon, and then tried to induce home owners to bring their properties in line with these goals. About twelve to fifteen hundred privately owned properties were renovated. The establishment of adequate schools was urged, and renewal funds were obtained for schools and community facilities and for the removal of junkyards and other objectionable conditions with which the community itself could not deal. All leaders had in common "a clear recognition of the need for action to prevent their neighborhood from sliding into deterioration, an unreserved acceptance of the principle that the citizens themselves must act to this end, and an abiding conviction that, so long as the city cooperated and supported the same objectives, citizen action could indeed save the neighborhood." [23] The goal of a widespread, effective, and essentially independent organization was more nearly reached in Haddington than elsewhere, with pride of ownership and awareness of neighborhood.

To improve an area beyond the redevelopment of individual homes, developers and private capital were needed, though dis-

22. Morton was one of the few projects spoken of with approval by Jane Jacobs because of its sensitive treatment of physical and social planning issues and its strong community involvement.

23. *Partnership for Renewal,* pp. 59–60.

appointingly slow in becoming available. The proximity of a declining area, or the number of dilapidated homes, might have been the reason in different cases. Individual homes in decaying areas may be successfully rehabilitated in some cases, but little overall profit can be expected to attract investors. If there is reason to expect that an entire area will change its character and receive a new lease on life, however, investors will be interested. This was the case in several areas of Center City (see chapter 8) —in some because of the revival of historic areas, in others because of the reflected "snob value" of the historic areas or because of the newly awakened demand for town houses.

If the "almost good" fringe areas had been saved, as was intended, conservation could have been demonstrated as successful. But the normal progress of blight from the center outward was hard to stop, especially since the suburbs provided little relief by absorbing low-income families, and there was not much new construction in Center City, which could give the "filtering" process (see below) new fillip. The tragedy of urban redevelopment is that few city areas actually get renewed, little new housing is built in the city, and thus the movement to "better" housing leads to more decay because still more people have occupied the same dwelling during its lifetime. Growing families add to the problem. Not only "bulldozer" clearance, but also new and more imaginative approaches to urban renewal have met with failure and, consequently, criticism.

## Code Enforcement

Code enforcement is a necessary underpinning for renewal. Ordinances to strengthen Philadelphia's code enforcement were continually being sought. Early achievements of the new administration were the creation of the Department of Licensing and Inspections, the adoption of new housing, building, and fire codes, and the passage of a new zoning ordinance. But without enough inspectors to respond to daily complaints, and magistrates willing to penalize home owners disregarding violation citations from the inspectors, the city could not prevent further deterioration, which was especially expected in areas designated for eventual renewal.

*New Legal Tools*

Code enforcement has different meanings depending on the kind of use home owners intend to make of their property. The owner-occupier's prime concern is to maintain his home in good condition for his own daily living comfort. The absentee landlord, an investor, usually owns enough real estate to effect economies of scale in management. He often finds himself renting to low-income tenants. A violation notice means a reduction of his profit on his investment in order to correct the violation. Since theoretically he is not permitted to rent the property until the violations have been corrected, its market value in its present condition is zero. The cost of the required improvements must then be equal to at least the capitalized value of the rent received after code violations are corrected. The landlord may try to pass part of this code correction cost on to the tenant, may abandon his property when faced with the need to put money into maintenance, or may try to sell the property before correcting the violations, leaving the inspectors to find the new owners and start violation proceedings from scratch. The Commonwealth of Pennsylvania required a certificate declaring the property to be in compliance with all regulations before sale could be consummated, but the extent to which this was actually enforced is questionable.

Thus, one effect of code enforcement is to depreciate the value of substandard properties. But whether the owner ultimately pays for the required improvements depends on the supply in the particular housing submarket involved. If the market is tight, the cost will be passed on to the tenant, and that may mean displacement or doubling up if he is unable to bear the additional rent any other way. Philadelphia has designed the following measures to make code-enforcement more effective.

1. Magistrates are urged not to grant landlords a long period for compliance, or to permit those owning a number of properties in violation to improve them one at a time according to *the owners'* priorities.

2. Through a 1956 ordinance, the city has the right to enforce its orders by correcting the violations using its own crews, or by

contracting out the work and assessing the cost of repairs against the property. For several years Clark tried unsuccessfully to get such a law passed by the state. The lien can also be taken out of the rent paid, collected at the time of the owner's death if he cannot afford it earlier without serious hardship, or obtained by selling the house at sheriff's sale, all depending on individual circumstances. "All funds expended should be collected promptly, so as not to subsidize slum owners indirectly," says the Philadelphia Housing Association. "Use of the City's abatement power might be a most effective way of dealing with the problem of low income owners who cannot comply with the code. . . . [The lien] would be collected when the property is sold or transferred to another owner." [24] Unfortunately, this device has been used only sparingly, largely because the ordinance providing for it was never funded sufficiently to be fully effective.

3. A tax-delinquent property can be put up for sheriff's sale, and the city has the right to "buy in" for the amount of the tax owed. This is especially useful if a violation notice has induced the owner to stop paying taxes. Then it is up to the city to rehabilitate the property, use it for low-income families, or demolish it. Vacant lots or boarded-up buildings can also be acquired by the public, rehabilitated where possible and used by city, redevelopment, or housing authorities. Since 1965, vacant structures can be declared a public nuisance if the owner refuses to repair them, and can be rehabilitated or demolished.

4. Another method of exerting pressure on a landlord is through a 1966 state law which, in line with similar attempts in other states, provides for the withholding of rent from the landlord if he is in violation of the code. The rent is paid into an escrow account if the house is declared "unfit for habitation." The city can use the money to carry out the repairs, and after these have been made, the balance of the escrow account is turned over to the landlord. Alternatively, arrangements can be made with a contractor to receive the money and carry out the needed repairs, or the tenant can get his rent back if nothing has happened in six months, so that he can make a down payment on a newly

24. Philadelphia Housing Association, "Housing Programs for the Poverty Areas," *Issues,* February 1966, pp. 4–5.

renovated home. The rent escrow idea has begun to catch on in Philadelphia, and in some other areas; the city informs every tenant of his right under this legislation.

Code enforcement during much of the reform period was rarely effective in inducing home owners to rehabilitate. Still, the availability of the legal tools had the advantage that scarce urban renewal funds (both city and federal) did not have to be used to get rid of buildings in violation of the code.

## Relocation

Congestion is clearly one of the causes of blight; yet the displacement of residents from one area to another sometimes leads to further congestion. "Where people are moved from squalid dwellings in congested areas to decent homes in healthy neighborhoods, the renewal of the areas they have left can be augmented by the renewal of the people themselves." [25]

A central relocation service was provided by the Rehousing Bureau of the Redevelopment Authority assisting all those displaced by slum clearance, code enforcement, and other public purpose projects including highways. One of its main problems was to motivate those displaced so that they would understand the physical and social advantages to be gained by being relocated, as well as the resources available to them making it possible for them to benefit from this action. In 1958 the Philadelphia Housing Association undertook a survey which indicated that only three out of ten displaced families moved to satisfactory housing, seven of them relocating in housing below code standards. When Philadelphia was compared with other cities, it was concluded that other cities "have done far better," although Philadelphia was "an acknowledged leader in many phases of urban renewal." [26] The survey recommended that the Housing Bureau convince and relocate into proper quarters those who had found housing on their own which was below acceptable code standards. It further recommended that dislocated families be given first priority for public housing, and that, in addition to a

25. "A Relocation Policy for Philadelphia" (statement by the office of development coordinator, May 1960).

26. Philadelphia Housing Association, "Relocation—The Human Side of Urban Renewal," *Issues*, November 1958, p. 2.

certificate to this effect being issued by the bureau, responsibility be assumed for seeing that the family was accepted for public housing. Furthermore, the bureau should obtain help from social agencies for families "unable to cope with their problems in personal or social adjustment." [27]

Three studies of relocation problems were carried out by Elizabeth Wood, the last two in 1963 and 1965 for the Community Renewal Program. She concluded that "the question the City must face is whether it should try to unite social and physical rehabilitation in its renewal program, and if so, how such an agency should be constituted. This is a question that no city in the country has answered. . . . In time there will come into existence in every large city . . . a social welfare structure that will bring about a systematic rehabilitation of the City's deprived and underprivileged." [28] The Wood report recommended that a socially oriented Relocation Bureau explore with other public agencies the possibilities of common programs for "social rehabilitation of families affected by urban renewal and Code Enforcement." Although more research and thought was devoted to the question of relocation in Philadelphia than in many other cities, it is possible that what was needed was less research but more dedicated individuals to help the dislocated find decent dwellings.

## Housing for Low-Income Families

From the end of World War II, the avowed purpose of federal housing policy was to provide a decent, safe, and sanitary home for every American family. The first priority seemed obviously to belong to the low-income families; that is, to those who could not obtain a decent home in the private housing market. The classic way in which shelter in the private market becomes available to low-income families is through the filtering process (whereby vacated homes are taken over by progressively lower-income families).[29] Working from the top, this process is seldom effective in

27. Ibid., pp. 4, 5.
28. Elizabeth Wood, *The Needs of People Affected by Relocation*, CRP Technical Report, no. 17 (October 1965), pp. 50, 54.
29. The most extensive treatment of that phenomenon can be found in William Grigsby, *Housing Market and Public Policy* (University of Pennsylvania Press, 1963), chaps. 2 and 3.

providing decent housing for those at the lower end of the economic ladder, though those obtaining housing may still be better off than they were before. The low-income family is not likely to have enough money to maintain its new home. Hence it becomes a public responsibility to provide safe, sanitary, and uncrowded homes to those whose incomes are too low to obtain it through the private housing market. Different measures to this end were tried in Philadelphia.

In analyzing the 1956 housing inventory of Philadelphia, and comparing it with the 1950 census, William Grigsby found that the housing stock for low-income families had noticeably improved through the regular market process, due in part to the fact that better-off white families had moved to the suburbs, permitting poorer families to move to a limited degree into better housing.[30] But this statement needs explanation. The 1960 census reported that one-sixth of U.S. households lived in substandard housing. If code violations and overcrowding were also considered, about one-fourth of the country's population lived in housing that was less than "decent." The *percentage* of substandard units in the steeply increased (by 23 percent) U.S. housing stock, however, had *dropped* during the 1950–60 decade by about half. This apparent improvement, at variance with the general belief that slum housing conditions were getting worse, was counteracted by a simultaneous *increase* in the number of substandard dwelling units actually occupied, as well as an increase in the number of people living in those houses. In addition, those pushed into these high-density living areas were, at least in Philadelphia, primarily nonwhite. Thus the problem of low-income housing was still considerable during the reform period.

*Public Housing*

The oldest program designed to mitigate the housing problem of the poor has been public housing, first provided for by the Housing Act of 1937, which authorized construction of housing projects at federal expense. Philadelphia soon availed itself of this opportunity. Even this early depression-born remedy tied together slum clearance and rehousing of the dislocated. The first

30. Ibid., pp. 261 ff.

clearance projects under the urban renewal laws provided vacant sites, which were used in the fifties for building high-rise public housing projects. As early as April 1951, the Philadelphia Housing Authority commissioned a sociologist from the University of Pennsylvania to study the human, social, and "livability" consequences of elevator-type public housing apartments.[31] He suggested that density beyond twenty dwelling units per acre was detrimental to the formation of a community among the tenants; that social stresses resulted if the individual felt unable to control his own environment; that each family should be responsible for its own yard and other outdoor space, as this increased the status and dignity of all its residents, and that as incomes increased, tenants should not be required to leave the project, since this group would obviously include those with leadership potential whose departure would adversely affect any burgeoning community cohesiveness. In other words, public housing should not be built beyond a height of two or three stories if at all possible, and should be of low density.

The members of the Philadelphia Housing Authority are not all appointed by the mayor: the mayor and the city controller each appoint two members, and these four select a fifth. This gave Joseph Clark, when he was controller, the chance to appoint Walter M. Phillips, who changed the authority's image from that of an instrument of political patronage to one of an agency of social concern, as manifested by the commissioning of the 1951 study. The authority saw public housing as an opportunity for dealing with social problems and for strengthening the neighborhoods in which projects are being built. To mark twenty years of public housing, the Citizens' Council on City Planning and the Philadelphia Housing Association established a Committee on Public Housing in 1957, to review Philadelphia's program. Among the suggestions of the resulting report was "that public housing projects consist mainly of one or two story houses with private yards . . . and so designed as to appear not too different from the houses in the surrounding neighborhood . . . [and] that community facilities be available in public housing projects, and be available also to residents of the surrounding

31. Anthony F. C. Wallace, "Housing and Social Structure" (Philadelphia Housing Authority, 1952, mimeo).

neighborhood." [32] The report also proposed the purchasing of "existing houses on the private market for operation as low-rent public housing"—an experiment that became the "used house" program.

Unless a site had already been cleared as an urban renewal project, it became ever more difficult to find new sites that were acceptable for public housing, although the federal government allocated comparatively large numbers of housing units to Philadelphia. Rafsky complained: "There is a chronic shortage of sites which will meet the needs of public housing . . . [without] occasioning such a storm of protest as to make erection of projects there virtually impossible." [33] It soon became a racial-political question. Part of the problem was the objection of white politicians to integration in the projects, which they disliked even more than all-Negro projects. Negro leaders increasingly objected that all-Negro projects perpetuated segregation. However, realizing that the city needed public housing, if only to make other renewal projects possible by providing alternative shelter for those displaced, members of the council were apt to persuade the particular councilman in whose ward some units were proposed that it was "his turn." One year in the late 1950s, this situation led to a surprising result. The housing coordinator suggested instead that only a few inconspicuous low-rise units be built in each ward, so that no single ward and thus no single councilman would be appreciably affected. To a man the entire council revolted; without the possibility for logrolling, *all* refused to accept the plan, and, as no alternative was available at short notice, no public housing sites whatever were approved that year.

In 1954, the Interagency Committee on Housing and a subcommittee were charged with devising a weighted formula for public housing sites. They agreed on the following criteria: contribution to an urban renewal activity; net addition to housing supply; relation to community facilities and services; minimized

32. "Basic Policies for Public Housing for Low-income Families in Philadelphia" (report of the Committee on Public Housing Policy). Summary in *Issues,* November 1957.

33. William L. Rafsky, statement to National Association of Intergroup Relations Officials, November 29, 1956.

need for relocation; good environment; neighborhood acceptance; low site costs. Then all potential sites in the city were sur-
veyed, scored, and rated, and the committee made its recommendations on the basis of the scores. Although the final decision
probably had to be a political compromise, it was much more apt
to withstand political onslaught if careful reasoning stood behind the recommendations. The evaluation tried "to define 'desirability' from the broad viewpoint of the total city welfare," a
question on which "no clearcut guidelines existed." [34] But the
result was that, each year (except the one just mentioned), a
number of public housing sites were approved.

Clearly, public housing was a necessity for the lowest-income
families. But the reluctance of many home owners to accept
public housing in their own neighborhoods, and the fact that it
was increasingly hedged about with federal restrictive regulations,
prevented its functioning adequately. The Housing Authority
tried to increase public housing to a thousand units annually. But
it reached that goal only in 1963 and did not even come close in
any of the other years. By 1966, only about 14,000 public housing
units all told were in existence in Philadelphia; the law permitting their construction had been passed in 1937! [35] In 1967,
Mayor Tate set a "four year goal of 47,000 low and moderate income public housing units." Deputy Managing Director Gordon
Cavanaugh said in his annual report for 1970 that only slightly
more than 13,000 units had been built and fewer than 2,500 were
planned for 1971. The Philadelphia chapter of the Americans
for Democratic Action said that the battle for low-income housing was being lost.

Both the reform administration in Philadelphia and the civic
groups concerned with the housing problem tried to change local
and federal regulations to aid the families who needed help.
Many changes and devices were new in the Philadelphia reform
era, though they seem routine today. Of these devices probably
the best known is the Philadelphia "used house" program.

34. William L. Rafsky, "Our Changing City" (address to Sixth Ontario
Housing Conference, June 2, 1958).
35. Charles Abrams, "The Negro Housing Problem: A Program for Philadelphia," CRP Technical Report, no. 18 (December 1966), p. 92.

### *"Used House" and Other Alternatives*

"Public housing . . . is required as a concomitant to the renewal program. . . . But other programs are simultaneously necessary . . . because people are a diverse lot with individual likes and dislikes." [36] Philadelphia's Housing Authority was the first to get Washington's permission, in 1958, to buy privately constructed or rehabilitated houses for subsidized tenancy—what is today called "turnkey" housing in the case of new houses.

Buying and rehabilitating existing houses for subsidized rental to low-income families was suggested by the Philadelphia Housing Association and the Citizens' Council on City Planning through its Committee on Public Housing (mentioned above). Compared to new construction, these units are reasonably priced, especially those with space enough for large families. The program gives the Housing Authority more for its dollar, although it sets up detailed specifications for the rehabilitation before agreeing to the "take-out" after the completion of the work. The rehabilitation aspect also has a beneficial effect on the neighborhood and the housing environment, which is more apt to lead to social rehabilitation of the families involved. A survey in 1963 "showed that 'used house' tenants are accepted without reservation by their neighbors, including owner-occupants, [who] consider the program to have improved the neighborhood. There seems to be no social distinction made between a 'public housing' family and his better-off neighbors. (Some of this may be due simply to the uniformity of row housing. . . . One really can't tell the publicly owned house from the private house in the row without being told.)" [37]

The Haddington area was chosen as best suited for this experiment, partly because of the interest and strength of the Haddington Leadership Organization. Also, prices of houses there seemed comparatively reasonable for a pilot project. The Philadelphia Housing Association suggested that these houses be bought *anywhere* within the large Central Urban Renewal Area, in order not to upset market values in an isolated smaller

36. Ibid., pp. 93–94.
37. Philadelphia Housing Association, "Success for Experiment—The Used House Program," *Issues*, April 1963, p. 5.

area; but it strongly advised against purchase in areas considered to be in the "A" category—slums or near slums—lest social rehabilitation be too difficult. In effect, the authority restricted the area for the demonstration "used house." Although the program was held up for several years by a taxpayer's lawsuit, when it could be pursued again after 1962 it was considered a moderate success.

Citizen groups had long maintained that the rule which forced tenants out of public housing units when their income increased beyond the maximum permitted, had an overall detrimental effect. The Pennsylvania Economy League–Bureau of Municipal Research proved this by a survey of public housing tenants.[38] If the tenant were permitted to remain and pay a higher rent as his income rose, the public housing community as a whole would benefit. A "lease-purchase" plan was permitted by the Housing Authority under the 1965 Federal Public Housing Leasing Program. Tenants could apply part of their subsidized rent as equity under a purchase-option plan which enabled those with increased incomes to remain. The 1968 Housing Act also made it possible for those living in "used houses" to avail themselves of this option.[39]

## The Philadelphia Housing Development Corporation

Public housing, even in the newer forms introduced in Philadelphia, was essentially an undertaking to subsidize the rents of low-income families. To make home ownership more accessible to such families, however, the forging of new devices was needed—specifically, the availability of mortgages. It became apparent that low-income families could most likely achieve home ownership through another quasi-public corporation.

Various staff members of the development coordinator's office had urged such a corporation,[40] and it was agreed to as an important innovation at the October 1963 meeting of the Interagency Committee on Housing. The new organization's first task

38. Pennsylvania Economy League–Bureau of Municipal Research, *Retaining Tenant Leaders in Philadelphia Public Housing*, April 1966.

39. The deputy managing director for housing called this development a "great breakthrough," Philadelphia *Bulletin*, June 14, 1969.

40. Interoffice memoranda, August 16 and 21, and October 17 and 22, 1963 (in City Archives).

was seen to be that of helping neighborhood organizations acquire and rehabilitate homes to sell to low-income families, advancing funds to them for this purpose, and instituting a program of mortgage guarantees for those "whose low income would ordinarily prevent their obtaining credit from regular lending establishments." [41] The program would thus become a cooperative venture with these neighborhood organizations. In addition, the new corporation would stimulate the establishment of new neighborhood groups, which could similarly be helped to make home ownership possible for low-income families.

The Philadelphia Housing Development Corporation (PHDC) was started in the summer of 1964.[42] The city granted it a $2 million revolving fund, and the corporation's administrative expenses were covered by a grant from the antipoverty program. Four Philadelphia savings banks suggested setting up a $20 million mortgage and home improvement fund to provide financing in normally unmortgageable areas. This, they felt, would stimulate both rehabilitation and new construction. Even before the corporation was started, it had been suggested in a report to the CRP that a "Neighborhood Renewal and Rehabilitation Insurance Fund" be set up for similar purposes.[43]

The new corporation was to acquire properties through direct purchase, donation, or transfers from the city of tax-delinquent real estate (acquired at sheriff's sales), to rehabilitate such properties if they were structurally sound, and to build new, single-family dwellings on vacant lots. Both types of property were to be offered directly to prospective low-income owners for low prices, or to the Housing Authority in "move in" condition.

The PHDC's program of selling rehabilitated used houses was not to be limited to areas where the Housing Authority operated the "used house" program, although the two programs would

41. Pennsylvania Economy League–Bureau of Municipal Research, *Citizens' Business*, January 11, 1965.

42. Statement of development coordinator, March 13, 1964. Memorandum from City Solicitor Edward Bauer to Mayor Tate, July 6, 1964. Committee for the Formation of a Nonprofit Housing Corporation minutes, August 27, 1964.

43. *Proposal for a Neighborhood Renewal and Rehabilitation Insurance Fund—N—Double R—Insurance*, July 1, 1964 (prepared for the CRP by Bernard Meltzer and Edward Simon of the firm of A. M. Greenfield and Company).

strengthen each other. The PHDC would sell such houses in all parts of the city, particularly in older but still sound neighborhoods. In fact, it could extend its activities beyond the city limits.

The bylaws of the PHDC called for ten city directors, specifically named in terms of the official position they held, and twenty-five directors from the public at large, representing citywide organizations, to be named by the mayor. The directors were authorized to approve acquisition, sale, lease, or other disposition of land and other property, and their development, improvement, and maintenance. They were empowered to guarantee loans and mortgages.

The basic philosophy of this nonprofit corporation was that rehabilitation of substandard housing, stabilization of neighborhoods and promotion of owner-occupancy among low-income families would undergird any efforts of urban renewal in the affected area. PHDC seems, according to newspaper reports, to have found the turnover in single-family dwellings slower than expected, the needed repairs more arduous than anticipated, and the banks' $20-million revolving fund too slow in becoming available.

*Financing "Lower-Middle-Income" Housing*

Mastering financing problems was almost the only way to provide proper shelter for the low-to-middle income families, so long neglected. They were the people too "rich" to qualify for public housing, but too "poor" to obtain standard housing on the open market. Philadelphia struggled with the problem for years, both by trying to change the attitude of local banks (and local FHA representatives) and by suggesting changes in federal legislation.

The 1961 Housing Act made FHA insurance available for lower-middle-income families at below-market interest rates, if the housing was built by nonprofit organizations such as churches, cooperatives, or quasi-public corporations (like PHDC). Gradually, settlement houses, church groups, and civic organizations began to sponsor housing developments for these groups, but the total number of units built in Philadelphia was disappointing. PHDC worked assiduously at bringing decent homes within the reach of lower-middle-income families. FHA was supposed to insure mortgages for such undertakings on a long-term basis, up to forty years. Despite the guarantee, it was often difficult to find a lending institution willing to grant a loan, perhaps because of the kind of neighborhood involved, the income or age of the applicant, or the fact that the bank had no confidence in the future of the area. Philadelphia banks were slow in coming across with the $20-million revolving fund, so that PHDC was hampered in its attempts to aid these lower-middle-income families.

Appearing before the U.S. Senate Banking Committee, Mayor Dilworth stated that "once you go into the older neighborhoods, it is virtually impossible to get a really long-term mortgage—and the problem of the value set on the house arises immediately. . . . Our experience has suggested that the lengthened term is not enough. Reduction in the interest rate is needed as well, and we have therefore advocated—and still do favor—a program of direct government lending for this purpose." [44]

Philadelpha officials had long cast envious glances at New York, where the Mitchell-Lama law permitted hundreds of millions of dollars to be funneled into the low- and low-middle-income housing market. The city of New York issued tax-exempt bonds, secured by the rents and guaranteed by the city and hence cheaper than revenue bonds. Because of the tax-exempt status of the bonds, the issue was usually bought up quickly, mainly by insurance companies interested in financing construction for low- and middle-income families. The fact that the construction was carried out by limited-dividend corporations or cooperatives made it possible to take advantage of federal laws to obtain mortgages at a below-market interest rate.

In spite of frequent urging by the Philadelphia city administration, the Pennsylvania legislature refused to pass a law to permit the exclusion of such bonds from the calculation of city credit, given the fact that their interest was slightly higher than that on general obligation bonds. While these bonds were still a good investment for insurance companies in New York, they were not issued in Pennsylvania. As they had to be counted against the city's credit, it was feared that they might increase the interest paid on *all* the city's bonds.

Late in 1967, a new plan was adopted in Philadelphia: a development can now be sponsored by a nonprofit corporation

44. See n. 19 above, p. 19 of Dilworth's statement.

which will mix public-housing families and moderate-income families, some units with and some without a rent subsidy. Families can move from either category into the other, without having to move from the project.

## Minority Housing

According to the 1960 census, two-thirds of the inhabitants of substandard dwellings in Philadelphia were nonwhite. While the supply of standard housing had increased along with the declining density, the nonwhite low-income population had increased. This increased the pressure on substandard housing. Hence, rents and prices went up, raising the percentage of their income that poor nonwhites had to pay for shelter.[45]

In 1960, half of the nonwhite families were located in census tracts more than 80 percent nonwhite, and with their population increase the number living in extended segregated areas also rose. Though the rate of this population increase declined, their movement out of the ghetto remained slow, so that in the Philadelphia area the suburban percentage of nonwhites actually declined.[46] The philosophy of the reform government was clearly that, unless Negroes (or other minority groups) could be enabled to live anywhere within the metropolitan area according to their desires, one of the socially most important purposes of urban renewal would be missed. Mobility must be coupled with the attainment of standard housing. For that reason much of the effort of the period was directed at furthering integration and expanding choice.

Among many civic groups attempting to help were the Fellowship Commission, the Fair Housing Council of Delaware Valley, Friends' Suburban Housing, and (the latter's creation) the Philadelphia Metropolitan Housing Program, as well as some thirty suburban fair housing councils. Mayor Dilworth spoke of the

45. One-half of Negro families with incomes below $4,000 spent 35 percent *or more* for shelter, as compared to the 25 percent suggested as the maximum to be spent. At the same time, the percentage for the other income groups declined. (See appendix 3, Technical Report No. 14, pp. 48 ff.)

46. This is not true of most other large cities: the percentage in the suburbs of New York, Chicago, San Francisco, and Los Angeles increased by 50 percent or more from 1950 to 1960 (Harry Sharp and Leo Schnor, "The Changing Color Composition of Metropolitan Areas," *Land Economics*, May 1962).

need to break the suburban "white noose" around the city with the help of these civic groups, but he rarely spoke of those parts of the city which insisted on remaining "lily-white" (such as the northeast), for he was not sanguine about changing their attitudes. It was hard to accomplish Negro mobility in the metropolitan area, even if whites could be persuaded not to flee the city. Only a limited number of black families could afford the price of suburban houses; those who could, might not "fit" into the cultural and occupational environment there, even if civic groups worked hard to effect their acceptance; nor would they necessarily want to leave their accustomed neighborhoods, their friends, their churches, and go through the struggle of integrating a neighborhood.[47]

The charter had established, for the first time, an official Commission on Human Relations, one of whose tasks was to help Negroes to settle in formerly all-white areas within the city. The commission had been given the right to investigate and to use law enforcement when persuasion failed—but it tried to avoid this for fear of increasing racial tensions. "It is the Commission's practice in many cases to eliminate discrimination through conference and conciliation. Extended counselling, neighborhood organization work and surveillance are often required to counter rumors, provide factual information and guide local leaders dealing with neighborhood change."[48] When a Negro moved (or wanted to move) into a white neighborhood, the commission expended great efforts in organizing neighborhood groups and in trying to make the residents understand that there was no reason to fear a quick Negro invasion and, most important, that property values would not be affected unless white home owners tried to sell in panic. The commission's executive director, George Schermer, who had headed the Detroit commission, had the ability to persuade and influence, while remaining tough if necessary. Both mayors Clark and Dilworth stood firmly behind him, but in 1964, lacking Tate's full support, Schermer resigned.

A small number of private builders in Philadelphia deliberately set out to construct developments for integrated occupancy.

47. Eunice and George Grier, *Privately Developed Interracial Housing* (University of California Press, 1960).

48. "Intergroup Problems in Housing" (prepared for the Commission on Human Relations by Dennis Clark, August 1961) (mimeo), p. 7.

Many of them were influenced by the philosophy of the Quakers, who had so long been deeply involved in the problem of integrated housing for minorities. While these builders were moderately successful, their total impact on the Philadelphia real estate market was not great.

One large urban renewal area seemed to provide Philadelphia with a magnificent chance to build from scratch a new, well-integrated community: the Eastwick area. This covered 2,000 acres of swampy, low-lying land occupied by few homes. The city hoped to build it into an entirely new community, occupied by both residences and industry. The "New Town in-Town" would eventually house about fifty thousand persons. Konstantine Doxiadis, the well-known Greek city planner, won the architectural contest; his plan included parks, green belts, buffer zones, shopping centers, churches, and interesting small residential communities built around cul-de-sacs.

The Institute of Urban Studies of the University of Pennsylvania, under the direction of William Wheaton, was commissioned to conduct a detailed economic feasibility analysis.[49] The study suggested that the project was indeed feasible. It tried to anticipate whether the demand for homes would decrease when it became known that integration was a clear condition of the development, and to arrive at some recommendations for the best strategy. Later, that part of the study was worked out in greater detail, under the auspices of the National Commission on Race and Housing, by Chester Rapkin and William Grigsby.[50]

What happened at Eastwick was disappointing and much slower than city planners and consultants had anticipated. Builders of homes in different parts of Eastwick used various stratagems, none of which was adequate to establish racial integration in new communities or maintain a stably integrated level.[51] Eastwick was slow in being built and occupied, possibly because it was not made clear to potential buyers how the entire area would

49. "Program for Eastwick Housing Market Development Analysis" (mimeo), completed in 1954. Among the scholars involved were Chester Rapkin, Louis Winnick, Ernest Fisher, and Ned Shilling.

50. Chester Rapkin and William Grigsby, *The Demand for Housing in Racially Mixed Areas* (University of California Press, 1960).

51. By 1968, of 1,200 completed dwelling units, 940 were occupied by whites and 260 by nonwhites. Only 16 percent of expected new construction had been built by redevelopers, and the consultants did not seem to be agreed on any clear reason for this deficiency.

be physically changed from its previous poor environmental condition, which included burning dumps, oil refineries, and swamp land. Some observers blame an ineffective sales force; others claim that neither white nor black potential owners knew what racial composition to expect; still others attribute the project's sluggishness to a changed attitude on the part of some Negroes regarding the desirability of racial integration. Whatever the reason, Eastwick did not achieve what it seemed to promise and could hardly serve as an example of a stably integrated development. This one-time chance to show the feasibility of large-scale integration appears to have passed Philadelphia by.

It was reluctantly concluded that what had been suggested for Eastwick could not be carried out without some kind of "quota system." Whether this would be legal was an issue for the courts to decide. The point really is that it is impossible to stick to the concept that color makes no difference when the object is to desegregate. Abrams argues convincingly that the purpose of a quota system is to *exclude*, not to *include*.[52] Only the first is prohibited by law. The motive (good faith of the agency) must be considered when two principles conflict, he maintains. But Philadelphia's Commission on Human Relations disagreed. "The major civil rights decisions of our courts, which have, in recent years, broken many of the chains of discrimination, were forged under the Rule of Law. . . . Now to destroy this, and revert to a government of, not law, but 'good faith,' would be a disastrous step back, even though proposed by honorable men who are attempting to step forward."[53]

## The Concepts: A Brief Appraisal

During the reform period, Philadelphia was clearly ahead of the redevelopment attempts of most other cities in the breadth of its policies, the tie-in with broader developmental programs, and the imaginative approaches used. Yet Philadelphia's renewal policies could not be imitated by other cities without evaluating their circumstances carefully.

Philadelphia realized earlier than other cities that rehabilitation is more effective than clearance. If conservation had been

52. Abrams, "Negro Housing Problem," pp. 47–48.
53. Letter to Charles Abrams, December 1966. Quoted in Abrams, pp. 48–49.

given more of a chance and been allocated more funds, it would have been more successful in helping home owners to improve their environment. But the question of dealing with the worst areas kept being raised—and that question was going to lead to yet another change in renewal priorities. Civic groups argued that areas chosen were too small; they would have preferred to concentrate on larger areas with more public improvements. To what extent could community organizations be relied on to act as catalysts? How could private developers be induced to invest in neighborhood renewal, and was there a way to persuade financial institutions to support the future of specific neighborhoods with loans and mortgages? Even more important questions are raised by today's observation that all the efforts spent do not seem to have resulted in less blight in Philadelphia than in other cities. Were the tools not effective, in the long run, to withstand the onrushing forces of blight? Had those forces become stronger over time, so that the measures of the reform ceased to be enough? Or had the measures lost some of their effect as the elan of the reform waned? Should Philadelphia's experiments be repeated under other conditions and in other times? Or have enough of its experiments been tried in other cities to show how much they can achieve? Are the problems too overwhelming to make the expectation of finding *any* solutions realistic?

Even after passing in review different aspects of policy-making in urban renewal in Philadelphia, it is difficult to come up with unequivocal answers. Some popular journals, from the *Saturday Evening Post* to *Time* magazine, praised Philadelphia's renewal efforts as characteristic of the achievements of the renaissance, while others condemned them as total failures.[54] The growing national literature about renewal efforts across the country reveals the same range of opinion.[55]

54. E.g., *Time* magazine of November 6, 1964, attributed the entire success to Edmund Bacon. Articles in *Architectural Forum* and *Saturday Evening Post* also praised the entire Philadelphia government. A series of feature articles in the Philadelphia *Inquirer*, on the other hand, attacked the city's renewal efforts. The *Greater Philadelphia Magazine* published an article, "Requiem for a Renaissance," in November 1964, in which Rafsky was blamed for the total failure of renewal and, to even the scales, another one in July 1968 ("Paradise Lost") in which Bacon was blamed for all that went wrong with redevelopment.

55. Many of these arguments are summarized in James Q. Wilson (ed.), *Urban Renewal: The Record and the Controversy* (M.I.T Press, 1966). Other

The apparently changing goals of urban renewal in Philadelphia caused the greatest controversy: the program was created for providing decent homes for families of all income groups, yet often slums were cleared and the poor displaced to make room for economically profitable luxury apartments. The law permitted increasing portions of renewal funds to be used, not for housing, but for industry, commerce, and educational institutions. The effect of this use on those families whose housing supply failed to keep up with the population was only gradually realized during the 1950s, and led to increasing attacks on urban renewal efforts which seemed to have betrayed the originally intended beneficiaries.

Paul Davidoff, addressing the Citizens' Council on City Planning, considered which groups were helped and which were harmed by the city's actions. "During the 1950's and the 1960's, the reformers, the elite groups . . . supported programs which, at best, maintained the status quo in regard to poverty and, at worst, increased the problem. . . . It is quite clear that renewal as we have known it has little place in a great society, a society in which major governmental attention will be devoted to providing for the needs of those denied equality of opportunity. . . . The future urban renewal program for Philadelphia must be directed towards [this] basic goal." [56] In the early 1960s not many Philadelphians saw the problem in terms of the war on poverty, as Davidoff did. He felt that the local powers had given in to those who wanted to rebuild the obsolescent parts of the central business district, increase the tax base, and attract more industry, at the expense of devoting most renewal funds to better housing. In line with Davidoff's argument one valid critique could be leveled against the federal government: in the 1961 amendments to the Housing Act and in the antipoverty program in 1964, Washington failed to attach the kind of strings to urban renewal funds which would ensure their being utilized in line

scholarly books on this topic are: Jerome Rothenberg, *Economic Evaluation of Urban Renewal* (Brookings, 1967); William Grigsby, *Housing Markets and Public Policy* (University of Pennsylvania Press, 1963); Scott Greer, *Urban Renewal in American Cities* (Bobbs Merrill, 1965).

56. Paul Davidoff, "Renewing Renewal: Making Renewal Work for Equal Opportunities" (speech to the Citizens' Council on City Planning, February 5, 1965).

with the purposes of the poverty program. As we have seen at the beginning of this chapter, one choice to be made among the variety of goals for urban renewal was whether to look at renewal from the viewpoint of the city or from that of the metropolitan area. The choice which would ultimately be made, and which would decide the mix between residential and nonresidential uses, depended on the kind of pressure which potential beneficiaries could exert, or which concerned civic groups could muster on their behalf. The most obvious choice always demanded is for a "higher" (that is, more economical) use of the land, which would bring in higher profits for the owner. But this option ignores the social cost, and thus was not likely to be decisive for Philadelphia's reform government, which tried to consider benefits and costs to society at large before deciding on the use of the land. In this connection it is interesting to consider the protests of residents, students, and civic groups, who objected to the clearance of some older, low-middle-income and even slum housing to make way for a new University Science Center (see chapter 9). Though plans for the center finally prevailed, it took all the pressure the Establishment could muster to see that the long-term advantages of such a center for the city and the whole area should be allowed to outweigh the losses to the individuals to be displaced. Arguments of this kind increased in fervor as time went on.

The increasing restiveness of those most directly and adversely affected by the demolition of their homes, and the growing awareness of this restiveness by influential citizens, led to the realization that the 1957 policy needed reviewing. The principle of moving from the further outlying good areas toward the slums seemed now questionable: it seemed increasingly impossible to keep the worst areas waiting, possibly until some of the homes were abandoned and could thus be cheaply acquired for clearance. On the other hand, it now seemed possible to take advantage of newly available "poverty" funds to combat some of the social problems made visible by renewal activities. The stage thus seemed set for new approaches.

The 1959 Housing Act had promised funds for cities which desired to take a fresh look at urban renewal. When Philadelphia received the funds to conduct such a Community Renewal Program (CRP), it was in a good position to undertake this task, because its earlier policy discussions, its concern about renewal priorities, and its experiments with all kinds of new tools had laid the groundwork for a sophisticated reappraisal.

A small policy committee under the chairmanship of William L. Rafsky was appointed in 1961, with Edmund Bacon as vice-chairman. The executive directors of the Redevelopment Authority and the Housing Authority, and the commissioner of licenses and inspections were members. Placed organizationally within the Redevelopment Authority, the staff of twenty professionals was directed by Graham Finney, assistant executive director of the City Planning Commission, as well as by a technical director. This staff was supplemented by professionals working for other city agencies, as well as by outside consultants. Nineteen technical reports as well as staff papers and consultant reports were issued (see appendix 3). A technical advisory committee was also formed, which included directors of civic groups and nonprofit corporations with related interests. In February 1967, a final report was issued, representing a basic consensus between the staff and the political leadership.

## Evaluation of Renewal

### Interdependence

Although different aspects of development had been seen as separate but related facets of a broad problem, the CRP was more inclined to view all development comprehensively rather than as the sum of disparate programs. An examination of the effects of some renewal problems upon others revealed new insights. The CRP was "based on a comprehensive set of goals of a variety of programs [and] their relationships." [57] Under this new approach it seemed, for example, that a family's housing problem would not necessarily be solved if the interest rate on its mortgage were lowered; rather, the family might be better helped in the long run by having its income raised, the educational level of all its members and thus their opportunities increased, eventually making it possible for the family to filter up to better housing. Poor

57. CRP Final Report, *Major Policies and Proposals* (1967). Letter of transmittal.

families have fewer educational opportunities, which widens the gap between their need for better jobs and a higher income, and their ability to attain them. Because their income stays low, they cannot afford or maintain good housing; so it deteriorates and governmental action becomes necessary.

It was the strength of Philadelphia's CRP that all the different social problems and their solutions were seen as different aspects of the same phenomenon. Some in the city were afraid that this comprehensiveness might hide a lack of understanding of how relevant each part was individually for bringing about the total result. But the CRP staff felt that this danger could be avoided if it continually focused on specific development decisions.

## Trial Alternative

It was first necessary to spell out how far the different renewal programs would improve environment, housing, education, choices, jobs, income, and so forth. Each element would be affected by *any* chosen strategy, but they could not all be maximized at the same time. Hence a price had to be paid in terms of one goal for pursuing another (for example, cutting down housing quality in order to improve the family's educational opportunities, or acceptance of a less interesting job in order to live in a better neighborhood). Several strategies were explored.

The first strategy was a continuation of the present division of funds among residential, industrial, and Center City development. Increased income and tax returns, residences for families in different income groups, commerical and office development, and industrial expansion—these were the other key elements of this first alternative, which was dubbed the "City in Renaissance."

The second strategy was to see the city as the regional capital, "economically, culturally, and symbolically." Employment and income and the city's economic assets were emphasized. Investments would be concentrated in nonresidential projects, and residential activities would take a back seat, the argument being that economic prosperity would provide housing solutions over the long run. This alternative was called the "Regional City."

The third strategy used urban renewal dollars to improve personal opportunities for the citizenry; substantial departures from present policies were assumed. Schools and other community facilities would be built, new housing would be constructed, activities would be spread over a larger area. "Noncash credit" would be emphasized, as would a variety of programs throughout the inner areas of the city. Investments would be used to foster growth, so as to maximize personal opportunities for all citizens. This alternative was referred to as the "City of Opportunity." Since this alternative was at variance with existing legal conditions of the federal program, a legislative or at least an administrative change in both Washington and Philadelphia would become necessary.

The CRP staff discussed a number of questions about these strategies: did all strategies enhance job opportunities and income? Did equal opportunity and social mobility underlie each alternative? Would inner city residential areas be given new emphasis? And, finally, the crucial questions: how far would each strategy go in developing programs with social rather than only physical results, and to what extent would personal well-being and increased opportunity lead to an improved "quality of urban living"? This thinking later led to three different "program packages," dealing respectively with housing, job opportunities and income, and education.

The CRP evaluation brought out the fact that urban renewal activities too infrequently asked "for whom" they were undertaken and which group of the population was to benefit, at the cost of which other group. These questions became even more important; for whom were jobs created, and what kinds of opportunities should they be? How was additional income to be created? What kind of education was being considered? All this meant that the new element of social planning was added to the discussion—a concern that grew both locally and nationally while the CRP study was underway, and became a major challenge to public policy. Human and social concerns were recognized as being basic to renewal problems.

When Arthur Row was asked in the Interagency Committee on Housing in 1956 whether the comprehensive plan he was working on would also spell out the underlying social plan, he indicated that it would not, although a good environment for all income groups would be basic to it. Several years later, however, a consultant to the CRP stated that if "the primary objective of planning is investment in people, then major decisions and investments are . . . determined by human and social needs. Physical and economic planning are but a means to achieving human and social objectives." [58] In line with this thinking, the CRP studies tried to identify the criteria for determining the social needs of residents of different neighborhoods, which could determine the right "mix" of developmental remedies for each environment. Those carrying out the study tried to use a social cost-benefit analysis as the basis for deciding on specific programs —much as is done in economic cost-benefit studies. But they found that they had to learn much more about the needs and value systems of different income groups. Despite some effort, the CRP was unable to get much beyond the realization of that need and could not yet synthesize social planning and urban renewal.

## Changing the Renewal Policy Once More

The CRP professional staff insisted that the problems posed by identification of social goals, including education, training, jobs, and income, should be the concern of the CRP. This became the center of many a heated discussion within the CRP committee. The members of the committee did not agree with the staff. Its two most prominent members, Rafsky and Bacon, took issue with the staff position for different reasons. Rafsky stuck to the purpose of studying renewal strategy. He thought that studies heretofore largely neglected (such as cost-benefit studies or housing market studies) would undergird renewal priorities more firmly, and that the CRP had been created primarily for studies of this kind. He was disappointed that the CRP staff failed to look more intensively into possible new devices in the housing field, and he felt it was getting too exclusively involved in social aspects. Rafsky also was leery of CRP involvement with programs of groups and agencies other than city departments, or with decisions of private groups. He thought the CRP should identify *where*

58. Richard H. Uhlig, *Planning in the Urban Environment: Next Steps in Social Research and in Social Planning*, CRP Technical Report, no. 16 (July 1965), p. 2.

policy-making should take place, but not itself make policy decisions.[59]

In some ways it is surprising that Rafsky, always so firm an adherent of the broad viewpoint, showed himself so reluctant to take an even broader, more modern approach. He was afraid that lack of success of the proposed remedies either as social change or as improved renewal strategy might result in the staff's sitting between two stools. Also, he did not believe that Mayor Tate would accept the broad approach. But after listening to the determined and systematic reasoning of the CRP staff, Rafsky was eventually won over, largely by the CRP's soft-spoken director, Graham Finney.

Bacon's bias in favor of physical planning was to be expected. The secondary position he had assigned to social problems was emphasized by statements of his associates. Nevertheless, possibly influenced by the CRP staff, his public utterances gradually seemed to indicate increased awareness of the social issues. (In 1968, he asked a social scientist to join his staff to start a social research unit, but the appointment lasted only a few months.)

All of the CRP's thinking implied a deviation from previous policies, specifically the 1957 policy. One of the younger staff men, recently a member of the CRP committee, charged that the CRP had simply failed to touch on the central problem. "It is impossible," said Richard Buford, "to wait ten years to work from the outside in" and "to brush the social problems under the rug. . . . What's more, it is morally wrong." [60] One of the reasons for the 1957 decision not to try to renew slums near the center of the city had been the thought that a higher vacancy rate in time would make clearance cheaper. Now again the CRP, forced to use scarce funds most economically, proposed that poverty funds be used where needed—where there were the poorest people, the worst schools, the most dilapidated housing. A CRP report states the dilemma succinctly: "It became clear that resources must again be directed to the inner area. Some who discussed the mat-

59. CRP Committee minutes, June 17, 1964.
60. Interview with author, January 13, 1965. At that time Buford was commissioner of licenses and inspection, and as such a member of the CRP Committee. However, before that he had been for quite some time a member of its staff. Subsequently, he left Philadelphia to join Mayor Lindsay's administration in New York City.

ter took the moral position that the worst areas of blight and poverty warrant the greatest attention. Others argued pragmatically that failure to act there might jeopardize other portions of the total program." [61]

In accordance with the city administration's continuing approach to minority housing, it became clear that social and economic mobility of the city's residents would be essential for developmental programs, a fact which seems to permeate all aspects of alternative programs. "Unlike classrooms, jobs or houses, the goal of unrestricted entry to new neighborhoods and new communities is in the nature of extending an option that *may or may not* be exercised by the minority family. . . . [The importance lies in] the attainment of conditions that *permit* minority groups to locate along the entire social and economic continuum enjoyed by other residents of the city." [62]

### *The "Program Packages"*

The "program package" most clearly related to social issues was that dealing with educational opportunity. (It had been debated at the time the new Educational Home Rule Charter was discussed and eventually adopted—see chapter 2). The new Board of Education's president, Richardson Dilworth, had appointed several task forces in 1965 to report when the board took office. One of them, on "Capital Program and Physical Plant," was chaired by Rafsky and had Graham Finney as a member; they were working hard on it while the CRP strategy was being hammered out.

A year earlier Finney had drafted a proposal for a demonstration grant for the schools in one area of the city (Germantown).[63] The study, to be funded by the grant, was supposed to find out whether the presence of quality urban schools would encourage private investment and lead to maintenance of good housing, as

61. "Findings and Recommendations" (draft), 1965, by Graham Finney, p. 33. In the present chapter this draft has sometimes been cited rather than the final report because the draft shows more imagination and better reflects the CRP's thinking. The final report is more the result of political compromises.

62. "Findings and Recommendations" (draft), p. 15. Emphasis added.

63. "The Schools of Germantown: A Proposal for Urban Schools in a Renewing Community" (draft), February 1964.

well as to stability of racial integration. Are school facilities and education a positive force in renewing urban neighborhoods? "To what degree can good schools help to counter the outward movement of whites and contribute to a continuing balance in racially changing areas?" Finney planned to use the Germantown experience as a basis for a hypothesis about the effects of schools on the environment, so that this theory could be built into the structure of the CRP.

The idea behind the CRP's emphasis on educational opportunities was that renewal of the school environment would affect the extent to which the schools were able to carry out their goals of educational excellence. The impact on the total environment of the areas where the new schools would be located could be substantial, affecting the total attractiveness of life in the city. The task forces' reports [64] urged that school plans be directly related to the city's development plan, capital program, and urban renewal program, and, where feasible, that "education and welfare be planned and constructed together in a functional cluster." [65]

The housing program package was perhaps the cornerstone of the CRP strategy. As "the pivotal goal of the proposed development program," [66] it focused on three interdependent elements: (1) low-income households and their problems of shelter, services, and income—"*recovery*"; (2) lower-middle-income households and their needs for deconcentration, ownership, and better exertion of choice—"*dispersion*"; and (3) new, improved environments to retain and attract middle- and upper-income households—"*replacement*."

In a reversal of the 1957 policy, the CRP in 1967 advocated that the entire inner city become a theater of renewal action, within which all existing tools would be used, including broad environmental improvement and rehabilitation and conservation tools which had previously been considered mainly for preservation of better areas. It was now felt, first, that massive applications of all these tools, even well beyond code enforcement, would

64. Reports of the task forces to the incoming Board of Education, submitted November 8, 1965 (John N. Patterson, William Rafsky, Donald Rappaport, chairmen).
65. Task force report on capital program and physical plant, p. 20.
66. "Findings and Recommendations" (draft), p. 83.

change the character of the inner city. Second, as the relative cost of housing for low-income groups had increased to a disproportionate share of their incomes, the CRP recommended income supplementation in the form of rent certificates, which could be used throughout the city and possibly even the metropolitan area, not alone for those dislocated by public action but also to help the total housing supply. "This is the only device that can assure an uninterrupted program of renewal actions vital to economic growth and other development objectives . . . [and] stimulate required rehabilitation and construction activity." [67] Third, the CRP asserted that "the entire income of impoverished households has to be adequate and in balance, if other measures of recovery are to take hold. . . . [They also] require jobs and medical care as well as income." [68] Hence the questions of education, jobs, and income had to be tied into the problem of housing. Physical renewal must "be paralleled by programs dealing with the economic and social problems of the population that is affected. This means that social planning must share in framing any development." [69] Part of the housing strategy would be to improve housing choices for minority groups; but that effort was most likely to be successful if tackled in conjunction with problems of employment, income, and education.

The third program package, job opportunity, had an entirely different focus. In the first place, most of its problems originated in national economic forces, over which Philadelphia had little control. The task was to improve the city's employment problem, which had plagued it for a long time. Elements of this package include industrial renewal and economic growth, Center City development, and institutional expansion. Though most of that strategy is beyond the scope of the present chapter (see chapters 7, 8, 9, and 11), it is important here to note how employment and income were related at every turn to the housing problem in the CRP package.

"The CRP flows from and builds upon the City's comprehensive Plan, the Central Urban Renewal Area study . . . and a continuing series of studies by City agencies, business and civic

67. Ibid., p. 112.
68. Ibid., p. 97.
69. Ibid., p. 110.

groups and the universities," states the foreword of the CRP's final report.[70] "It differs [from earlier analyses] in its greater emphasis on social and economic implications of renewal, and in the use of sophisticated methodology. . . . The concept of renewal in this report includes job-training as well as land for industry, family counselling services as well as neighborhood parks, expanded educational programs as well as new school buildings, equal opportunity and mobility in housing choice."

The CRP's major contribution to methodology was to try out—or "trace out" with the help of computers—the effect of specific changes on all parts of the regional system. Several hypothetical programs could be prepared (it was done with different capital programs, for example) and then compared with each other in terms of resources used. Going one step farther, the CRP simulated the progress of the three trial strategies over a period of eighteen years (three capital program periods) to measure different development objectives. The results showed that degrees of achievement varied as a result of different resource inputs—in terms of better homes or skills or jobs or incomes of the population affected. On this basis specific objectives of future development programs could be considered. (This approach was similar to the method used in testing alternative total transportation plans in area transportation studies—the "Penn-Jersey" transportation study had tried it, for example.) Though the CRP staff used this method for some of the preliminary strategies, they decided against using it in the preparation of the final recommendations, as their emphasis was on the social aspects and hence on elements not subject to exact measurement. CRP mathematicians and operations researchers recommended instead a continuing use of cost-benefit analysis.[71]

### How Practical Are the Proposals?

The consequences for practical application were somewhat surprising: the final CRP report in 1967 proposed *not* to concentrate all its renewal tools on the inner city as the staff had earlier

70. *Major Policies and Proposals* (1967).
71. CRP report by George Tucker, *Phase 1, Months 1–30, Progress Report*, no. 15 (July 1965), pp. 20–21, quoting from *The Application of Network Scheduling to the CRP Program*, CRP Technical Report, no. 7 (July 1963).

suggested, but to extend the area for renewal treatment considerably beyond what the older policy had envisaged. This recommendation was called the "distributed approach," which proposed directing all public investment to a "single large theater of operations," the "community improvement area." This challenged previous ideas about the size of urban renewal areas—it even contradicted existing federal legislation. Previously an attempt had been made to relate separate programs to each other by a careful set of priorities, and to assure that renewal areas were large enough to make a meaningful impact. Dorothy Montgomery's attempt to enlarge the area, however (partly in order to take noncash credit advantage of more capital projects), had, it will be remembered, been rejected by the city administration. The community improvement area went way beyond her suggestions and included almost the entire city; specifically, it covered those residential areas that were so bad that they needed "reconstruction" and the better areas which could be helped only by "renovation," but not those which needed primarily "maintenance." It also included industrial areas and institutions. (Essentially, the only parts of the city excluded from the community improvement area were the northwest and the northeast, which are suburban-type areas.) The broad geographic distribution would permit the application of renewal treatment to any part of the area, though under a detailed plan for the entire large area. The distributed approach would mean limited treatment in dispersed areas, each part of the area receiving the particular kind of assistance its residents needed. The CRP report's affirmation that its actions would be "focused directly on areas which are likely to be readily responsive or in which public or private market forces are clearly favorable" [72] sounds strangely like a reference to the "opportunity areas" chosen in the pre-reform era for renewal wherever a private investor was interested. In this respect, at least, renewal policy in Philadelphia seemed to have come full circle.

"Added flexibility is one of the major reasons for changing to the distributed approach," the report explained. "Renewal programs involving physical change can be coordinated more closely with related programs for improved education facilities, anti-

72. *Major Policies and Proposals*, p. 10.

poverty action, physical and mental health services, recreational facilities, and a host of others." [73] The rather surprising recommendation, however, sounded more like a compromise between the conclusions of the CRP studies and an attempt to state a practical renewal policy. Concentration on the inner city would have been a possibility in harmony with CRP thinking. But what happened was that breadth was dispersed into geographic width, which made it politically feasible to satisfy all potential claimants for renewal treatment. The practical suggestions of the final report appeared to be added—without much relation—to previous staff recommendations, thus in effect negating some of the new thoughts of the CRP staff.

The suggested administrative device for implementing both the trial strategies and the program packages for a particular period was an Annual Development Program. Through this program, public and private investments could be channeled into functional categories: people, housing and physical environment, property, economic growth, and transportation. The Development Program would spell out the goals of each specific program, and the possible alternatives toward reaching these goals. It would then be up to the city administration to choose among the alternatives according to its predilections.

One of the problems of the Development Program was that it dealt with decisions by the city itself, while many influential kinds of investments lie outside local policy control: hence even a comprehensive presentation of the various city programs would cover only a part of all investment influences. But the CRP staff wanted to present a program which would achieve an overview of all operations in the city, whether or not they were carried out *by* the city, thus making it possible for the staff to view the sets of policies simultaneously as a whole, so that they could see the interrelationships among the different programs.

The Development Program was intended to become a new pattern for decision-making, by expressing long-range policies and their methods of implementation. The city council was supposed to regard it as a companion document to the capital program. The idea of incorporating all these elements in the new Development Program was excellent. But unfortunately, like

73. Ibid., p. 11.

most of the new approaches of the CRP, it came in the last stages of the reform era, too late to be of practical significance. Although a "Community Development Program" was prepared during 1967, which divided all activities of city agencies and nonprofit corporations into specific program elements, it was never carried out in detail. But the CRP studies (though not the final suggestions) still represent the capstone of the deliberations on Philadelphia's renewal program and might well prove useful at another time and another place.[74]

74. See appendix 3 for a list of the CRP studies and reports.

# 7  *Industrial Development*

In seeking new industries—whether to increase employment, expand the tax base, or for any other reason—cities rarely count the long-range well-being of the community. Few cities have tackled the problem systematically. Philadelphia is an exception. As early as 1954, the administration began to approach the problem in a new way, and its methods have since been imitated in part by other cities.

During his mayoral campaign and in his inaugural address, Joseph S. Clark began referring to the great need for new jobs and increased economic activity. The impact of unemployment on the city, exacerbated by the post-Korean depression, was apparent to him. His first request of the newly appointed city economist was for regular reports on employment and unemployment statistics for the city itself—rather than for the metropolitan area—and for analyses of what these figures implied for possible economic strategies.

Clark was also aware of how much new taxables could do for the city. He knew that many of its basic economic problems could not be solved without the help of federal funds or large amounts of private investment. Hence, he hoped to induce new industry to move in and existing industry to expand, which would alleviate both the tax and the employment problem. Furthermore, new jobs would increase the spending power of those newly employed, and this over time would further improve the local economy and indirectly help others as the effects multiplied. Meanwhile, many urgent needs pressed in on the mayor: could these more long-range economic problems be allowed to detract from his concern for the immediate visible needs of so many people? Immediate expectations were for better health care, reliable police protection, and new playgrounds. Could such social needs be postponed, so that they could be dealt with more effectively after the attraction of economic activities had improved the city's fiscal capability?

Economic problems had long been submerged. The "climate" generated by a corrupt city government had driven firms out of the area. The migration to the South of many textile firms created unemployment among low-paid workers. The city itself felt the weaknesses more acutely than did the surrounding metropolitan area. In recoveries following recessions, Philadelphia seemed unable to return to prerecession employment levels.

The new administration was changing the values and expectations of the citizenry: instead of patronage and payoff, performance was the currency for attaining one's goal. Honesty and merit took the place of connections. The citizens expected action. But long and careful preparations are needed for economic improvement and the attraction of new economic activities, and results are not seen as quickly as are those in social services. Before private investment could be stimulated, a new attitude by business toward its city had to be generated.

Elected officials are perennially cursed by the time lag between the inauguration of a plan or program and the result; this is especially true of developmental programs. Clark told the author that while the long awaited demolition of the "Chinese Wall" took place early in his term, "my symbolic act solemnified the action of my predecessor. When Dick Dilworth turned the first shovel of earth for the Dock Street Food Market, he finished what I fought for, and started a new era in Center City." Similarly, much of the momentum of the Tate administration has been due to the fact that Tate did not actively halt the natural progress of Dilworth's projects.

## The Food Distribution Center

The first undertaking of the Clark administration in the industrial field, before any plans for industry in general had been conceived, dealt with a specialized facility for one industry only —food distribution. The project—long contemplated—was undertaken by a top private business group for the general welfare of the community, with (increasing) help from the city government. This enterprise was unique in its sponsorship, its breadth of concept in a special area, and its pioneering involvement of both private and public spheres.

## The Rationale

The old market, grown up since William Penn's days near the port in Center City, was overcrowded, unsanitary, and inefficient and lacked good access routes. All types of wholesale food—fruits and vegetables, poultry, seafood, dairy foods, meat, and dry groceries—were handled there. Its relocation would allow historic areas near Independence Hall to be opened up and restored. Center City traffic would be eased, while freeways near the new market would permit wide distribution of goods. More efficient operation for handling would lower costs.

As early as 1950, the GPM, barely weaned, had considered such a possibility—in fact, the idea developed not long after a federal park near the Independence Hall buildings had been approved by Congress, thus bringing restoration of historic areas closer to reality. Philadelphia was urged by Congress and the Department of Agriculture seriously to consider undertaking the relocation of the old market. In 1951, Robert Sawyer, then GPM executive director (he soon was to take office as the city's new managing director), predicted that it would be done. GPM set up a special committee, chaired by a prominent banker, to consider the project, but the fight to get the Home Rule charter approved kept the GPM from devoting its major effort to this enterprise at that time.

In 1953, Mayor Clark addressed the GPM executive committee and pleaded with its members to get involved in governmental cooperation beyond the city's boundaries, and to promote a metropolitan approach. But the GPM turned down the mayor's request to undertake an overall project. Their earlier interest in the wholesale food center, from which the entire region would benefit, seemed to answer part of the mayor's plea.

The office window of Harry Batten, president of the advertising firm of N. W. Ayer, and instigator of the original group starting GPM, looked out over the decrepit shacks of the oldest part of the produce market. Batten, who was devoted to the old parts of the city, convinced the other members of the GPM board that the relocation of the food merchants was worthwhile, if only because it would make redevelopment of the old city possible.

After a number of feasibility studies had been conducted (including one by the U.S. Department of Agriculture—spurred by the GPM), a model of a center was unveiled at the 1954 GPM annual dinner, attended by representatives of forty national food concerns. Mayor Clark pledged the city's full cooperation for such a private undertaking, but the GPM still failed to see it as a city-private endeavor which it was to become. The fact that the city owned the land the GPM had chosen for the facility, and the need for the city to provide the expensive infrastructure, should have convinced the GPM early that close cooperation was necessary.

On February 15, 1955, the nonprofit Food Distribution Center (FDC) Corporation was chartered by the GPM. The board included GPM board members, other prominent businessmen, and three city officials. To start the corporation, GPM raised $250,000 from forty business and industrial corporations, only a few of which were connected with the food industry. The private Fels Foundation also granted the GPM $100,000 for this purpose.

### Feasibility of the Food Center

The site chosen was unfilled swampland, much of it owned by the city, which had been using it as a dump site. In the spring of 1955 the Redevelopment Authority prepared a detailed redevelopment plan. Land would have to be filled before it could be sold to the new corporation, and streets, sewers, and water mains would have to be built. This involved considerable public money. Of course, assessments would recoup some of the cost in time, and part of the cost would be absorbed by the budgets of the Streets and Water departments, since these expenses would be incurred if the land was to be developed at all, no matter for what purpose. Therefore, while not all this could be called "specific" FDC investment, an estimated $14 million had to be counted as the public cost of equipping the land for food center use. The costs of utilities and their special installation in individual buildings would not be incurred until each building was ready for occupancy and the tenants were secured, so that some expenditure could be delayed. It was planned (and eventually so contracted) that, after amortizing its debt to the Redevelopment Authority and meeting its other long-term obligations, the FDC Corporation would turn over the completed facility to the city, which would then be able to derive revenues from it. Still, the large public expenditures, suggested at a time when public improvements were so necessary, and funds for them so scarce, caused some raised eyebrows. The argument that greatly increased tax revenues could be anticipated was hypothetical, as it was based on the supposition that the center would be successful.

To find out whether the center would be a success, and what tax revenues would accrue, the GPM and the Redevelopment Authority commissioned a "re-use appraisal" by a real estate consultant (really an economic feasibility study). The appraisal assumed an eventual private investment of $85 million—although the original Department of Agriculture study had assumed that initially only $38 million would be spent. Actually, refrigeration and modern handling techniques had changed the economics of the food business. If it had been only a consolidation and relocation of food wholesalers, the food center may not have been economical; it was the modern techniques which made it so. On the basis of full occupancy of completed buildings, the rentals paid by merchant-tenants had to amortize the capital cost of land and buildings, and cover operating costs of the FDC and the facilities it provided as well as those of the specialized merchants' association renting and managing each of the buildings. The increase in rentals per square foot would be more than made up by the up-to-date handling equipment; the decrease in the amount of labor required; the savings on cartage and porterage, spoilage and damage; and the elimination of traffic delays.[1]

The appraisal concluded that, after completion of the center, the city would receive additional real estate taxes of over $1 million annually. Tax returns actually reached this figure in 1966 and were expected to go up to $1.5 million within five years. In addition, a sizable increase in business transacted at the new location had been estimated, generating business taxes as well as wage taxes from new employees to this growth. This calculation did not even include the secondary generation of activity and the multiplier effect of having more people employed as the demand for food and processing increased; this would push up the center's feasibility even further.

1. "Wholesale Food Distribution Facilities for Philadelphia, Pennsylvania," U.S. Department of Agriculture, *Marketing Research Report*, no. 201.

Financing the buildings themselves was not easy. City credit for wholesalers without enough equity was mentioned as a possible solution to the problem. It was suggested that the city's capital program funds be used to finance some specific facilities, since all of them would eventually become public facilities. However, city officials questioned such an arrangement. Bacon, for example, wondered whether the GPM was "asking the city to assume all risks." [2] The dangers of a loose arrangement between private effort and government support were becoming clear; both sides had to learn gradually how such a partnership could be forged.

## Power Battle

While matters were still in the discussion stage, a major battle broke out. Albert M. Greenfield, who had been called "the most powerful single individual in the City," [3] was the most prominent real estate broker in town. He was an important Democrat who helped raise money for the party, and hence he commanded power in the city council. As a result of their personal evaluation dating back to the Depression, directors of the GPM steadfastly refused to involve Greenfield in their undertakings. (Greenfield's bank, like so many others, had been in financial trouble during the Depression. When the run on his bank started, says Russell Davenport in *Fortune* [1936], Greenfield was first helped by the bankers, but "when they had loaned $7 million, it was obvious that the dyke would not hold and . . . they unexpectedly decided to let the bank go." The GPM believed, as did others, that he might have saved his own fortune at the expense of his depositors.)

What ensued was a "battle of the giants," revolving around prestige and personalities rather than the merits of the FDC proposal. The battle went to the roots of the public-private relationship, for Greenfield was a private businessman who tried to use his real estate knowledge as well as his political muscle to stop the proposal of a group he did not like and who had excluded him from participation.

2. Report to Mayor Joseph S. Clark, March 1954 (in managing director's files).

3. E. Digby Baltzell, *Philadelphia Gentlemen* (Free Press, 1958), p. 379.

Greenfield's arguments were twofold: he contended that city representation in the FDC Corporation was too small to safeguard the public interest, and that the economics of the enterprise had not been sufficiently investigated. These factors would halt the project unless it was bailed out by still more public money.

Mayor Clark and his managing director, Vernon Northrop, could not let the challenge pass, as the commitment of public funds was involved. They asked for a report from the city economist, whose conclusions were as follows: (1) The value of the improved land would far exceed the cost of improvements and would yield an attractive tax return even compared to any other industrial use. (2) Business at the new site would be much greater than at the present location, as customers would be attracted from a wider area. (3) On the basis of anticipated operating expenses compared with revenues from tenants, capitalized income would result in a value clearly exceeding the facility's cost. (4) The FDC would be constructed gradually, as the need became apparent and when food merchants were ready to sign leases at rentals high enough to amortize the costs; that way space for expansion and for additional facilities (for example, cold storage) would be saved and risk minimized. (5) Savings for merchants through less spoilage, and lower cartage and loading costs, could be considerable (estimated by the Department of Agriculture as $3.5 million annually for the produce market). These savings might be partly passed on to the consumer. (6) As far as returns to the city were concerned, real estate taxes would increase with each completed building, and wage taxes with each additional employee. Savings because of fewer fire hazards, less policing, and less health inspection would mount up in time. Urban renewal on the site of the old market would increase tax receipts there above costs. Finally, when the facility reverted to the city at the end of the stipulated period, it would still be partially productive and thus would get revenues into the city's coffers.[4]

This report did not stop the power play, however. A mediation meeting on July 28, 1955, was unsuccessful. The GPM was still

---

4. Memoranda from the city economist to Mayor Joseph S. Clark, September 12, 1955, and to Director of Commerce Walter M. Phillips, June 20 and September 20, 1955.

adamant about opposing additional city representation on the FDC board. Finally, Harry Batten called the GPM executive committee on August 22 for a meeting and got them to call a halt to any further FDC development, in view of Greenfield's adamant opposition. The committee clearly wanted to place the blame—and did so in time for the afternoon papers! Several conciliatory attempts were made by Mayor Clark, Richardson Dilworth (then in the middle of his campaign for mayor), and Governor Leader. The governor, for example, called the parties to his office. Tempers flared; even Clark lost his patience. Finally, Greenfield's promise to acquiesce in the erection of the food center was obtained. His appointment by Dilworth as chairman of the City Planning Commission the following year—whether or not there was any connection—gave him more influence on the city's development than he was able to exert in the food center controversy. On the basis of the city economist's evaluation, the managing director and the director of commerce testified before the city council in December 1955 in favor of the FDC. An ordinance was passed while Clark was still mayor, approving the redevelopment proposal and the contract with the new FDC Corporation as developer, and the city council appropriated money for utilities and other land improvements. Vernon Northrop, who as managing director had carefully safeguarded the city's interests when negotiating the contract, soon parted company with Dilworth, the new mayor, over appointments, and became the new corporation's executive vice-president.

## The Nuts and Bolts

The construction of the various buildings had to be financed separately in each case. The equity of the ultimate user was decisive. An excellent credit rating made financing simple; but where the equity of the final user (the produce firm, for example) was not sufficient for the needed loan, the FDC gave the financial institution its own 5 percent bonds as security. While that somewhat reduced the need for equity, the firm itself always had to provide a share of the cost. The FDC retained title and fixed the rental so that it covered both the amortization of the loan and the 5 percent interest paid on the bonds by the FDC. After amortizing the building, the firm could use the option provided in its agreement to buy the land. To finance multiple store buildings, outside loans (often from New York insurance firms) had to be obtained, because of the uncertain equity situation.

Nonetheless, city money was still needed. For the produce and seafood building, the city made $1 million available to the FDC in 1958. Later on, when buildings to house the stalls for individual meat processors and meat wholesalers were to be constructed, $3 million was made available to the FDC out of the city's industrial revolving fund, against the issuance of FDC bonds.

Each group of merchants was urged to form its own organization to negotiate for the group; it was hoped the merchants would appreciate the need for one voice to speak in their common interest. Such organizations could also provide channels of communication to the dealers to convince them that they really had to move from their old quarters. This would avoid the specter which haunted them all of simultaneously having two markets in different places. An organization for each group of food dealers emerged. However, it was next to impossible to convince individuals involved that the city was serious about redeveloping the old market. The timing of the condemnation of the old properties to jibe with the completion of the new building was not enough. Distribution of separate stalls to the tenants in the new building could not proceed until it was certain whether and when everybody would be willing to move. The wrecker's ball had begun its work before some would give in.

All this required much planning and policy coordination at two levels. The Interagency committees on Center City and on Industry and Commerce brought the FDC's executive vice-president together with representatives of city agencies and other nonprofit corporations whose actions had to be dovetailed with those of the FDC. Below this level, a technical committee, the Food Center Coordinating Committee, brought together all those concerned with building large projects in the center, including those needing private utilities. This committee's actions were described in a Philadelphia *Bulletin* editorial at that time as "the top coordinating job of complex public works in the city's history." The moving spirit of that committee was the city's deputy managing director, John Bailey.

Synchronization of actions in the old and new markets was not easy; different business groups and public agencies had to complete a variety of activities—and the completion of all of these activities had to coincide. For example, the problems of meat dealers and processors, whose location was spread at random through two redevelopment areas other than the old market in Center City, had to be considered carefully. Should they be forced to relocate in the FDC or permitted to move elsewhere? Could redevelopment proceed deliberately to dislocate the largest number of meat dealers early, so that a building for them in the FDC would become economical? This question was discussed in many meetings of the Interagency Committee on Industry and Commerce.

Early in 1956, the land of the old market was condemned. By mid-1958, the first phase of the new FDC was ready, including utilities and streets; and in June 1959, the produce wholesalers moved in; the dovetailing between the two markets worked perfectly. As soon as each subsequent parcel of land was made available, there were food merchants ready to start building processing plants, warehouses, distribution points, and so forth. The FDC used the time from 1958 to early 1966 to conduct its sale and lease operations. In 1966 it had virtually completed its mission —earlier than had been anticipated. The total investment had been $62 million, of which about $40 million had come from property owners or as mortgages. Most of the expected $100 million in private investment was committed. In 1967, the management of the FDC was taken over by the Philadelphia Industrial Development Corporation. In June 1969, FDC board chairman Stewart Rauch announced that all the short-term debts had been paid off, that all but two of the center's 358 acres were occupied or committed, that $75 million of private capital had been invested, and that food firms in the center were employing 9,000 persons.

The FDC endeavor had moved a step beyond the Penn Center Development (see chapter 8), which had often left the government powerless to influence decisions affecting what it considered to be in the public interest. By contrast, the public was directly involved in the FDC, not merely as an observer, although not yet as a partner. But it was not until the start of the Philadelphia

Industrial Development Corporation, covering all aspects of industrial development, that full partnership led to a different approach on complex policy issues.

## Establishing the Principles for Industrial Development

Early in the term of the new administration, industrial and business groups made Clark's director of commerce, Walter Phillips, aware of the dearth of available land suitable for industry within the city's boundaries. Land on which to expand firms or attract new ones could not be obtained in large enough parcels. The city had built to its limits, and modern industry needed more space.

### Importance for the Local Economy

Phillips quickly recognized the importance of the problem, not only in terms of jobs and taxes, but also to justify the confidence that business had shown in the renaissance. There was no question of the benefit to be derived from successful industrial activities.[5] Did this mean attracting more industry of no matter what kind? Should those firms be attracted which would best fit into the existing local "mix" of economic activities and contribute to their growth? The region's potentialities had to be clearly understood before suggestions could be made on the types of economic activities the city wanted to attract, or on the best way in which to proceed.

There seemed little purpose in full-page ads extolling Philadelphia's virtues. "Saturation bombing" was rejected as expensive and ineffective; instead, carefully designed pinpoint attacks would be employed. Relatively little had been done in any cities in this direction. Without any guidelines, all efforts at industrial development could result in inefficient and wasteful use of scarce resources. Whether an industry would be considered a "desirable" addition could be decided only on an areawide basis; the criteria also would vary from region to region. The existing industry mix in Philadelphia with its strong textile component would probably not respond as well to the addition of machine tools as would an

5. Cabinet meetings, December 21, 1953, and October 25, 1954. See Walter M. Phillips to Mayor Joseph S. Clark, December 23, 1954.

area in which the fabricated metal industry was already well represented. Linkages between existing activities and new ones entering the region could give considerable impetus to the economic health of the area, including additional income and employment generated through the multiplier effect created by the new interrelationships. In many cities entirely new industrial complexes have been created by the careful addition of selected industries.[6]

## Desirable Industries

Which additions to Philadelphia's economic activities could be considered "desirable"? A preliminary test was run by the city economist's office.[7] Without benefit of a special survey, the national 1947 input-output matrix had to be used as a first approximation, and, given Philadelphia's diversification (which to some degree paralleled that of the nation), this was not as inapplicable as it might have been for some areas. After studies had been made of such factors as likely linkages, growth trends, and cyclical stability, it was recommended that a limited number of industries, properly "disaggregated" into small subgroups, should be further investigated. The mayor's Economic Advisory Committee suggested a detailed study to find out which industries the city would woo. The study was designed by faculty members of the University of Pennsylvania but was never carried out, because the money for it was never contributed by the Industrial Development Corporation, which had been the expected source. The results would have constrained the Industrial Development Corporation and its executive director in the exercise of much discretionary power. The other reason was the corporation's shortage of funds.

In trying to maximize the city's economic health, two separate concepts had to be identified. The first was the locational attrac-

6. Walter Isard, *Industrial Complex Analysis* (Technology Press, 1959), or *Methods of Regional Analysis* (Wiley, 1960). For Philadelphia itself, a study "Linkages and Industrial Complexes," by James McNulty (University of Pennsylvania) was carried out for the office of the city economist.

7. "Most Desirable Industries for Philadelphia's Development" (memoranda from the city economist), February 25 and June 10, 1955. See also Kirk R. Petshek, "Issues in Metropolitan Economic Development," *Journal of the American Institute of Planners*, July 1966, pp. 244–45.

tiveness. What kinds of industries would be most likely to respond readily to efforts to attract them to Philadelphia? To whom would Philadelphia's locational advantages be most attractive? Second, what goals should the city try to maximize in selecting "desirable" firms or industries among those which might be attracted? Unless the firm would find the Philadelphia area attractive, there was obviously no point in analyzing its "desirability." Hence it was important to keep these concepts clearly separated in the minds of the city's economic analysts. Nor was it always simple to determine desirability. For instance, a particular industry might be attracted to the area and its entry considered helpful to the area's well-being, but it might still, on balance, be a liability by consuming resources (for example, occupying land) which could be better used to attract a different kind of firm. Also, the respective costs to the city in terms of needed facilities, congestion, police, air pollution, or other social costs had to be considered along with the overall benefit of alternative industries.

The Economic Advisory Committee tried to decide on criteria against which to measure different economic activities and individual firms. Some of the following were held to be important factors: (1) wage level or total payroll, (2) number of employees per acre, (3) employment stability, (4) kind of labor utilized, (5) likelihood of growth, (6) tax receipts, (7) linkages with suppliers and customers in the area, and (8) generation of secondary income and employment.

A criterion not considered at the time, but which undoubtedly would be added today, is the question of how many hard-core unemployed could be absorbed by the industry, and whether the industry would be willing to participate in federal programs to assure their frictionless employment by the firm.

## Ranking Desirability Criteria

Objective methods of weighing these criteria for purposes of comparison were not available in the early fifties. Environmental conditions change over the longer run, as does the relative desirability of an individual industry within any industrial group, so that a valid comparison of types of economic activities may not be possible. What was important, however, was determination of the kinds of activities likely to do the most good for the economic well-being of the whole community. Industrial development efforts could be concentrated on those individual firms, within the industry groups designated as beneficial for the area which might be attracted. Efforts to influence economic development were worked out in the later 1950s to provide guidelines rather than an exact formula for obtaining the desired results. More recently, simulation models have been developed for use in transportation and other areas. As we have seen, the principle was applied in the CRP studies of alternative renewal strategies. Similarly detailed and comprehensive data about the city would make it possible to see what effects different industries would show if they were added to the existing Philadelphia economy. For example, when Philadelphia realized the potential impact of scientific research (the "knowledge industry") on its development, provided university talent could be harnessed, its University City Corporation commissioned just such an investigation (see chapter 9).

The amount of leeway a city administration really has and how much influence it is able to exert in shaping economic development may be questioned. Linkages of an industry to other activities in the area are, of course, the easiest criterion by which to judge a firm's potential or actual contribution to the region and the price worth paying to attract or retain it. This method can be a discriminating device to use on different firms competing for a choice spot. Usually, however, it is difficult to reject a firm, no matter how low the aggregate benefit to the area appears to be. A government with discrimination and courage can decide to wait for another activity which has more to offer in economic benefits to the area, but this is a hard principle to follow.[8]

## Industrial Renewal

There are different ways of furthering industrial activities. One is to use vacant land, as was done in the case of city-owned tracts (see next section), the Food Distribution Center, or that part of the Eastwick development designed for industry. Since these parcels of land could not be called blighted (unless the land is

8. See Kirk R. Petshek, "Can Industrial Development Be Systematically Approached?" *Land Economics*, May 1968, pp. 256 ff. (Copyright 1968 by the Regents of the University of Wisconsin. Portions of this article were used with permission of the University of Wisconsin Press.)

not useable without being improved), federal urban renewal funds could not be used. The other method involves making more land available for industrial use by clearing out slum housing (or possibly obsolete industrial buildings). This kind of redevelopment can obviously use federal funds and competes for them with other claimants. Industrial renewal was applied in several areas of Philadelphia, but especially at the densely settled land near the center (for example, the "Franklin" and "Callowhill" projects not far from the State Independence Mall), which freed land for economic activities in an area for which there was prime demand. The first application for federal funding was made in mid-1958, but it was only accepted in 1961 and was approved in 1965 (see chapter 8). Some land was cleared in areas of mixed land uses to permit existing firms to expand on site. This device induced a number of firms to stay in Philadelphia; they were, in fact, willing to repay every cent the city had laid out for assembling the land.

Industrial renewal was considered an important tool in the economic arsenal of the city, for "the City's most important assets are the approximately 40,000 business establishments presently located" in Philadelphia, and the administration "must give first priority to keeping these firms in the City." [9] By the mid-1960s, Philadelphia not only had to make up the 90,000 jobs it had lost during the 1950s and early sixties, but had to gain an additional 75,000 to bring the unemployment rate down to the national average of 6 percent, and another 25,000 to lower the rate to the "full employment" rate of 4 percent.

In the capital programs of the decade 1953–63, about $54 million or about 24 percent of all urban renewal funds—federal, state, and local—were allocated to industrial renewal. This figure obviously did not include money spent on preparing vacant land for industrial use. But it did include the provision for utilities, parking and loading space, and any other facilities the newly cleared land needed to make it useful for attracting new industries, or for expanding old ones. The industrial developer must know—to a greater extent than the residential developer—the kind of tenant he has, and have detailed specifications before con-

9. Elizabeth Deutermann, *Economic Development,* CRP Technical Report, no. 13 (December 1964), p. 30.

struction can begin. Finding such users for land planned for clearance may well delay the renewal process.

In the case of residential development, blight—a condition for receiving federal funds—is largely a matter of structural deterioration or the absence of specific amenities, both of which can be easily demonstrated. In designating industrial buildings for demolition, it must be proved that they are functionally or locationally obsolete, which means that no firm can be found which considers these buildings useful.[10] Whether it is worthwhile to rehabilitate them also has to be carefully examined in terms of their other potential uses—essentially an economic judgment. Before deciding that a building should be demolished, it must be shown "that an investor probably could not make a profit by repairing or remodeling it." [11]

After a long series of meetings between city officials, businessmen, members of the mayor's Economic Advisory Committee, and others, the city commissioned the firm of Arthur D. Little to conduct a study of the problem of industrial obsolescence. The study was supposed to "determine the status of Philadelphia's present industrial plant on the basis of an objective scale of obsolescence, to recommend a strategy framework for a redevelopment program, and to suggest redevelopment priorities in the light of Philadelphia's long term economic prospects." [12] It defined obsolescence as the factors that could impair the current and potential usefulness of industrial sites and buildings in Philadelphia. The study was divided into a physical and an economic part— the supply of and the demand for industrial facilities, respectively. The first part classified the characteristics of industrial structures in relation to their potential usefulness for industry, resulting in a "profile" of existing old buildings in the various industrial areas of the city. The study's economic part identified those factors which determined building requirements of specific industries in Philadelphia: seven major industry groups (com-

10. Probably the best discussion of industrial obsolescence is contained in Chester Rapkin and Associates, *Industrial Renewal* (New York State Division of Housing and Community Renewal, 1963).

11. Harold Wise, *Industrial Renewal: Requirements and Outlook for Philadelphia*, CRP Technical Report (not numbered) (December 1964), p. 21.

12. Arthur D. Little, *The Usefulness of Philadelphia's Industrial Plant* (January 1960).

prising about 50 percent of Philadelphia's industrial employment and their subgroups) were reviewed to determine future technology and needs for labor, materials, supplies, and physical requirements. This then made it possible to match industrial demand for, and supply of, buildings available. Finally, the report recommended the kind of renewal treatment advisable for Philadelphia's different industrial areas.

The recommendations were stated in very general terms, leaving many decisions to the judgment of city officials. But they gave a much clearer picture of what considerations should enter such decisions. For instance, the study helped officials to make determinations about the buildings to be demolished in the areas of Center City which had been assigned redevelopment priority. The study also laid the basis for later detailed evaluations by the city of the kinds of uses best fitted for particular areas.[13]

The study showed that many of the old buildings could still be used. This was especially true of loft buildings near the center of Philadelphia, a location where modern buildings were expensive to buy or even to rent. Loft buildings made it possible for small firms and "incubator" industries to afford a near-center location; often several of them could combine to occupy a single building. Also, because industrial firms normally count cost of location simply in terms of out-of-pocket expenses per square foot, old, but rehabilitated, buildings in the city could often serve a firm as well, but more reasonably, than suburban locations. Being able to compete in this way with the suburbs was an important advantage for Philadelphia.

As mentioned earlier, the percentage of urban renewal funds permitted for outright use for nonresidential purposes had gradually increased from 0 in the 1949 act to 30 percent in the 1961 act. In 1961 President Kennedy stated: "Our urban renewal efforts must be substantially re-oriented from slum clearance and prevention into positive programs for economic and social regeneration." Given its high level of unemployment, Philadelphia was able to move a step further. The federal government certified

13. Discussion in Interagency Committee on Industry and Commerce, May 20, June 17, 1959, and January 13, August 10, 1960. Some of the studies decided on as a result of Arthur Little's recommendations were of the "Callowhill Redevelopment Area" and the "Independence Mall Urban Renewal Area," the latter carried out by Larry Smith Associates.

in 1964 that, as industrial renewal would enable Philadelphia to improve its economy substantially, it would be permitted to use a different provision of the Urban Renewal Act, which would free the city entirely from even the 30 percent limitation. Hence economic criteria actually determined how much use Philadelphia could make of industrial renewal funds.

## Another Quasi-Public Corporation

In 1953, when the Philadelphia administration became aware of the industrial land shortage, it began to consider the device of an industrial park, which was already being used elsewhere in the country. This device seemed the more appropriate because the city owned some land which could be declared surplus and disposed of for industrial parks in such a way that both public benefits and private profits would result. (During World War II the federal government thought it advisable to have a second airport available in Philadelphia, especially for military use. Hence land was condemned for that purpose in Northeast Philadelphia, and an airport for freight handling was constructed, but not much used. When the war was over, most of the North Philadelphia airport could be declared surplus by the city.)

### The City as Trustee for Industrial Land

The essential device was to view the city as trustee of the city land to be managed "to the best interest of the people of Philadelphia as beneficiaries." [14] Directly disposing of the land to a private developer might not have served this purpose. Speculators might have left it unused, to await appreciation. Circumstances may prompt an industrial developer to sell the land quickly and realize the greatest profit *for him,* and this may not coincide with the greatest benefit for the city's economy. Even if land is used for industry, selection of firms by a private developer may ignore long-term economic benefits. It cannot be guaranteed that the goal of stability will be considered even if it were possible to stipulate the minimum employment which the developer has to

14. Walter M. Phillips, *A Program for Industrial Land Development within the Corporate Limits of Philadelphia* (Department of Commerce, September 20, 1954), p. 2. Similar proposals were submitted by him June 3, 1954, and January 14, 1955.

generate. It is likely that the effect of secondary economic activities will be overlooked. It would be very hard to induce a private developer to wait for what might be, from the public's viewpoint, the most desirable user of the land.

Could not the fact that the land was in the hands of a public agency be used to devise an industrial development policy which would halt the deterioration of the city's economic base? If industry's modern-day demands for land were taken into account— for example, single-floor production, attractive surroundings for research, and employee parking—an industrial district with transportation, city facilities, compatible industrial tenants, and all kinds of shared services might compete effectively with industrial parks in the suburbs. To accomplish this, the land could be transferred to the Redevelopment Authority, which would install streets and public utilities, demolish useless structures, divide the land into saleable parcels, and sell it.

## Using the Redevelopment Authority as Conduit

The Redevelopment Authority was empowered, unlike other city departments, to sell land on the basis of negotiated terms, free from the competitive bidding which is required of other public agencies. This, however, is a requirement which business finds hard to live with. Flexibility is so necessary for business firms' own operation that it is important for them to have publicity avoided (also for the sake of their employees' morale). If the transaction were handled through the Redevelopment Authority, it would then contract (through industrial brokers) with industrial developers to prepare and market the land and sell it to an industrial development nonprofit corporation. Thus the Redevelopment Authority would serve as a "conduit" from the city to a new development corporation. The creation of such a community-organized, nonprofit corporation, dedicated to the strengthening of the local economy, could then share with the Redevelopment Authority the task of deciding on the economic activities which were in the public interest. This, however, was a hard pill to swallow for those who considered the market the most reliable indicator of the public interest—Albert M. Greenfield was again among the dissenters. Greenfield felt that his many years of experience in disposing of land should be more valuable in deciding what was best for the city than some theoretical ideas! He objected in principle to the use of the public authority when the matter could be handled by private business. Also, he felt that, if the city could convert the land to industrial use, so could private business, and make a profit on it (see below).

On Mayor Clark's suggestion, advice was sought from practical men and members of the power elite in the community. The proposal was submitted informally to a committee of the Chamber of Commerce, the Society of Industrial Realtors, and the development divisions of the utility companies. While the reactions were favorable, the question of who would be willing to sponsor the nonprofit corporation was left in limbo, and postponement was suggested.[15] Meanwhile, the lawyers had found the legal aspects of this complicated proposition in order. Housing coordinator William Rafsky saw the importance of industrial land for the city as a whole and helped greatly in getting the idea accepted. Not everybody was convinced. Edmund Bacon, for instance, said in a report to Mayor Clark: "You should know that I disagree with Walter [Phillips's] idea of creating a special nonprofit organization. . . . Any agency must be either definitely governmental or definitely private, and . . . an attempt to straddle the two . . . will inevitably result in disaster." [16]

## *More Practical Power Roadblocks*

When the issues of economic and industrial revival finally came to the fore, the mayor was preoccupied with many other problems which he hoped to bring closer to solution before his term ended. Thus, when Phillips brought up his novel and unorthodox proposal for industrial development in cabinet, he got scant encouragement. The time may not have been quite ripe for his ideas to be sold to the public. Other concerns were paramount, priorities

15. Meetings with these groups took place on May 28, June 18, 1954, and May 6, 1955. See also Phillips's weekly reports of May 7 and August 13, 1954, to the mayor, and his memorandum to Clark (undated), "Industrial Land Program." Also memorandum from Peter Schauffler to Joseph S. Clark, October 26, 1954.

16. Weekly reports to the mayor, July 2, 1954 (in managing director's files).

had already been set, and objections to the new approach made it unlikely that, at a time when the battle was raging over the Food Distribution Center, Clark would be willing to take on yet another fight.

Again, Greenfield was implacably opposed to the idea. It ran counter to his economic philosophy. Eight hundred acres of the city's surplus land would make a neat parcel for private development. In fact, before Phillips had completed his proposal, he received (as he told this author) a visit in his office from members of the Greenfield firm who wanted to discuss with him the sale of the land: he told them very firmly that the city had other ideas about its use.

The importance of Greenfield's political power in the Democratic party and in the city council, as well as the fortune he had accumulated throughout his life's business ventures, enabled him to persuade other affluent individuals to contribute to the Democratic war chest. This ability gave him influence among councilmen, forever dependent on party contributions for their reelection, and hence the administration could not disregard his views. (Later, he also used his influence to obtain additional appropriations for the City Planning Commission.) Greenfield continued to believe that the virtues of unfettered enterprise would indirectly take care of the benefits to the public, and that nothing should interfere with a man's ability to make money in the private market. On the other hand, the professionals working in the administration firmly held that, where private action did not help individuals or groups who could not help themselves, the government would have to intervene. Since Clark and Dilworth, as well as Walter Phillips and William Rafsky, saw the need to attract industry in order to improve business climate, employment, and tax base, they regarded the proposal for industrial development as worth fighting for.

When Clark finally decided to submit the ordinance to the city council in 1955, the councilmen, knowing that Greenfield opposed it, let it languish in committee. Although Greenfield did not prevent ultimate adoption of the program, he managed to postpone its execution for three years. The basic policy question —who would be responsible for developing the land—was never solved during Mayor Clark's term.

*The New Corporation*

When Dilworth took office in 1956, the blueprint was ready for industrial development, and much of the business world was favorably disposed. But the means of translation into reality were still unclear. Was the corporation to be, as most documents of the period reported it, a private-public partnership? The Pennsylvania Economy League–Bureau of Municipal Research made a careful study for the city's Commerce Department.[17] Fredric Mann, a flamboyant businessman with a predilection for "wheeling and dealing," had succeeded Walter Phillips as commerce director. Mann left most of the city's business to his staff, thereby remaining free to continue his own business pursuits from his city office. He believed that it should be a partnership such as the bureau had advocated. He took over Phillips's ideas in toto, as well as the credit for his methods. Even then, passage of the ordinance was not easy. Mayor Dilworth and Mann's deputy negotiated with Greenfield along with Rafsky who, as mentioned, had long seen the great need for the ordinance. The ordinance was finally passed, as it had been worked out, with only minor deviations in structure and functions of the Industrial Development Corporation. The essential features of Phillips's proposal remained intact.

The Chamber of Commerce seemed the right vehicle to join the city in founding the quasi-public corporation for developing industrial land. Lennox Moak convinced the new president of the chamber in 1956, Robert Sessions, that this was the time to grasp the nettle of industrial development. Sessions had worked in the TVA and believed its philosophy. He had come to town as senior partner of a major consulting firm. His desire to cooperate with the city administration in this matter led to a novel enterprise, which involved both the public landowner acting with the public purpose in mind, and private business underwriting some of the risks. The nonprofit Philadelphia Industrial Development Corporation (PIDC) was formed by the city and the Cham-

17. Pennsylvania Economy League–Bureau of Municipal Research, *An Approach to Philadelphia's Industrial Renewal Program* (1956), p. 11; also, their *Elements of a Comprehensive Industrial Renewal Program for Philadelphia* (1957).

ber of Commerce in early 1958. As the city's industrial development agency (so designated by the council), it could receive state funds earmarked for industrial purposes. Advice and help by experienced businessmen on its board proved invaluable.

The PIDC's executive director, Richard Graves, promised to bring into the new corporation not only experience with the real estate business but also the "public" approach to it all. Graves's political sense (he had once run for governor of California) led Richardson Dilworth to ask his advice and to invite him to attend many cabinet meetings. The newly established Interagency Committee on Industry and Commerce presented a welcome vehicle for him to bring the different public agencies, departments, and other nonprofit corporations together to jointly decide on the policy to guide the actions of the corporation. As we have seen (chapter 4), this committee had as its regular members the City Planning Commission, the Redevelopment Authority, all cabinet members, individual departments if involved, the PIDC, the FDC, and the Old Philadelphia Development Corporation. Representatives of three nonprofit corporations discussed policy with cabinet-level representatives and independent authorities, so that all voices could be heard, misunderstandings clarified, individual city departments instructed, and policy set for dovetailing development plans of the city, the Redevelopment Authority, and the various nonprofit corporations.

Graves spoke the businessmen's language. With his imagination and charm he was a colorful figure who inspired the confidence of business as he brought forth new ideas. Business began to feel that the city was really concerned about its problems, and that the PIDC was actually the place to go for help. Graves never turned down any firm that came to him, whether or not he was able eventually to solve its problems. The PIDC tried to be all things to all people—but that gave business the feeling of spirit, encouragement, and initiative. Graves lit fires in the minds of Philadelphia firms, who became less inclined to leave the city. The "climate" seemed to change, although it was hard to prove the difference statistically in just a few years. When Graves left, an entirely different executive was needed, who would put system and logic into the PIDC's operations, establish guidelines and follow them, consolidate the corporation's gains, carefully extend them in an orderly fashion, and limit its role.

## Various Devices for Help to Industry

### The IRS Ruling

The most important tool for the PIDC was a ruling from the Internal Revenue Service declaring its obligations to be tax-exempt (July 1959), presumably because the PIDC was regarded as an instrument of government. The PIDC was thus able to supplement a firm's insufficient equity by adding its obligations as further guarantee for a "package deal," or to help finance buildings by supplementing a mortgage. The grantors of these loans did not have to pay federal tax on the interest received. For recipients in high tax brackets this meant that the actual interest rate might in effect be doubled. The feeling of "getting a good deal" without living in an area which openly subsidized industry, as was the case in other parts of the country, was a powerful incentive for firms to locate in the Philadelphia area. Efforts of the PIDC would have been impossible without the tax-free interest inducement, at least until the corporation was firmly established. The momentum established and the confidence returned would not be totally lost even if the tax ruling were revoked.

An IRS ruling in 1966 actually discontinued the tax-free status, but the PIDC, then under its new executive, weathered the blow. The Redevelopment Authority agreed to use its tax-exempt bonds to help clients of the PIDC with financing problems, thus continuing some of the advantages lost. But since the authority is a public body, the publicity necessarily attendant on its activities slowed down the PIDC's ability to act quietly and promptly.

### Finding Financing for Firms without Equity

One of the most difficult problems was to get financing for industry. Two different types of firms needed it. A minority of businesses had enough equity and a sufficient credit rating to obtain a mortgage or commercial loan without any difficulty; the vast majority had neither. They were too newly established, had too narrow a profit margin, or needed too much operating capital to have built up any substantial equity. Their net worth was too low for a commercial loan, which usually is granted on the basis of past profits and balance sheets. The problem was basically the same as was experienced with Food Distribution Center customers, but it was more acute.

In terms of private investment, industrial development is not very attractive, since the demand is specialized, depending upon a variety of technical specifications. The best a speculator can do, as we saw earlier, is to put up a shell for an unspecified industrial client—but even that is by far less attractive as an investment than a residential subdivision and therefore needs higher profits to counteract the greater risk.

Certainly a mortgage can be financed on the basis of ownership of such assets as land and buildings. But who will finance the other involved firms—possibly some 30 percent of them—who are unable to borrow on their own equity? The need for secondary financing thus was great. Almost every one of the PIDC's clients was in need of investments which could not be fully secured—junior financing. Risk money, therefore, was of the essence to get all these firms located or relocated.

If the PIDC could have lent the money against its own credit to close the gap, how much would it have been wise for the PIDC to advance? The firm would have to repay both the mortgage and the unsecured loan from its own profits, which might have made the annual cost prohibitive. The PIDC felt that a reasonable figure for a firm without equity (say, $1 a square foot) would be too low a return to make financing likely.

These problems soon became the PIDC's primary preoccupation. It tried meetings with public utilities and banks to stimulate the creation of risk pools by financial institutions. Because at that time only a small portion of urban renewal money was available for nonresidential purposes, it was suggested that *private* urban renewal for industry be used through such a financial pool. It was argued that the necessary "write-down" (the difference between cost of acquisition and of disposition) could be covered if the city loaned the money on the basis of the additional tax returns expected from the completed project. But the city council was afraid of such an arrangement.

The PIDC then advocated using the unusual device of a "definitive loan," as contained in federal legislation (up to forty-year mortgages at an interest rate close to the one paid by the federal government). Such a loan involves a land lease for a reasonably long term. Not having to purchase land and being able to get a fast tax write-off on the buildings gives the industry more flexibility in case of technological change. The PIDC tried hard and for a considerable period to sell industry on this seldom-used device, but in vain. Finally, condominium arrangements between several small firms were suggested, in which they would pool their resources to jointly rehabilitate an older building. But no developer willing to take the risk could be found.

Yet another plan, formally proposed to the PIDC board, called for the PIDC to acquire special industrial buildings for dislocated firms or newly formed small businesses patently without sufficient equity. The PIDC would execute long-term leases with the tenants and negotiate mortgage financing, providing it could find 25 percent equity money for a secondary mortgage, if need be, against tax-exempt interest payments to bridge the gap between the cost of the building and the mortgage. But even under the favorable conditions of the PIDC's tax-exempt interest payments, no such lender could be found: Philadelphia was just beginning to put risk capital into new investments. The financial underpinning of the banks was in conservatively invested trusts, not available for such undertakings. Seed money to trigger new investments was only available from less established sources, money gained from an earlier risk having been undertaken, and in the Philadelphia of the late 1950s such money was not plentiful.

## Revolving Fund and Sales Prices

The foremost task of the PIDC was to sell land to industry. It soon became clear, however, that using the city's surplus land could not be a one-shot proposition. It was decided to keep the money obtained from the sale of some of this land in a special revolving fund in order to acquire more land for industry. Considerations of public interest thus could enter into still other transactions. As more city land became available, PIDC had to compete with other agencies who wanted it for their own purposes. As newly acquired parcels were added to the city's economic "arsenal," the "land bank" came to contain a variety of parcels at different locations, and of different sizes and potential uses, thus making its "window display" more varied and attractive to business. Land suitable for eventual use thus was available even if no immediate developer was in sight, and it could be kept until the best use from the public viewpoint could be found. The interim tax loss was the price the city was willing to pay for the eventual benefit it would derive from this kind of use.

The revolving fund was also used as local matching money for federally aided projects or, in cases in which an immediate public "push" became necessary, to get some major development started. An example was the rehabilitation of an old loft building for "incubator" firms lacking equity, a step which might lead to attracting major research firms. It soon became clear, however, that the "revolving" nature of the fund had to be preserved. If the fund were spent when there was no likely source for repayment, it would soon be exhausted and would cease to revolve. Hence it was reserved for cases—and its use became carefully circumscribed —in which private firms or the federal government would guarantee repayment. It could thus not be used for a "write-down" of the land, but only for buying and improving land which would later be sold for industrial use. The most spectacular use of the fund was for "prior acquisition," a procedure specifically authorized in federal legislation. This is the early purchase of industrial land in redevelopment areas, to enable a firm to move to a new location earlier than would normally be possible if the firm were paid for the old property only after regular urban renewal procedures. Because it was important for a displaced firm to be able to dispose of its old plant early, this device was used to mitigate some of the adverse effects of urban renewal.[18]

Selling land to industry was the purpose of the PIDC, but it was not clear what price the PIDC should ask. Owners of private land, trying to avoid underbidding by quasi-public agencies, tried to have the price set at what the prevailing market asked. The city's aim of helping industry made it necessary to be competitive with land elsewhere, such as in the suburbs, rather than to maximize the one-time revenue from the sale of land.

18. The federal government had to issue a letter of "prior consent." The city's capital budget had to contain funds for early acquisition (Interagency Committee on Industry and Commerce, August 1960 and April 1961). The Redevelopment Authority, Food Distribution Center, and Philadelphia Industrial Development Corporation agreed on the type of cases for which money for "prior consent" expenditures should be reserved. These expenditures had to include, among others, the costs of the transportation of expensive equipment (Center City Coordinating Committee, August 20, 1958).

A high-level committee recommended "bellweather" sales prices—what retailers call "loss leaders." Such prices were arrived at in order to build up demand for land in an industrial district. After the establishment of desirable firms made the remaining parcels increasingly more attractive, prices could be raised. This had been the practice of private developers for some time. As a nonprofit corporation, PIDC had only to cover its own costs. Even after calculating costs of tranferring the land to the city, making improvements (for example, installing public utilities) and computing the assessments, the total cost was still well below normal prices for suburban land. Given the original commitment that the land would be sold at fair market value, the bellweather policy seemed a reasonable compromise because it meant that, on the average, each parcel would have been sold at fair market value. It also led to the possibility of attracting firms in competition with other regions—or, for that matter, with the suburbs.[19]

## Regional Approach versus Visible Results

This last point raised another thorny problem: was it the mandate of the city administration (or the PIDC) to keep firms in the *city* or merely to keep them in the *area?* Citizens of Philadelphia could profit from increased employment or income in either case—they would benefit, via the multiplier effect, to a certain extent from every activity within the area. Should the PIDC's concern be so parochial or so tax-oriented that it was only interested in city location, or should its partnership with business give it a metropolitan outlook? How much effort was warranted to keep firms from moving to the suburbs, or to lure them to the city from the surrounding area?

City officials pushed hard for the broader view. The managing director urged cooperation with the suburbs. "We are just beginning to develop a wholesome spirit of cooperation. . . . We cannot overlook the fact that a great many of our taxpayers either live in the city and work in the suburbs or vice versa." But the

19. "Industrial Land Policy" (memorandum from Mayor Richardson Dilworth), January 23, 1959. PIDC board meetings, December 12, 1958, and March 25, 1960, and again September 13, 1961. Food Distribution Center Executive Committee, November 12, 1958, and February 25, 1959. Mayor Dilworth to William Kelly, then president of the PIDC, September 13, 1961.

PIDC's executive director countered that he had to guard the city from "industrial pirating by the suburbs, who are using the very lands which the city's extension of water and sewer services makes it possible to develop." [20]

Graves's position of keeping as many firms as possible on city-owned land reflected more "spectacular" successes, easily visible to the man in the street. In Graves's desire to start the ball rolling, "spectacular" became his byword. A "first" which showed banks, brokerage houses, and other firms that it could be done would start a chain reaction, Graves thought. Thus, firms that either could not have left the city anyway, given the nature of their businesses, or that added only a negligible number of jobs, were established on scarce city-owned land. A number of well-known firms were brought in to make the business community take notice. More important, the PIDC was afraid that if well-known firms could *not* be persuaded to stay in the city, there might be created a negative attitude which would snowball. Some of these steps to gain industry were clearly necessary, especially at the beginning of the PIDC's operation. But this attitude was likely to play havoc with the basic principles which some city officials had attempted to lay down.

Firms which wanted help crowded the PIDC's offices, demanding an immediate decision or an assessment of the long-term advantages to city or area. It was tempting to show daily "results" in responding to these demands, and Richard Graves found it hard to stay within theoretical guidelines, no matter how sound they were. The Interagency Committee and the PIDC board were often engaged in ratifying actions already taken rather than evaluating future activities.

## A Contract with an Outside Developer

A broad new proposal was finally made. Having been unsuccessful in obtaining equity financing in any of the directions indicated, the PIDC suggested calling in a New York developer, the firm of Tishman, Inc., which had connections with many national firms and enjoyed a nationwide reputation. Having erected many office buildings, the firm was now interested in

20. Managing director to Richard Graves, July 29, 1959, and Graves's answer August 3, 1959 (in managing director's files).

getting into industrial investment. Under the proposal, Tishman would have the right to acquire a large portion of the city-owned land and dispose of it to industrial firms. Each tract of land would be sold to Tishman at the *appraised* price (the bellweather principle would not be followed), and he would erect buildings, mostly for lease to industrial tenants. Graves requested him to lease 40 percent of the rental space to small firms with financing problems. Tishman agreed to supply financing for these buildings, investing his own equity.[21] This would solve the primary problem the PIDC had been struggling with, how to take care of small firms with little net worth.

## The Economists' Arguments

Some time before the contract was to be signed, different individuals and groups had raised serious doubts. The plan meant, for one thing, that one more layer was being added between the city and the final industrial user (city–Redevelopment Authority–PIDC–developer–final user). Many leaders in the city, including the man who later became chairman of the Redevelopment Authority and executives of nonprofit corporations, voiced concern. But the most thoughtful statement came from the mayor's Economic Advisory Committee.[22] In February 1961, a delegation from the committee presented to Mayor Dilworth the committee's recommendations. They found him responsive.

The burden of their argument was that this "finest piece of industrial land" should be developed for the benefit of the city's overall economic goals, including "the maximum generation of additional economic opportunities." Having operational control over a wide variety of properties of different characteristics would strengthen the city in working on a broad economic program, whereas giving up prime industrial land to a private developer would weaken it. Profit pressure on a private developer might force him to carry out transactions rapidly, with little attention to selecting the type of industry which would be best for the community's economic health. The committee asked whether the

21. Exchange of letters between Graves and Tishman, March 23, 1961 (in PIDC files).

22. Economic Advisory Committee, "Use of Private Developer for North Philadelphia Airport" and "Statement of Criteria for Industrial Park Development at North Philadelphia Airport," December 9, 1960.

PIDC had tried to get financing for an entire package of diversified parcels, rather than for individual pieces of land. Could this not be accomplished on the basis of backing by the business community, and some pooling of resources? And, if an industrial developer with national contacts was considered essential, why not retain him on a fee basis to bring in new industry?

The committee further suggested that some of the criteria for the selection of industrial tenants be included in the contract with Tishman, Inc., as general, but flexible, guidelines, with discretion vested in the PIDC board's evaluation. Such criteria might include the amount of land the developer should be required to reserve for incoming firms, or for low-net-worth firms, or for expansion of existing firms; the number of workers to be employed per acre; the types of workers the firm would tend to employ; economic growth potential; cyclical stability; and linkages within the area and complementarity of firms. The committee's statement included guidelines for determining Philadelphia's growth potential, cyclical stability, and industrial complex possibilities.

The PIDC board appointed a special committee to scrutinize the contract with the developer. The city economist submitted several questions about the Tishman contract to the committee, in line with the deliberations of the mayor's Economic Advisory Committee, for example: (1) Will prices be in line with the earlier policy on industrial land pricing? If not, should not the public (through the PIDC or the city's revolving fund) share in the higher price charged? (2) The developer would benefit as financier from PIDC's tax-exempt status by receiving higher interest; as contractor he would receive a cost-plus fee; as lessor he would charge what the market would bear; and for the land he would pay only slightly more than actual cost to the city, which would be less than a private developer would have paid before the industrial park was built. Was this a fair share between the private and public sectors? (3) Most of the functions would be performed within the developer's organization: would this not mean a brokerage fee for him as real estate agent, a financing fee as banker, a contractor's profit, a management fee for administering the buildings and obtaining tenants—plus, of course, a developer's normal profit? (4) What assurance was there that the developer would himself finance an appreciable number of industries with low equity, one of the main purposes of engaging him in the first place? (5) Was it not possible to negotiate a contract with fees stipulated only for those services which the PIDC was unable to provide? [23]

In spite of all these questions, the contract was signed. The PIDC board felt that any other decision would reflect a vote of no confidence in Graves. Graves believed strongly that a nationally known developer who could make the advantages of Philadelphia's industrial land generally known would break the ice, and that the developer could help solve the problem of small firms with little net worth.

One of Graves's main purposes in bringing in Tishman was to support the weak credit rating of marginal firms. However, instead of providing credit so that such firms could buy the land and build their own plants, Tishman usually acquired the land himself, built the plants, and leased them to the clients. Since he himself was leasing the land with an option to buy from the PIDC, he was actually subletting the finished facilities. He used his own equity only rarely, partly because many of the new firms he brought in had A-1 financial ratings—a situation which PIDC could have handled comfortably.

In the original contract, the developer was given exclusive rights of development in 75 percent of the land under discussion, unless a company could afford to buy land directly from the PIDC. A change in the contract renewal, however, provided that the PIDC could itself finance all companies wanting to own their own facilities without being able to afford the immediate outlay. That left the developer with exclusive rights only if the company did not want to become the owner.

A number of interviews carried out by this author with persons involved indicated that Tishman's success was anything but spectacular. By 1967, he had developed and owned only about half a dozen parcels, about 3 million square feet of plant space out of 600 acres available in the Northeast industrial park, or a little more than 8 percent. PIDC, on the other hand, had disposed of a considerable portion of the land. Comparatively few

23. Memorandum from the city economist, October 27, 1960, and minutes of several subcommittee meetings.

of the companies now occupying the industrial park are the financially marginal ones the PIDC worried so much about. It appears that the majority of these firms wanted to own their own facilities, and with some help from the PIDC (often temporary) they were able to acquire them. The developer's services were needed only where the plant desired to lease. The firms with poor equity, however, who wanted to own their facilities, have essentially not been served.

This experience made Philadelphia's business community doubly aware of their responsibility as trustees of the public interest. Businessmen did not want to let aggressive promotion methods gain ascendance over carefully evolved ideas for Philadelphia's economic development—whether or not they individually agreed with those ideas. Within a year of the signing of the contract, after four years as executive director of the PIDC, Richard Graves left Philadelphia to start his own consulting and land development business in California. He had succeeded in restoring business confidence, and the time was ripe for a different, more systematic kind of management. This change in tone was effected when Richard McConnell, the city finance director, took over in early 1962 and united the direction of the FDC with that of the PIDC. He regularized the PIDC's responsibility and pulled it out of situations where it could not fulfill its obligations.

It had been necessary effectively to convince Philadelphia firms with space problems that they might find what they needed without moving out. Now that business was improving, a professional organization was needed which could see to it that planner, broker, banker, and lawyer were brought into every transaction. McConnell undertook the task.

## The New Executive

The PIDC acts as liaison in obtaining financing for industrial firms, even where credit and equity are poor. If firms are referred to a financial institution, the PIDC staff has carefully prepared the application to make certain that the client is a good risk. Similarly, policy questions are prepared and discussed prior to any recommendation to the board.

One outcome of this professional approach is that the PIDC has a staff with expertise in various facets of management, so that it can help firms improve their efficiency, their accounting methods, and their management practices, or show them how to present a favorable picture to the bank. Since the PIDC staff investigates its clients carefully, they may advise, for example, that renting would be more advantageous than buying because the cost ceases to be a capital investment and becomes an operating expenditure. They can tell where the firm's weaknesses are, and what can be done about them. Staff engineers are often able to show that a new location, a different physical arrangement, and added integration of different phases of production could make money for a firm and hence make mortgage financing feasible. The staff often suggests that a firm hire a management consultant. Those firms not willing to do so, or to change their system to achieve greater efficiency, find the PIDC's attention waning.

Another aspect of this new approach is a more scientific method of attracting new firms. The basis for economic development—for more jobs and private investment—is a guide for the PIDC's activities. The potential of firms can be measured against this framework. The PIDC can now determine, knowing the alternatives open to a firm, what its prospective employment, income, taxes, and the like, are and hence whether the firm is worth assisting.

The PIDC's bid for a firm now may be successful, but this could not have happened without the long gestation period— the thinking time under Joseph S. Clark, the successful partnership with business under Mayor Dilworth and Richard Graves, and the maturing under Richard McConnell.

Statistics seem to bear out the need for this long period, and the final success under a more businesslike management. While the first annual report of the PIDC (February 1960) named only six firms already in new quarters and six more in process, the 1965 report, issued at the end of the year, spoke of seventy new buildings, over $110 million total investment, and 35,000 new jobs created.[24] The 1966 record speaks of 11,500 jobs retained or

24. The only figures for the amount of investment contained in the 1960 annual report refer to initial investments of over $10 million. The number of added jobs is not mentioned in the report. By December 1962, 81 buildings had been acquired or erected for a total of 5.7 million square feet. Close

created and $35 million private capital committed during 1966 alone. The 1967 report states that during 1967 $30 million in private investment was committed and almost 5,000 new jobs created. Cumulatively, this means $179 million in investment, over 51,000 new jobs, and 24 million square feet of plant space through 1967.[25] The ten-year report, through 1968, speaks of 54,000 new jobs, $194 million private investment, and six industrial parks in addition to the one on the North Philadelphia Airport.[26]

All across the country areas are competing for industry. There is no a priori reason to assume that this competition is beneficial to net national growth. The very fact that such an assumption cannot be made may be the reason for the current doubts about the wisdom of the Internal Revenue Service in granting tax privileges for this activity.

Systematic efforts in Philadelphia attempted to direct industrial development into channels to benefit the entire area. Other cities could learn from Philadelphia's experience—as much from its failures as from its successes.[27] Of special interest are the joint public-private partnership institutions, which contributed actively to policy-making, and the variety of financial devices that were tried. An important lesson is the one that was learned from the controversy about the inclusion of an outside developer, uncommitted to and perhaps unaware of the broad reasoning by which citizen groups intended to benefit the community at large.

to 15,000 jobs had been created for an investment of almost $37 million. During 1963, another 39 buildings for over 2 million square feet had been added, and another 4,500 jobs and $20 million investment. Two years later, the total expenditure had risen to $113 million, 244 buildings, 17 million square feet, and over 35,000 new industrial jobs (Report of Activities, November 1958 through February 1960; 1963 and 1965 PIDC Summary Statements).

25. *1967, PIDC's Big Year in New Plant Construction.*
26. *PIDC 1968: Ten Years of Progress in Philadelphia.*
27. Kirk R. Petshek, "Industrial Development," especially pp. 267 ff.

# 8    *Rebuilding Center City*

The arrangement of Philadelphia's Center City into quadrants, each around a gardenlike square, has been maintained almost unchanged from the days of William Penn's "greene Countrie Towne." A good commutation and mass transportation network has preserved Center City as the focus of many activities. Philadelphia's special importance in the nation's history gives extra impetus to centripetal tendencies, which have kept community leaders in town long after their counterparts in other cities have fled to the suburbs. Tradition has helped maintain a wide variety of activities in this core area.

Many periods in Philadelphia's history find their focus in some part of Center City. Historical buildings, once spurned as only obsolete, are being restored. Cultural and commercial activities which have withstood the general gravitation toward the western part of the city include commuting and mass transit terminals. New office space is being added and occupied, in spite of realtor forebodings. The reestablishment of such activities near the core and the building of special types of residential facilities have encouraged a number of the area's leaders to abandon suburbia and even the periphery of the city, and to return to the center to live.

It is difficult to assign credit for the reawakening of Philadelphia's Center City to any specific influence; it was probably due to a combination of factors. The restoration of historic areas and rehabilitation of historic homes and other residences for different income groups; improved mass transportation into and within the core; revival of financial, insurance, and headquarters services, the addition of open places and public plazas—all combined to make Philadelphia's core attractive for twentieth-century living.

## The Railroad Builds Penn Center

Few believed that Philadelphia's "Chinese wall" would ever come down. The Pennsylvania Railroad had decided in 1925 to shift its terminal back to the west side of the river; but before it began demolishing the wall, depression and war intervened. When the Broad Street railroad station was finally demolished with the Chinese wall, not long after Joseph Clark became mayor, new development could open up both at the very center of the city near City Hall and in the corridor between the old and new stations. The railroad, owning most of that land, decided to build an office center and an underground shopping development near City Hall.

It was a strictly private endeavor, though morally supported by the city administration. Mayor Clark wanted the plans for Penn Center—as the project was to be named—to have a maximum impact on the city's development. Since the city did not participate financially, he had to resort to a variety of indirect pressures, which were not very successful. He appointed a Citizens' Advisory Committee to protect the public interest. An Art Commission already existed which had jurisdiction over a part of Penn Center, but it had power only to delay development despite Clark's efforts to get it strengthened. The railroad, however, appointed an Advisory Board of Design.

The selection of a New York developer of office buildings (Uris Brothers) troubled some of Philadelphia's civic groups, such as the Citizens' Council on City Planning, for they were afraid that the profit motive would transcend the developer's concern for the improvement of Philadelphia. In fact, the Advisory Board of Design rejected Uris Brothers' first building plans, and the Citizens' Advisory Committee sharply criticized them. Instead of changing its approach, the development firm bypassed the Art Commission: commission members were shown the plans only after the steel already had been ordered.

Edmund Bacon had worked on ideas and plans for Penn Center ever since he was in architectural school. His design, including a sunken plaza, a shopping arcade, and open spaces showed imagination, but the developer was loath to sacrifice financial return to excellence of design. Bacon, by then executive director of the City Planning Commission, pressed for a unified design for the entire development, rather than a piecemeal approach. On many points, however, he had to compromise with financial and real estate arguments that demonstrated a lack of interest in the city's total development. Fortunately for the city, the new president of the Pennsylvania Railroad (appointed in 1954), James Symes, was in favor of an overall approach. He preferred a Rockefeller Plaza-type development and tried to give play to broad public views, provided they were economically feasible.

Faced with the intransigence of the developer and the powerlessness of the Art Commission, Clark called all concerned parties together for an emergency meeting: the railroad, its Advisory Board of Design, the Art Commission, the developer, and Ed Bacon. He managed to wring some compromises in the public interest from the parties. Still, the argument that, this early in the city's rebuilding, private action should not be discouraged by too stringent public controls carried the day. The Citizens' Advisory Committee had tried to arouse the civic conscience, but in spite of Clark's help, it met with indifferent success.[1]

The total investment of $100 million in Penn Center was not lost on the rebuilding of Center City: one office building after another was being built in the area between the Pennsylvania Railroad's new and old stations, and the offices were quickly occupied. This development continued through the years, stimulating the improvement of many of the adjacent areas. Over time, some concessions—though not enough—were made to design and imagination at the expense of greater earnings.

In spite of the frustrations of getting Penn Center built the way it finally emerged, Clark called it "the best effort that the free enterprise system can make to combine the acquisitive instinct and the public good." [2] But this experience, early in his term, taught him how important it is to have chips before getting involved in a poker game: in subsequent undertakings he insisted on entirely different public-private partnerships.

1. See the chapter "Penn Center" in Cyril Roseman, "The Public-Private Cooperation and Negotiation in Downtown Redevelopment Decision Process in Philadelphia" (Ph.D. dissertation, Princeton University, 1963).
2. Philadelphia *Bulletin*, January 28, 1953.

## The Old Philadelphia Development Corporation

Richardson Dilworth publicly designated Center City as one of his primary interests as soon as he became mayor in 1956. After extensive cabinet discussions about implementing renewal of the "old city," the mayor called a special joint meeting of the City Planning Commission and the Redevelopment Authority for formal approval of the idea. The coordinator (not yet "development coordinator") suggested that he request the Greater Philadelphia Movement "to bring together all the interested business and civic groups" to explore with them "their interest and willingness to participate." Some type of permanent organization under the GPM's leadership would emerge, Rafsky believed.[3] But this is not what happened.

On July 2, 1956, the cream of the power structure, fifty-four men strong, appeared in the mayor's reception room by his invitation. The meeting opened with a film, "The Heart of the City," which depicted the parallel between a human heart and the core of an area. The words of the new chairman of the City Planning Commission, Albert M. Greenfield, were moving. Meeting and film were his idea. The message was clear to all that, if nothing were done to revitalize the city's center, the entire city would fall apart.

At a GPM luncheon early in 1956, Harry Batten had spoken feelingly for Center City renewal. The birth of the Old Philadelphia Development Corporation (OPDC) took place at a meeting in Mayor Dilworth's office a few months later, attended by Dilworth, Batten, and Greenfield. In mid-1956, shortly after he showed the film "The Heart of the City," Greenfield publicly announced the corporation's founding and promised that it would be capitalized at $250 million. Actually, only half a million was raised in the first half-decade—but that was all that was needed. Batten even suggested that Greenfield be made chairman of the nominating committee for officers of the OPDC. At the funeral of U.S. Senator Francis Myers, Batten and Greenfield appeared arm-in-arm for the first time, to the unconcealed surprise

3. Memorandum from William Rafsky to Mayor Dilworth, January 26, 1956.

of many who remembered their very recent and very bitter Food Distribution Center fight.

Batten evidently appreciated that Greenfield was embracing Center City renewal, which included the Society Hill area, so close to Batten's heart. Batten also realized that Greenfield, who had been effectively excluded from the two other big projects, Penn Center and the Food Distribution Center, was anxious to ride a horse he could call his own. It also suited Batten to help Greenfield to put his brand on it, since Batten's own pet ideas were being advanced.

William Day, chairman of the First Pennsylvania Banking and Trust Company, was elected president. A quiet man of humility and great charm, he held the position for many years. A criterion for membership on the OPDC board is that the member be the president or board chairman of his own firm. This gives assurance of the board's continuance as one of the most high-powered of all the quasi-public corporations. The purpose of the organization's incorporation is to "aid and assist in the redevelopment, renewal, replanning, and general improvement" of Center City.

At the first board meeting, Greenfield suggested Jack Robin as executive and promised to go after him personally—an assignment not viewed with much hope by those present who, like this author, did not believe that Robin could be persuaded. He had moved from the position of secretary to Mayor David Lawrence of Pittsburgh to membership in the Redevelopment Authority there and chairman of the Parking Authority. He had then become state secretary of commerce and chairman of the state Planning Board. While holding this position, he had started Pittsburgh's Industrial Development Corporation. To everybody's astonishment, he agreed to come. As executive vice-president, he started as a member of the OPDC board, and thus on the level of the elite itself.

Looking over the city officials who excelled as professionals, Robin soon picked Rafsky as the most brilliant and effective operator. These two attacked many problems together, though via entirely different routes; eventually Rafsky became Robin's successor.

Robin took over his new job early in 1957, a year after

Northrop had become director of the FDC and just before Graves began his activities at the PIDC. He was soon a member of the Philadelphia Parking Authority, which he quietly reorganized from within—as Dilworth had hoped he would. Robin was invited to sit in on the cabinet, to be a member of the city's Parking Policy Committee, and to participate in city-state discussions on expressways. In his new duties, he put to good use his chairmanship of the state Planning Board and his considerable past experience in political discussions. His position as ghost writer for David Lawrence (who later became governor of Pennsylvania) from the time Lawrence was mayor became important for Philadelphia.

Greenfield was soon persuaded that the southeast quadrangle was the most promising area for redevelopment. Bacon's interest in the historic area may have been partly responsible for arousing the interest of the Planning Commission's chairman, but Greenfield's interest was not surprising, as his firm also owned sizable parcels of land in the southeast quadrant. Although he had resigned from the firm upon his appointment, he knew better than most that if new development could make money anywhere in Center City it would be in Society Hill,[4] and more specifically in the southeast quadrant as a whole.

## Society Hill

The second interagency committee, the Center City Coordinating Committee, had been started before Robin was on the job. Its first informal meeting, in July 1956, was attended by city officials, architects, engineering consultants, and executives of the quasi-public corporations. On May 29, 1957, Robin attended his first session, where he made it clear that the OPDC's main purpose was "to obtain potential redevelopers, . . . to get action both private and public in this area, and to engage in some special projects." [5] The OPDC itself would not engage in redevelopment but intended "to act primarily as a catalyst. . . . The OPDC is a nonprofit citizens' organization. It has no public powers. Its strength comes from its acceptance by public officials as a disinterested associate in seeking what is best for Philadel-

4. So named for an early commercial group, the Society of Free Traders.
5. Center City Coordinating Committee minutes, May 29, 1957.

phia." [6] Robin's next action was to invite all professionals involved in the redevelopment of Center City East, for which the federal government had just announced the reservation of $11 million, to a monthly luncheon meeting for detailed Center City planning. In two hours of hard work, a great number of detailed decisions were made. (Under Rafsky's chairmanship, a maximum of five minutes was permitted at the start to order the meal and for personal conversation.) Representatives of other nonprofit corporations, city officials (including the City Planning Commission and the Redevelopment Authority), representatives of the Independence National Historical Park, and occasionally state representatives and different consultants were present. While the topic was related to that of the Interagency Committee on Center City, the subject was narrower and the expertise of the participants clearer: architects and designers played a large role in determining what the renewed area should look like and how a market for sale and rental of residences could be assured. (Later, when industrial areas in Center City were to be renewed, the question of their economic feasibility was discussed.) Although Rafsky chaired these meetings, Robin's ideas, appraisals, and evaluations left a clear imprint on the deliberations of the group and strongly influenced its decisions.

## The Historic Area

The area in which a number of historic houses stood, near the shrine of Independence Hall, had been too long neglected. The area in front of Independence Hall and other federal buildings had become a mass of dilapidated warehouses, so that it was next to impossible to find the Hall, let alone view it from a distance. In 1944, the American Institute of Architects had identified about 150 buildings, mostly in private hands, as having historical significance. By 1958, half of them had been destroyed. In spite of that, the physical remnants of the nation's early history were saved.

Two public actions were taken before the city began to show an interest. After the war, the Commonwealth of Pennsylvania began to demolish all buildings in front of Independence Hall in order to free it from obstruction so that a State Mall approaching

6. OPDC Second Annual Report (1958), p. 1.

it from the north could be built. In 1948, Congress designated the Independence Hall buildings and areas to the east up to the river, which contained many other historic buildings like the First and Second National Banks, as Independence National Historical Park. The whole area was to be restored, preserved, and administered by the Department of the Interior. The city administration and the City Planning Commission were, after 1952, close to these undertakings. Special civic groups (for example, the Society for Historic Landmarks and the Independence Hall Association) had long been concerned and, led by Judge Edwin Lewis, helped all they could. Judge Lewis almost single-handedly persuaded the state to undertake the building of the State Mall.

Appropriations for the Independence National Historical Park had to be fought for annually. Over the years this became more difficult, because every year additional small historic areas were proposed for acquisition by the park, thus pushing up the appropriation needed.

The first stage of the city's redevelopment project in the historic area (Washington Square East) was approved by the federal Urban Renewal Administration in 1957; it was designed to preserve and restore the remaining historic houses and to rehabilitate the rest of the area, thus recapturing some of its latent value. It was clear that the cost of this historic reconstruction would far exceed its economic return, so that it had to be made viable by being combined with the construction of new apartment houses and town houses. Some of these new dwellings could be erected where the old food market had stood (see chapter 6). The town houses were supposed to be designed in the historic tradition, reflecting a time when these homes were an alternative to several hours' horse-and-buggy ride to an owner's country estate. Yet they were to be modern enough for today's living— a difficult architectural task of blending the old with the new. (The relative merits of faithful historic reproduction compared with building twentieth-century houses, externally blending into their surroundings, were debated in a famous discussion between architects Edwin Brumbaugh and Lou Kahn.)

*Ensuring Preservation*

While public condemnation normally is used with caution, in this case the danger of further destruction of historic buildings demanded boldness. Eminent domain was applied in 1957 to this area in such a way that every building in the redevelopment area would become public property with a stroke of the pen, the price to be negotiated later. Architectural consultants to the Redevelopment Authority and the OPDC had carefully scrutinized each building and decided which ones should be demolished, either because of their structural condition or in view of the overall plan. For those houses that were to remain, detailed architectural standards were worked out in Robin's monthly luncheon meetings. Every former owner was approached and offered the chance to have his property conveyed back to him, provided he signed an agreement to renovate in accordance with the architectural standards decided on. On the OPDC's suggestion, the Redevelopment Authority also hired its own architect to help former owners by preparing plans for their homes in line with these standards.[7] If the owners did not want to sign the agreement, the OPDC was empowered to find a new buyer willing to do the restoration.

For new owners the standards for restoration were more rigid than those permitted the original owners. If an individual buyer could not be found, the next step was to offer the property to interested civic groups with concern for historic buildings who could restore it in line with historic plans. Only if all these efforts failed was the house turned over to the redeveloper for the entire area (from whose redevelopment area it had originally been excluded), who would not be likely to have the house rehabilitated. However, he was permitted to demolish it only if he could prove to the satisfaction of the Redevelopment Authority that rehabilitation was economically unfeasible.[8]

This elaborate attempt to preserve buildings was successful beyond expectations. Of 567 owners, 470 signed the agreement to restore.[9] Interest shown by community leaders—the emerging

7. Ibid., p. 5.
8. Statement by Redevelopment Authority, February 6, 1959.
9. OPDC Fifth Annual Report (1961)

"snob appeal"—helped the rehabilitation effort. Dilworth started this effort by building a handsome family home in colonial style, though with modern conveniences, on Washington Square. A GPM director, an editor of the *Saturday Evening Post,* and the owner of a radio station followed. Since prices kept rising, the group continued to be exclusive.

## Selecting the Redeveloper of Luxury Residences

The redevelopment contract for this area brought about keen competition with bidders from all over the country. While the City Planning Commission's suggestions for the area were the general basis for the proposals, they had to be judged by the developer's ability to blend the old and the new imaginatively. The "historicity and preservation" of the area, not the price for the land, was the overriding issue. The city was determined not to let the pressure of competitive land prices defeat the purposes of the redevelopment for this area. (Still, proof of financial responsibility and the likelihood of the agreement's being fulfilled remained important criteria for the contract.)

Eight nationally known developers showed an interest. A carefully selected small group consisting of city officials, board members of commissions, authorities, and quasi-public bodies, as well as civic association representatives and civic leaders watched the presentations of some imaginative models. Each presentation took the better part of a day. After all the presentations were completed, considerable time was spent on discussion. Finally, the decision went to Webb and Knapp from New York (Zeckendorf's firm) and to a Boston developer (who soon after was bought out by Webb and Knapp).

Financing became an important consideration. Consultants from the University of Pennsylvania studied the demand for residences in Society Hill, drawing their conclusions from past evidence of renters' preferences for Center City living. They felt there was a sufficient—but not plentiful—demand for high-rise apartments, town houses, and rehabilitated homes.[10] Thus, when other private apartment houses (unrelated to this project) were

10. This study was published in 1960 as *Residential Renewal in the Urban Core,* by Chester Rapkin and William G. Grigsby (University of Pennsylvania Press).

proposed, FHA was afraid that the projected demand would be absorbed by them, and stalled on the loan to Webb and Knapp, so that building could not begin until July 1962; meantime, city officials kept nervously watching the Center City housing market.

The aim had been to attract families to Center City, which would help reestablish it as the dominant section of the metropolitan area. But the high rent needed to offset rising costs, both for high-rise buildings and the restoration and new construction of town houses, left only high-income families eligible. Construction primarily for the "wealthy, poodled families" [11] raised objections. Even if it would be possible thus to attract some of the leadership back into town, was it socially justified? Fiscally, the redevelopment project meant higher returns, but socially it meant displacing the poor—and some small businessmen—to make room for the rich. Some critics, after listening to complaints of individual home owners, questioned whether Society Hill justified the expenditure of public money at all. Civic groups were concerned, and so were members of the city council.[12] In fact, the council held back approval of the plan while the fate of six small businessmen, whose stores were out of keeping with the refurbished area, was being decided.[13]

The city could not retrace its steps, however. The Webb and Knapp firm was not permitted to solve its financial problems by replacing the planned high-rise towers with square slabs, and it built them as proposed—they look today much like the model originally presented. The OPDC put it this way: "Time is worth everything except a loss of quality. . . . It is time, the more leisurely time of the 18th and early 19th centuries, which gives the area of Old Philadelphia its unique flavor and interest. . . . The end result must be something in which Philadelphia will take pride for generations." [14]

Meanwhile, Dilworth felt that the city should also rehabilitate its own property to show its concern. A small neighborhood park

11. Philadelphia *Bulletin*, April 28, 1958.

12. Interview with Councilman Harry Norwitch, January 22, 1965.

13. The final compromise was that a barber, a tailor, and a real estate operator could stay for the rest of their lives, provided they rehabilitated their stores in line with the new style of the area.

14. *The Art of the Possible*, OPDC Third Annual Report (1959), p. 4.

appeared where an abandoned police station had stood. A nineteenth-century market (curiously called the "Head House") was
painstakingly reconstructed from old drawings, to show that it
could be done with care—though not without ample funds! Such
a demonstration was the key to the success of "restoring the whole
area and interest[ing] private people in doing restoration with
their own funds," Bacon had said earlier.[15] Citizen response was
encouraging. And with the help of the OPDC, many private and
group efforts enriched the area.

Interest in the area as a whole also led the OPDC to try to
attract to the Mall area other kinds of national shrines and landmarks. Different ethnic groups were stimulated to start special
buildings. The area of Old Swedes' Church was added to the
Independence National Park as a historic monument (although it
is about a mile away). The oldest Jewish congregation in the
United States, Mikveh Israel, was to get its synagogue reconstructed on the Mall. In 1960, the OPDC proposed the establishment of a National Shrines Commission, which would be a truly
national organization and focus interest on this historic area.[16]

## Priorities in Center City

In 1961, as soon as renewal in Society Hill could begin (the first
application having been piloted through local and federal offices
and approved, the existing buildings demolished, the plans
drawn, and the land condemned and conveyed), the difficult decision had to be made on the next priorities in Center City redevelopment.

To appreciate this difficulty, it may help to realize, as shown in
table 2, what amount of time elapsed even in a project like Society Hill, which had been given top priority.

The possibilities were these: (1) Redevelopment could be extended west from Society Hill into the middle-income residential
area immediately adjacent. There were few historic buildings in
that area, but there were two hospitals, hoping to expand. (2) A
commercial and office center also seemed indicated. This implied
a careful redevelopment of areas somewhere east of City Hall,

15. Edmund Bacon to Joseph S. Clark, March 23, 1955 (in City Archives).
16. Memorandum from Robin to OPDC, 1960. Also Center City Coordinating Committee, April 11, 1960.

TABLE 2                    Schedule for a Center City Urban Renewal
                           Project in Philadelphia: Washington Square
                           East, Units 1 and 2

| *Original Survey and Planning Application* | Wash. Sq. East | |
| --- | --- | --- |
| Submitted | 6–57 | |
| Approved | 10–57 | |
| | | |
| *Loan and Grant I Application* | *Wash. Sq. East #1* | *Wash. Sq. East #2* |
| Submitted | 7–58 | 6–59 |
| Approved | 12–58 | 3–60 |
| | | |
| *Loan and Grant II Application* | | |
| Submitted | 4–59 | 12–61 |
| Approved | 5–59 | 7–62 |
| | | |
| *Land Acquired by Condemnation* | | |
| *First Redeveloper* | | |
| Site Conveyed | 9–61 [a] | 10–64 [c] |
| Construction Started | 1961 | 1964 |
| Construction Completed | 1962 | 1965 |
| | | |
| *First Large Development* | | |
| Site Conveyed | 1961 [b] | 1965 [d] |
| Construction Started | 1962 | 1965 |
| Construction Completed | 1964 | 1966 |

a. Webb and Knapp, Inc., and successors: town houses.
b. Society Hill Towers, Alcoa Residences, Inc.
c. Head House Square Corp.: shops and town houses.
d. Penn Towers Development Corp.: town houses.

after an analysis had been undertaken of what activities had the
greatest expectation of success. (3) The areas to the east and west
of the (virtually completed) State Mall, which were still dilapidated and thus threw a pall on the Independence Hall area,
could be redeveloped for new office and government buildings.
(4) The area further north might be redeveloped for light industry and wholesaling.

The final argument ran something like this: the demand for
high-income Center City housing would not be great after the
completion of Society Hill. Redevelopment of the adjacent residential area to the west—part of which was already being privately
redeveloped—would present competition for the thin demand for
Society Hill residences. After some time lapse, however, the redevelopment in Society Hill might encourage further private ef-

forts in the area to the west. Existing homes there were already being subdivided, creating apartments for middle-income families. It was not likely that redevelopment would accomplish much change in the kinds of dwelling units being made available and the income level of families who would live there—and in that case it was not worth spending public money. On the other hand, if redevelopment were indeed undertaken, it might raise the price of housing, causing the dislocation of even more families and thus compounding the social problems encountered in Society Hill. In that case, the demolition of houses would lead to cleared land which would not be used for building shelter but would be absorbed by the hospitals, and thus would be taken off the tax rolls.[17]

On the other hand, the two areas farther north would add new office buildings to the tax base, and the additional space for industry would attract new firms or permit existing firms to expand. The great demand for industrial land was especially acute in the center of the city. Locations near the market, near suppliers, and near the labor force were in great demand. Since this was expensive land, and the firms were small, it was a proper place for some redevelopment write-down. A sizable number of firms were being displaced by urban renewal and highways, so that there seemed little doubt that the area would soon be fully used. The influence on Center City of commercial and industrial activities in these areas (particularly if a new transportation terminal should materialize) would be likely to affect favorably the private development already taking place south and east of the Independence Mall. Finally, private investment should have varied, multipronged outlets. Residential developers had been attracted to the Society Hill area and its environs, and now it might be advisable to open up opportunities for commercial development on the one hand and for light industry on the other. Total private investment thus was likely to be more plentiful.[18]

The administration resolved, therefore, to accord priority to development in industrial and commercial areas. Bacon's prefer-

17. Memorandum from William L. Rafsky, early 1960, and his weekly report to the mayor, October 1959. Also Center City Coordinating Committee, September 16, 1959, and November 18, 1959.
18. Memorandum from city economist, early 1960.

ence for the residential area immediately west of Society Hill was not accommodated until November 1965, when an application was made for redevelopment of virtually the entire area of Washington Square West (twenty-five blocks). The city council approved the ordinance in September 1967, the demand for medium-income residences having greatly increased in the meantime. The council gave its approval, however, only after it had been assured that relocation housing would be built before residents were displaced, that they would be relocated in the same neighborhood, and that enough low- and medium-priced residences would be available. The deputy managing director for housing stated at that time that low-income housing must take precedence over upper- and moderate-priced housing and that housing should have priority over commercial and institutional development. In the meantime, however, the two industrial Center City areas to the north had begun to be redeveloped and had been allocated the necessary federal and local funds. They provided space for relocation for many small businesses dislocated by other redevelopment projects.

The question was: what *kinds* of activities should logically be located in the center of a metropolitan area? A "Policy Paper on Center City" tried to answer this question; it was composed, rewritten, discussed, and tried again over some period of time.[19] The emphasis was on the overall efficiency of such an area and the interrelationships of the many different kinds of activities in the center of a city. This discussion served an important function at the time, raising many questions which had not previously been asked, and pointing up reasons for location of activities within the city's core which most city officials had not considered. The nine-volume New York Economic Study, the CED pamphlet by Raymond Vernon, *The Changing Economic Structure of the Central City,* and other writings have superseded and clarified many of the points touched upon in Philadelphia's policy paper.

19. Presented first by the city economist, changed by the assistant director of the Traffic and Transportation Board, it was discussed with city officials and representatives of various nonprofit corporations throughout most of 1958. Center City Coordinating Committee minutes, particularly June 18, September 17, November 19, and December 17.

The paper suggested that those activities should locate at the center which served the metropolitan area as a whole, or which needed frequent contact with other centrally located activities. These two criteria are likely to determine the size of the city center. City policy can begin to increase the center's effectiveness by making access to it and mobility within it easier—especially important for industry and commerce.

The policy paper further pointed out that efficiency is the center's most important aspect. Efficiency is helped if different subcenters are logically distinguished from each other. For example, offices that need frequent face-to-face contacts should be located closer to the center than more self-contained offices like those of insurance companies or other large corporations. (Each of these subcenters should of course have enough space for auxiliary services like printing or drafting, as well as amenities like stores or restaurants.) The conviction that these two types of office activities must be located at different parts of Center City became an important subject of discussion. The need for efficiency had to be asserted against the arguments in favor of appearance irrespective of location. There was a parallel need for the shopping areas to have related activities cluster at one place. The separation of shopping catering to different income groups would occur sooner or later anyway, and storage and routinized activities could be located outside of the center on cheaper land. This would lead to a reduction in the spread of downtown, and thus to its increasing efficiency.

The development expected to add most to the city center's efficiency was the planned "Market Street East," a combination of various modes of transportation—railroads, subway, buses, and freeway lanes—with varied new shopping facilities, parking facilities, an air-conditioned mall, second-level glass-covered arcades, and a subway concourse (see chapter 5).

The city had decided that the area north of Society Hill (part of it called "Franklin Redevelopment Area"), which has easy access to Center City, should be rebuilt for light industrial and small commercial enterprises. But what kind of activity was most clearly in the public interest? Certainly, large land-using industries and warehousing were not a good use of the land, even if a potential user expected enough profit to be willing to pay the price the land commanded on the market. The function of Center City in relation to the entire area was crucial, and for this reason it was imperative that the city government carefully monitor the use of the land there, where necessary exercising its power of eminent domain. Likewise, in the case of firms located along the water's edge which had ceased to need the water in their production process, the land use could be declared obsolete, and eminent domain could be used by the city to ensure that the land be assigned to some more suitable use. Just as blight and misery can penetrate the hinterland, carried along by the centrifugal forces mentioned earlier, these same centrifugal forces can be the conduit for a healthy tax base and adequate shelter if the resources with which time and geography have endowed a central city are marshaled and put to their best use.

# 9 *The Universities and University City*

What did the universities contribute—and how could they have further contributed—to the new reform administration in Philadelphia and the solution of the problems it faced? A group as intellectually oriented as were the reformers could be presumed to enjoy a close relationship with the intellectual elite concentrated in the city's universities. Joseph Clark was an overseer of Harvard University, and Richardson Dilworth was a trustee of the University of Pittsburgh. Many intellectuals were to be found in their immediate entourage. Several holding top positions in Philadelphia's administration eventually left to assume important university posts. It would seem obvious, then, that part of the city's brain trust would be drawn from the universities to advise the reformers in office, and that these institutions would therefore be a source of help and sustenance to the city administration. Why, then, did this not happen?

Historical accident is only a part of the answer. When the reform was born, Harold Stassen as president of the University of Pennsylvania showed little interest in the local scene. Temple University had, as a commuter institution, more local concern and began to be interested in its environment, but it had at that time only few outstanding scholars in the social sciences. Harold Stassen and Robert Johnson (president of Temple) were deeply committed Republicans, and the new city administration was Democratic, no matter how much its approach differed from that of the traditional Democratic city machine. Drexel Institute of Technology, the smallest of the three main institutions of higher learning in Philadelphia, with a campus almost adjacent to the University of Pennsylvania's, specialized in the technical sciences and work-study programs. Not until a new president entered the picture at the University of Pennsylvania did a new era begin to dawn.

The change began when Dr. Gaylord Harnwell, a well-known scholar, took over as president of the University of Pennsylvania. Still, for upper class Philadelphians, it was too close to home and did not have the prestige of other eastern institutions. However, it was located in the middle of a busy and interesting city, with which some of its faculty members might want to get involved. Like other large urban universities, the University of Pennsylvania did not want to inhibit faculty members from helping to build the kind of community which might make their institution truly "urban"; yet at the same time it needed to keep abreast of new teaching methods and to excel in scholarship. Recognition had come, albeit belatedly, to the fact that for some faculty members there must be a choice between activities within the community and intellectual endeavors isolated from it.

University City could never have been established if Gaylord Harnwell had not been at the helm of the University of Pennsylvania at the right time. When he was appointed in 1956, the reform government had already been in office for four years. Despite the stimulation of new ideas, the exploring, discussion, and enthusiasm emanating from City Hall, the universities had stayed in their ivory towers, though their own institutions eventually benefited from the change in the civic climate. Neither Clark nor Dilworth was awarded a degree *honoris causa* by a home institution. Activities in City Hall and its rapport with the sophisticated civic groups drew some social science faculty members into its orbit, despite the absence of any official city-university relationship. In many ways the Philadelphia administration of that time provided a laboratory for social science tools, for legislation adopted by the federal government, and for experimentation with programs which became prototypes. The academics' early involvement therefore was as individuals working with civic groups and nonprofit corporations. No position taken by individual faculty members could be construed as a position taken by their university as an institution. Given the organizational structure and the administrative framework within which universities function, it would be inappropriate and highly improbable of achievement for a university to take a public stand, except on matters where a very clear consensus has emerged supporting a position held by both faculty and governing body. Until comparatively recently, however, when controversy has centered on two main issues, universities seldom took any kind of public stand. The two issues are: university identification through contractual arrangements with the national government's defense policies, and, locally, confrontations arising from the effects of physical university plant expansion.

## What Role Should a University Play?

Should an urban university be an active participant in its environment and assume responsibility for some of the specific urban problems which beset its host city? Obviously, a university's first duty is to its students and their education. While in the 1950s the students had not yet objected as strenuously to the impersonality of university teaching as they have since then, the need for improvements in the university's teaching obligations could clearly be seen. However, good teaching does not require that the teacher isolate himself from his metropolitan area. On the contrary, active participation in an innovative city, as in a laboratory, may enhance his teaching.

"A university that does not serve its community is not a university," wrote Robert Wood in 1965. "The involvement of university people in large civic ventures is already a fact of life in many metropolitan areas. . . . The universities and their faculties have an obligation to take stands on larger public issues of urban areas not immediately related to the organizational interests of the campus." [1] And Charles Haar, in 1968, remarked: "Involvement and commitment; a respect for the pragmatic; a willingness to engage in and with community issues—few urban universities would rate high marks in such tests. By contrast, consider the contribution of the land grant colleges to the development of American agriculture. . . . Is the urban university as concerned, as competent, as creative and as conscionable in its

1. Robert C. Wood, "The New Metropolis and the New University," *Educational Record*, Summer 1965, reprinted in Bernard J. Frieden and Robert Morris (eds.), *Urban Planning and Social Policy* (Basic Books, 1968), pp. 401–2.

pursuit of urbanity and understanding, acumen and aspiration?" [2]

The large-scale efforts of the Ford Foundation in the early 1960s to stimulate universities to serve urban areas were compared with the land grant college experience. But subsequent events proved that the agricultural experiment could not be transferred. Agricultural extension deals with a business rather than with social problems, with the family as a unit of production. The goal of economic profitability is clear-cut. How does a university desiring to contribute to its community express concern with broad problems and exert an impact on community development? A specific social problem may be of sufficient interest to the individual faculty member to induce him to spend his scarce time seeking a solution to it. Such involvement will increase his general knowledge of the community's problems and make him more useful for a variety of his activities. Innovative ideas may make his contribution important. Analytical ability and use of proper methodology might well render social experiments more conclusive and public and social relationships more effective.

A local government official may persuade university faculty with the appropriate expertise to examine the consequences of its long-range plans, and to suggest possible alternatives and strategies for putting them into effect. This is an assignment well adapted to most social science faculty interests. But even if the public official realizes the importance of such a service, he usually cannot afford to pay for it, and the university as a rule is unwilling (or unable) to underwrite faculty time as a community contribution; if it thus devolves upon faculty members to contribute these services without remuneration, their contribution will necessarily be limited. Universities usually were unwilling to consider community activities as a substitute for the more traditional professional activities of teaching and research. In the early 1960s, the Ford Foundation attempted to open up this area of endeavor to university faculty members and to make available to the hard-pressed local administrator resources previously de-

2. Charles H. Haar, "The Urban University: Challenge and Response" (Convocation Address, Lake Erie College, Painesville, Ohio, February 28, 1968).

nied him. The foundation funds awarded to a few urban-based universities were administered with varying degrees of competence and imagination. The university nearest Philadelphia which benefited from these grants was Rutgers. While the programs unquestionably opened up new avenues of cooperation and left their mark on the university-city relationship, many promising areas of experimentation ran afoul of politics and bureaucracy as practiced both in City Hall and on the campus.[3]

In some communities, of course, lack of imagination of both elected and civic leaders may inhibit them from seeing how a university could help them. They may feel that they can identify their community's problems better than can intellectuals, most of whom are not even natives of the area. This drastically limits the desire and enthusiasm of individual faculty members who would like to help.

Where there is receptivity to university advice, however (as there was in Philadelphia, at least in principle), academics can participate in watchdog groups for community interests, as advisers to community groups or official agencies in their development plans, as gadflies to public officials or civic groups, as catalysts—by inviting leaders to meet on the neutral ground of academe to make sure that they fully understand a problem—or as members of task forces bringing factual material and expert analysis to the deliberations of lay citizen groups.

Too close a relationship with the community, however, may lead to identification with its value system and to advice which may run counter to faculty conscience. Unless faculty members involved are in objective agreement with the goals of the community, a university might find it best to avoid a "client" relationship with community organizations. (Should, for example, a law faculty help a community to circumvent a Supreme Court decision?) When members of a university faculty feel that an

3. On the questions of foundation grants and extension programs see Kirk R. Petshek, "A New Role for City Universities—Urban Extension Programs," *Journal of the American Institute of Planners*, November 1964, esp. pp. 306–7; John Bebout, "Urban Extension: University Services to the Urban Community," *American Behavioral Scientist*, February 1963; and James Coke, "Ways and Means for Urban Universities to Exercise a Unique Function in Their Communities," in University and Community, *Proceedings*, April 1963.

action the community leaders are about to take is not in the best interests of the public, the values agreed upon by a faculty constitute a clear obligation for it to speak out as a group. A community seeking help from a university should ask for it with a clear understanding of these often ignored limitations.

Although the Ford Foundation experiment in the early sixties proved only partially successful, Robert Wood, then undersecretary of the Department of Housing and Urban Development, conceived the idea of urban observatories.[4] As institutes tied to urban universities but financed largely by federal funds, the observatories would encourage university experts to research the kinds of problems to which city halls needed answers. As the research would be carried out without bureaucratic pressure but mindful of the city's needs, it would be done with all deliberate speed. These observatories would work simultaneously, and in cooperation, in different cities, making comparison possible. The U.S. League of Cities took up the idea (while Milwaukee's mayor Henry W. Maier was president) and started ten urban observatories.

Philadelphia—not one of the cities whose mayor wanted an urban observatory located in it—still needed little persuasion to make use of university talent. It is true that, where concrete technical problems were posed for which the council was willing to appropriate funds, existing university talent was drawn upon through consultant contracts.[5] But the city administration also needed academic guidance in its long-term thinking, its search for better ways of determining priorities, its striving for an overall development program. At the beginning of the reform, it lacked such guidance.

## The University of Pennsylvania

In June 1956, Martin Meyerson wrote: "The University [of Pennsylvania] faces the alternative of . . . assuming leadership in

4. Wood, "New Metropolis."

5. Examples of such contracts are: The Demand for Racially Mixed Housing; Demand for Housing in the Urban Core; Determining County Income; Linkages and Complexes; Water-Based Industry; Operating Costs of Redevelopment Areas; Need for a Real Property Inventory; An Investigation of Skid Row. Many other more technical counseling contracts were handed out, e.g., in the field of transportation.

creating a desirable neighborhood in which a university can flourish. It is an urban university, benefiting from urban, cultural, and educational facilities, and serving the urban community. If the University is to capitalize on its urban advantages, it must take care to offset its urban disadvantages. Faculty and students prefer to cluster about the place which stimulates intellectual and social activities." [6] The University of Pennsylvania itself stated: "An urban University cannot ignore the fact that it is situated in a given community and is therefore part of the historical cultural life and economic and general social environment of that community." [7]

The question of the influence of the university faculty on the institution's community involvement was raised in the early 1950s. Robert Mitchell, of the Department of City Planning, suggested in a memorandum to both President Harold Stassen and Dean Holmes Perkins that a university agency (he mentioned as an example the Institute of Urban Studies) be endowed with special funds to enable its faculty to participate in the formulation of city policies. (The memorandum itself could no longer be found in the files.) Independently (and without knowing of this suggestion), several city professionals later raised the question whether some arrangement could be devised which would make it financially feasible to obtain faculty participation in the city's new programs and faculty advice for the city's reform leaders. In a number of interviews in 1964–65,[8] this author discussed the feasibility of the university's obtaining a grant from a foundation or government source which would make it possible for faculty experts in pertinent fields to act, as if on retainer, as consultants to top public officials. They would be available for ad hoc advice and for long-term thinking about some of the broad problems of development for which administration officials lacked the think-time. New York City was actually using faculty members of the University of Pennsylvania in some such manner as consultants.

6. Letter to President Harnwell and Dean Perkins, June 30, 1956 (made available by President Harnwell).

7. "The Role of the University of Pennsylvania in the Delaware Valley Community" (statement by the university to the Middle States Association, 1963).

8. E.g., with Gaylord Harnwell, Vice-President Hetherston, Dean Holmes Perkins, George Taylor, Robert Mitchell, William Wheaton, David Wallace, Paul Davidoff, Chester Rapkin, and William Grigsby.

But no such arrangement with the University of Pennsylvania was ever consummated for Philadelphia during the reform period.

Meanwhile a number of faculty members at the University of Pennsylvania, mostly in urban and planning fields, did what they could individually.[9] President Harnwell pointed out in an interview how difficult it was to evaluate the contribution of a faculty member who was active in community projects, particularly if he happened to get involved in an area outside his teaching competence. At the University of Pennsylvania, credit for such community participation was unlikely, unless perhaps the faculty member had started a new program of potential interest to other institutions or had shown innovative ability which might be widely recognized by his peers. Only then might his action be considered pertinent in evaluating his academic standing—while publication is always a matter of record.

In a 1963 statement to the Middle States Association, the University of Pennsylvania said: "The University can only participate if its own development is enhanced. The scholar-educator has an obligation to his local urban setting only to the extent that he finds that setting useful to his needs as a scholar and scientist."

## Other Philadelphia Institutions

Temple University, given its semipublic character, was more concerned with reaching into the community. But its faculty personnel policy was similar to that of the University of Pennsylvania, and its main community interest was concentrated in its immediate environment. The slums surrounding Temple University made its involvement more important, although even here it was sporadic. But Temple, like the University of Pennsylvania, did not at the time respond to the broad question of commitment to urban problems in general, nor did it help the city administration in solving them. It did, however, make a conscious effort to research a problem that could be of help to other cities in its evaluation of the Skid Row near Center City in 1960. In 1963, as a result of this study, it suggested and helped start the Diagnostic and Relocation Center for the men on Skid Row.[10] Temple

9. Men like Robert Mitchell, William Wheaton, John Dyckman, Martin Meyerson, Paul Davidoff, etc.

10. *The Men on Skid Row: A Study of Philadelphia's Homeless Man Population* (Temple University, 1960); *What to Do about the Men on Skid*

was also instrumental in starting the "grey areas" project, leading eventually to the foundation of the Philadelphia Anti-Poverty Action Committee (PAAC).

Finally, there were the "Main Line" Quaker colleges—Swarthmore, Haverford, and Bryn Mawr. One of Mayor Clark's early executive secretaries, Paul Ylvisaker, came on leave from Swarthmore. Other aid was made available to the city administration by individual faculty members of these institutions, mostly as individual consultants or as research scholars to study the city's administrative practices.

No matter how much individual faculty members may have contributed to the solution of specific city problems, the universities in the Philadelphia metropolitan area remained, as institutions, aloof from the city's problems. The Philadelphia experience indicates that until recently we could have expected little local participation from institutions of higher learning in the development of public policy in any city. The city administration of Philadelphia was ready to receive, but the universities were unwilling to give. Events across the nation since the days of Clark and Dilworth in Philadelphia, which concern minority groups, the poor, and the unemployed, have precipitated some searching self-evaluation on the part of all institutions of higher learning. Not to be discounted is the pressure applied by student bodies, particularly at colleges and universities located in urban areas. The student seems to have recognized and insisted on the institutions' assuming some commitment in a way that was previously denied by their administrations. Thus we see at the end of the period more involvement by individual faculty members, who often identified themselves publicly with their institution, even though acting as individuals. We can also see a greater willingness on the part of the institutions to make budgetary provisions for programs which reflect concern for the urban condition, and less rigidity on the part of administration and trustees concerning public service activities on the part of faculty members.

*Row* (GPM, 1961); *Philadelphia's Skid Row: A Demonstration in Human Renewal* (Diagnostic and Relocation Center, Temple University, 1963). See also Leonard Blumberg, Thomas E. Shipley, Jr., and Irving W. Shandler, *Skid Row and Its Alternatives: Research and Recommendations from Philadelphia* (Temple University Press, 1973).

## University Renewal and the
## West Philadelphia Corporation

Both the University of Pennsylvania and Temple University were concerned with the area which made up the immediate environment of their own institutions. There was concern to improve the community for their students and faculty, and at the same time fulfill a social obligation to improve the lot of those living nearby —particularly citizens who might suffer from the university's desire to expand.

Improvement of the immediate vicinity and institutional expansion, however, may easily be contradictory objectives—in the same sense in which citywide benefits and those of the university's immediate neighborhood might not coincide. Institutional expansion has always meant the dislocation of residents, the problem in recent years being complicated by their possible participation in formulating alternative plans for their own neighborhoods. A university may mitigate conflict by consulting its neighbors about its plans (or at least keeping them informed), although relocation even with the university's help can seldom be accomplished without some controversy. Where the issue becomes exacerbated, the disadvantaged and dislocated will read the university's actions to benefit the environment as, at best, efforts to ensure the thriving of the university community, or, at worst, attempts to pacify the nonuniversity neighbors. Examples of such conflicts in university communities abound. Columbia University in New York City and the University of Chicago come first to mind.

The first relationship between the city of Philadelphia and the universities was forged through urban renewal, but at that time it was a pedestrian negotiation, as the institutions (each in its own area) simply requested land from the Redevelopment Authority for institutional expansion. The areas had been certified for several years as urban renewal areas: Pennsylvania in 1948 and Temple in the early 1950s.[11] This matter of physical renewal

11. Redevelopment Area Plan, *University*, published September 1950, for the University of Pennsylvania; *Northwest Temple, Southwest Temple,* and *East Poplar,* published September 1950, July 1953, and March 1955 for Temple University.

for the institutions, however, brought to the fore the whole question of competition for scarce urban renewal dollars. Where, among the city's priorities, should institutions of higher education stand? (See chapter 6.) The universities were as committed to their desires for expansion as were other claimants, irrespective of competing demands upon the city. Furthermore, the tax-exempt status of universities always arouses the feeling that their contribution to a city's development in monetary terms is negligible and that using renewal funds for their expansion must be justified by such intangible benefits as culture, art, general education, and a more rarefied environment.

In 1966, the University of Pennsylvania had 12,000 employees, with a payroll of $74 million; this monetary sum could easily double in a decade or two. Temple and Drexel also added significantly to the area's payroll. The degree-granting institutions in the area served 100,000 students, of which about one-fourth came in from outside the area. An average annual expenditure of $1,200 per student pours about $22 million into the area's economy. By the time the economists' multiplier and accelerator effects are calculated, the impact from the students alone should be in the neighborhood of $100 million.[12] Together with an expected $200 million payroll in 1975, this places education among the leading ten employing industries in Philadelphia.[13] Capital improvements for the institutions in the ten years following 1956 accounted for over $891 million, and the income of institutionally related households was estimated at about $100 million. It was expected that about as much would be added by the income of other households in the area as a result of the environmental and conservation efforts of the West Philadelphia Corporation, discussed below.

The spark that ignited the West Philadelphia Corporation was struck by a new business vice-president of the University of Pennsylvania in 1958. He advised President Harnwell to call a meeting of representatives of several West Philadelphia insti-

12. *University and Community*, pamphlet discussing the University of Wisconsin-Milwaukee, published 1967. Also Ernest R. Bonner, "The Economic Impact of a University on Its Local Community" (Planners Notebook), *Journal of the American Institute of Planners*, September 1968.

13. Elizabeth Deutermann, *Economic Development*, CRP Technical Report, no. 13 (December 1964), p. 36.

tutions along with the University of Pennsylvania and Drexel Institute.[14] After about a year, the idea of a community devoted to learning and research had taken hold. A private consultant was hired to advise the University of Pennsylvania on how best to go about creating an environment conducive to institutional growth and faculty living.[15] In 1959 the West Philadelphia Corporation was formed.

The obvious choice for president was Harnwell, though his appointment was made only after much discussion, for the corporation strove to avoid university domination.

Early in 1960, Leo Molinaro was appointed executive director (he later became president). He had been an executive of AC-TION (American Council to Improve Our Neighborhoods—a privately sponsored national group), an experience which enabled him to deal comfortably with business and civil directors. At the time of his appointment his board had representatives from the five local institutions and three community groups, but an almost total lack of businessmen and civic leaders with citywide prestige. What Molinaro had in mind for the West Philadelphia Corporation would, he knew, require the help of many members of the power structure within the city. Gradually the board was changed.

Molinaro first concentrated on setting up the area of University City as a living and working "community of scholars." At the time, the faculties of the University of Pennsylvania and Drexel lived far from West Philadelphia, which made any kind of cohesive community impossible. To help change this, University of Pennsylvania financing was made available to staff and faculty at favorable rates for the purchase of homes. In the fall of 1959, about 10 percent of the University of Pennsylvania's faculty lived in the area; that figure had doubled by 1962. By the fall of 1964, it had further increased to 24 percent, and the trend has continued. Encouraging faculty to move into the area would

14. Other institutions were Presbyterian Hospital and the College of Pharmacy and Science.
15. The history of West Philadelphia as it developed through the years, and the gradual emergence of a University City and a nonprofit corporation backed by the area's institutions, is told interestingly in Leon S. Rosenthal, *A History of Philadelphia's University City*, published in 1963 by the West Philadelphia Corporation. Rosenthal was then a member of the corporation's board.

clearly complement the threefold collaboration of the university
with the city administration and civic groups.

At the same time, Molinaro strove to become accepted by the
community of civic professionals holding key positions both in the
city administration and in the citywide civic groups. He knew that
he had to get the support of the "movers and shakers." Given his
original board of directors, he had to gain the cooperation of the
civic professionals, so that through them he could reach the members of their boards. Although a newcomer, he soon earned the
respect of this small, select group. They were experienced in evaluating newly appointed professionals, and Molinaro's imagination,
positive attitude, and obvious ability in this difficult field soon
won them over. Never at a loss for a new idea, he was ingenious
in finding ways of getting things done and in presenting new interpretations of known facts. (In May 1968, Molinaro resigned to
become president of a new subsidiary of the Rouse Development
Corporation, charged with the building of the new town, Columbia, in Maryland.)

## University City as a New Environment

Molinaro believed fervently in the vital role a university must
play in the life of a city. He believed that the new ideas and approaches evolved in universities could keep city leadership dynamic and make innovations a daily experience. This was particularly true, he felt, where scientific training provided the basis
for new inventions—technical, administrative, social.

Molinaro suggested that the businessman's entrepreneurial
spirit be drawn into governmental affairs to help the city government better to serve the public interest. He thus underscored
—though with a technological emphasis—what was already happening in Philadelphia's public-private relationships. The revolution in communications, for instance, had affected every aspect of community life. Universities, Molinaro believed, could
provide the experts in technical developments such as systems
analysis who might lead cities to an earlier understanding of
their problems.

Molinaro tried to imbue the University of Pennsylvania and
it actions with this personal philosophy of his. He did not
succeed, however, in broadening the university's approach into

a concern with the total urban area, but he did extend its interest in institutional expansion to an interest in its own environment.

## Different Planning Concepts

Bacon's concept for West Philadelphia differed from that envisioned by the new corporation. Bacon thought West Philadelphia's Victorian brownstone houses could at best be made functional but were of no architectural significance. He had difficulty in seeing the potential of University City as a unique project. He was ready, however, to concentrate renewal on one district of Philadelphia, and he preferred that the district be West Philadelphia. Because of Bacon's interest in Center City, some believed that he saw the University area as an increasingly serious competitor for the attention of the administration. On the other hand, Rafsky saw the importance of University City for the region as a whole. He had long defended the allocation of urban renewal funds to the institutions, although they competed with residential and conservation areas to whose renewal he was committed. The Planning Commission's District Plan for West Philadelphia emphasized its status quo as a residential area. The West Philadelphia Corporation, however, claimed that the plan showed "little economic understanding" of the area's needs, which could benefit considerably by the economic vitality generated by alternative land uses. The corporation was disturbed by the narrowness of subsequent plans submitted and the concentration on architectural relationships instead of concern for the effect on adjacent areas.

## Improving the Environment

The University City area comprised several neighborhoods, which over time started their own organizations. The West Philadelphia Corporation helped these local civic groups in many ways, including rehabilitation of homes, and did everything possible to encourage vital, personal involvement of area residents. The extensive community participation (long predating the "maximum feasible participation" sanction accompanying federal aid) which was thus engendered was probably the most important aspect of these activities. Representatives of the civic groups (Cedar Park

Neighbors, Spruce Hill, Garden Court, Walnut Hill, Community Associations, and Powelton Neighbors) were made members of the corporation's board. "Who lives in University City is as important to the concept of University City as any other single factor," said Molinaro. "Let us make it clear that we fully expect and desire a thoroughly integrated community in racial, religious, and economic terms. We believe a monolithic community—even if it were possible to achieve—threatens the dynamic balance we seek as our primary objective." [16]

One example was Powelton Village, one of the areas of University City whose "country houses" of "proper Philadelphians" gradually deteriorated. During World War II a Quaker group bought individual houses to renovate them, partly for shelter for conscientious objectors. But progress was too slow to be effective. Some civic-minded individuals then got together a group of contributors to save the area, with its wide, tree-lined streets (a rarity near Center City) and early Victorian (pre-gingerbread) architecture, and to attempt to preserve it as an interracial and, given the student and faculty populations, an international enclave. The group, called Powelton Village Development Associates, did not include members of the city's power structure—although some of its individual members contributed financially. Only some of the members of the group were living in the area. They succeeded in obtaining enough "concerned money" to rehabilitate a number of houses for rent, and some for sale. The in-and-out migration of the area did not affect its racial composition, though it may have raised the average level of education. It was the first revitalized community of University City, which succeeded and could serve as a model for others. It continued to improve in physical condition and property values, while maintaining and even increasing its interracial character.

In this neighborhood, where interracial stability was being encouraged by many residents of the neighborhood as well as citizens in other parts of the area, the city administration and the Greater Philadelphia Movement sponsored a risk pool of banks and savings and loan institutions. Even this pool would not become effective unless rehabilitation loans were guaranteed by the

16. "The Concept of University City" (lecture, Community Leadership Seminar, January 9, 1962).

FHA. But in University City, as in other neighborhoods formerly on the decline, it was an uphill fight to gain the FHA's approval for loans. The West Philadelphia Corporation added its voice to the others which had for so long been fighting this battle from the ramparts of City Hall with little more success. In 1966, the West Philadelphia Corporation managed to acquire low-interest loans of 3 percent, under a different section of the law, for one neighborhood in West Philadelphia, and since that time other programs made possible by later provisions of housing legislation have been adopted.

Meantime, the corporation waged its own limited war on many fronts. (1) It formulated an active neighborhood improvement program, providing professional services to support the neighborhood associations in their efforts to rehabilitate homes in their areas. A renovated demonstration house in each area, showing records of the problems overcome, served as a model for others trying to rehabilitate their homes. A "clinic" for their problems included a home design consulting service. Information on experiences with individual contractors was passed on. The corporation kept track of progress made, homes improved, and problems encountered.

(2) The corporation's first attempt to guarantee good institutional development was a request for a Planned Institutional District as part of the new zoning code, in order to provide the flexibility considered essential to the growth of urban institutions. In 1967, the city council established such districts for the University of Pennsylvania and Drexel Institute of Technology to further orderly development according to prescribed standards and to eliminate conflicting zoning categories.[17] This was an important step forward in developing environments for universities. The corporation also persuaded each neighborhood group to prepare a revised zoning map taking into account its specific problems. These maps would be coordinated by the corporation, so that each area's problems, as well as those of University City as a whole, would be recognized before proposals were submitted to the City Planning Commission.

(3) The neighborhood schools were offered opportunities to upgrade themselves through pooled facilities made available by

17. *University City*, vol. 6, no. 4 (December 1967).

the universities. The focus first was on the area's largest elementary school, with children from various racial and economic backgrounds; by 1964, the program was in force in three more schools. This entire "Universities-Related Program" reached a total of 6,000 children, 80 percent of whom were black.[18]

(4) In 1960, only 2 percent of the area's land use was devoted to open spaces or parks, to the mounting concern of the neighborhood groups. With the availability of funds for planning "open space and urban beautification" provided in the 1965 Housing Act, each group went to work to plan small parks, greenways, and residential walkways. The West Philadelphia Corporation retained a firm of landscape architects who worked with each neighborhood for eighteen months and then produced a cohesive program for all of University City, approved by the Planning Commission.[19]

(5) Finally, a number of activities were furthered by the corporation to improve the residents' leisure time. The school board established the West Philadelphia Center for Cultural Studies to serve as a community center for children and adults interested in artistic and cultural experience. The University City Arts League was started to promote both appreciation of and participation in the arts. In addition, the Beautification Committee of University City was concerned about the quality of life there and sponsored activities the neighborhood desired.

## Research and Development and the Science Complex

The West Philadelphia Corporation not only sought residential improvement but fostered plans for the development of a research-based community. Any community which boasts a mature university complex has introduced an additional element to possible industrial attraction: scientific talent, engaged in teaching

18. Publication by West Philadelphia Corporation on program in Henry Lea School (undated). Also January 1965 mimeographed publication of the West Philadelphia Corporation, dealing with this school program, and West Philadelphia Corporation, Fourth (and subsequent) Annual Reports. The Seventh Annual Report (1967) contains much on the corporation's efforts in conjunction with the Board of Education.

19. *University, City* vol. 5, no. 2 (November 1966).

graduate students, can align their interests with those of industry. The research and development (R and D) complex has proved to be a valuable new departure for some areas, as it "spins off" new firms. Was Philadelphia's industrial base strong enough, and its scientific talent good enough, to lure R and D contracts from government and private sources? Until the 1950s, this would not have seemed important. But since mid-century, transistors and printed circuits have revised electronics, plastics have replaced other materials, and man-made fabrics have revolutionized textiles and leather and thereby the clothing and soft goods industries. The precision of the laser beam, the accomplishments of space science, the healing power of isotopes, and the impact on communications of satellites all illustrate the effect of scientific research on industrial accomplishment. The kinds of jobs needed to service these inventions continue to change radically.

In the late 1950s, research complexes in conjunction with institutions of higher learning were established and competition for the resulting industrial development was fierce. Links between university research and the business community were forged. "The universities and the R and D establishments are becoming the growth nuclei for the economy and the major absorbers of creative manpower," writes Melvin Webber.[20] Brain power is the necessary trigger for a research complex. "Brains . . . attract other brains. This is the beginning of the chain reaction which sets off the research complex," states Elizabeth Deutermann, also pointing out that in the nation as a whole, investment in R and D had grown threefold in a decade to $19 billion in 1965.[21] One Philadelphia example is the drug firm of Smith, Kline, and French, which in thirty years had increased its research team from 8 scientists to 850, and spent in 1967 about $26 million for research. But in 1965, the Federal Reserve Bank reported that in Philadelphia the "proportion of scientists with Ph.D.'s is not so high as in the average large city. . . . The importance of improved graduate and undergraduate education

20. Melvin M. Webber, "The New Urban Planning in America," *Journal of the Town Planning Institute,* vol. 54, no. 1 (January 1968).

21. Elizabeth Deutermann, "The Innovation Industry," *Business Review* (Federal Reserve Bank of Philadelphia, August 1965), p. 20.

. . . and the nurturing of environment to keep the graduates in the area, cannot be overstressed." [22]

## The Research Tower

As early as 1959, Allan Bonnell, vice-president of Drexel, representing the West Philadelphia Corporation, had met with Richard Graves of the Philadelphia Industrial Development Corporation. They intended that the two organizations would jointly concentrate on attracting research-oriented industry to Philadelphia—particularly to West Philadelphia. A twenty-five-story research tower to accommodate industrial and commercial research space was proposed. In addition to the tower, it was suggested that individual buildings would be desirable for firms wishing to identify their firm's name above a building for purposes of public relations. A survey made subsequently, however, showed that only a small minority was interested in such promotion.[23]

Eventually it was learned that no multistory, multitenant laboratory had ever been successful in the United States. Buildings should not be more than six stories high.[24] A tower for chemical and technical research would be a physical straightjacket and therefore would not be practical economically. There would be too much danger that the different firms would interfere with each other (especially possible in case one firm went on strike); experiments with new inventions would be inhibited by the presence of other firms in the same building. So the tower idea was quietly dropped.

In spite of this temporary setback, the Philadelphia Industrial Development Corporation and the West Philadelphia Corporation together continued to plan for the research center—only now it was to consist of a number of low-rise buildings which, naturally, would require much more cleared land. A consultant's report indicated a positive response, emphasizing that Philadelphia, with its medical schools, drug companies, and chemical

22. "Scientific Talent in the Third Federal Reserve District," *Business Review* (Federal Reserve Bank of Philadelphia, August 1965), p. 16.
23. Group for Planning and Research, Inc., *Trends in Research and Development* (July 1963), p. 84.
24. West Philadelphia Corporation board of directors' meeting, January 21, 1963; consultant's report, pp. 77–80.

firms, should easily attract medical, scientific, and service industries. The report confirmed that University City was an ideal spot
to absorb, by 1970, about two million square feet of the area's
projected R and D activities.

The consultants proposed these uses for the planned research
center: (1) a research institute, sponsored by the nearby academic institutions; (2) an industrial research and development
center for private and corporate research operations; and (3) a
conference center. The impact such development would have on
the growth of Philadelphia's economy was obvious.

Following the acceptance of the report, a University City Science Center Corporation was formed by the PIDC and the West
Philadelphia Corporation as a new quasi-public corporation for
the purpose of establishing a Science Research Institute.

### Dislocation or Science?

Most urban renewal plans in University City had been for conservation areas emphasizing rehabilitation, with only occasional
sore spots being cleared. But in the area proposed for the Science
Center complex the story was different. If a center of the dimensions projected was to be built near the university, total clearance would be necessary. However, most jobs created by the Science Center would require a great deal of education or training,
so that area residents, including those now to be displaced, would
rarely qualify. Nor was there alternative accommodation for
those displaced. An aggravating factor here was that there was
no possibility of saving structurally sound buildings or conserv-
ing a part of the area.

The idea of the Science Center continued to appeal to business
groups and the power structure. Those to lose their homes were
largely Negroes and unskilled. While sympathetic to their cause,
the administration hoped that the city as a whole would benefit
greatly from the new development through additional jobs, income, and taxes. Advantages accruing through R and D to industries already in the area were strongly emphasized by the civic
leadership. Allied with the residents and small storekeepers to be
dispossessed were not only those who objected to such homes and
stores being razed to make way for nonresidential development,
but also groups which by this time could be rallied to protect

dispossessed black home owners against an encroaching Establishment, including the students at the institutions in the area.

By 1962, the Citizens' Council on City Planning questioned the thoroughness of the inspection that had preceded condemnation, the essential nature of the goals to be achieved through this project, and the architectural imperative that would result in use of such a large land area. In 1963, a sit-in was staged in the mayor's office. By 1965, the most articulate opposing group had submitted an alternative plan for the area, prepared for them by an architect, suggesting high-rise residential homes and town houses. This plan too was rejected by other groups because such housing would be financially beyond the means of the present residents. While relationships, objectives, and loyalties were forever shifting among the groups making up the coalition of opposition, the proposed science complex and its most easily identified proponents, the University of Pennsylvania, Drexel, and the West Philadelphia Corporation, were always "the enemy." The issue was a difficult one for the city administration to decide, but the eventual accommodation seemed to satisfy the critics. The plan adopted included new and rehabilitated housing for low-income families within the area designated for the science complex development—though only two hundred such units were mentioned—and relocation of the stores within a two-block radius of the new Science Center.

In 1967, the West Philadelphia Corporation reported: "After five years of planning sessions and public hearings, involving at least a thousand participants, University City Urban Renewal Units #3, #4, and #5 [the areas under discussion] were accorded final approval by the City Planning Commission, the Redevelopment Authority, City Council and the U.S. Department of Housing and Urban Development." [25]

Philadelphia's business leadership and its power structure were well represented on the board of the University City Science Center Corporation, the developer of the Science Center. Of thirty-six members, thirteen were directors of the Greater Philadelphia Movement.

Some of the center's tenants point to a possible major medical center there, too. City hospitals, particularly those in Center City,

25. *University City*, vol. 6, no. 4.

consistently refused to cooperate with each other (for example, in sharing expensive equipment) or to respond to the city's pleas that they do so. West Philadelphia, on the other hand, was able to develop a new dimension for the city. What was not possible in Center City became a reality in West Philadelphia. Other hospitals transferred into the area of the university hospital and of Philadelphia General Hospital. The atmosphere of University City thus created the beginnings of a medical complex. The National Board of Medical Examiners constructed a headquarters building in University City. A seven-story apartment building for doctors and medical students is being built there for $2 million.

University City is an excellent example of the kind of cooperation for which Philadelphia is so well known. Molinaro puts it well: "Philadelphia is blessed in that it has forged a strong partnership of public agencies and private organizations dedicated to common objectives for rebuilding the city. University City shares in this blessing in many ways. The Greater Philadelphia Movement assisted in founding the West Philadelphia Corporation, helped arrange for the Powelton Rehabilitation project. . . . Philadelphia Industrial Development Corporation spearheaded much of the thinking for new research uses in University City and has given great effort to working out plans for the University Research Center. . . . Thus the University City concept has three local implementing forces—the citizenry, private interests, and the governmental agencies." [26]

26. "The Concept of University City" (see n. 16 above).

# III

Evaluation of
the Reform

# 10 Professionals, Civic and Public

Throughout the discussion in previous chapters, the existence of professionals in high public office and in staff positions with civic groups was given credit for many of the accomplishments of the Philadelphia renaissance. Clearly, nothing would have happened without strong leadership. The top leaders in both community and administration created the spirit which made professionals in both groups participate enthusiastically in innovative endeavors. Their enthusiasm, in turn, generated an atmosphere leading to community growth and development, and inspired the men in the power structure (the "movers and shakers") to put their prestige on the line for what they realized the community needed.

Both volunteers in civic groups and professionals working in civic agencies prepared the ground for the reform, helped engineer the change in public attitudes and in the legal framework for local government, and succeeded in getting the power structure involved.

A wide variety of individuals in Philadelphia fell within the category of "professionals": city staff members involved in making or implementing policy, and executives or board members of various civic groups. Both elected and appointed officials in Philadelphia as well as leaders of civic groups possessed many of the attributes (and often the training) of professionals. It was usually professionals who brought forth the innovations. For instance, methods of mass transit were developed by John Bailey and Charles Frazier; renewal policies by William Rafsky and Dorothy Montgomery; industrial development by Walter Phillips and Richard Graves; port improvements by an outside consultant and Peter Schauffler; university development by Leo Molinaro; and issues of fiscal development by Lennox Moak and Richard

McConnell. In each case, civic groups and their staffs were intimately involved. The Philadelphia Housing Association, the Greater Philadelphia Movement, the Bureau of Municipal Research, the Citizens' Council on City Planning—or, in personal terms, Dorothy Montgomery, Robert Sawyer, William Wilcox, Lennox Moak, Aaron Levine—were professionals who contributed greatly to the results in Philadelphia.

Priorities in all kinds of public investments were pushed by cabinet members and members of the Planning Commission. Professionals on the mayor's Economic Advisory Committee opposed some actions of the Philadelphia Industrial Development Corporation, which they felt was acting too one-sidedly in the short-term interest of business development; the committee was eventually proved to be correct. And young professionals with new approaches, and the support of some civic groups, prevailed in the Community Renewal Program over established city officials. Professionals in either the public or the civic bureaucracies usually managed to get their positions accepted, though it was unusual for them to have to engage in a power play, in the crude sense of this term. (An exception was the area of "poverty" agencies, where the staff could not rely on consensus of the many groups involved; hence they had to fight for the position the professionals on the staff advocated.)

Instead of a monolithic group of experts dominating the Philadelphia scene, we have the phenomenon of disagreement among a vigorous group of professionals acting as decision-makers. The outcome of any controversy, as we have seen in some of the cases presented, was by no means a foregone conclusion. And where such dissenters frustrated proposed actions, the challenge to professionals to find other means to achieve their purpose (for example, in the case of the "used house" or in making mass transportation viable) became the mother of new innovations.

## Characteristics of Professionals

What special attitudes are characteristic of professionals in civic life? Professor John Howard, speaking about professional planners,[1] describes them as "affected" with the public interest and

1. John T. Howard, *Journal of the American Institute of Planners*, Spring 1954, p. 58.

able to submerge their own interests to it, recognizing the community's stake in the manner in which they exercise their knowledge. They use their independent judgment of what constitutes the public interest; in other words, it is not only their substantive insight which matters, but also their moral approach to the public concern. The professional has a "right to decide how his function is to be performed, and to be free from lay restrictions" [2] —that means, he has a need for a high degree of self-determination. Occupational identification leads to some kind of detachment, for he "wants to think objectively about matters which to laymen may be fraught with sentiment and emotion." [3] Interest in the subject matter leads him "to pursue and systematize the pertinent knowledge. It leads to finding an intellectual base for the problem one handles." The professional takes problems "out of their particular setting and makes them part of some more universal order." [4] In this endeavor, he "expects to be trusted (not judged) by those to whom he makes available his specialized knowledge. Only a colleague is competent to say when he has made a mistake." [5] Bernard Barber puts it this way: "The generalized knowledge and the community orientation characteristic of professional behavior are indispensable in our society as we now know it and as we want it to be." [6] For professionals to operate satisfactorily, they have to be "the innovators, the people who push back the frontiers of theoretical and practical knowledge related to their professions." [7] Professionals are able to analyze problems in terms of what causes them. They are also able to apply new insights to differentiate among alternative solutions. In their role in guiding decision-makers to formulate policy, they are distinguished from technicians, who have the expertise to *carry out* already decided policies, to handle day-to-day problems, and to apply existing knowledge to them. But the line

2. George Strauss, "Professionalism and Occupational Associations," *Industrial Relations*, vol. 2 (May 1963), p. 8.

3. Archie Kleingartner, *Professionalism and Salaried Worker Organization* (University of Wisconsin, Industrial Relations Research Institute, 1967), p. 82.

4. Everett C. Hughes, "Professions," *Daedalus*, vol. 92, no. 4 (fall 1963), p. 660.

5. Kleingartner, *Professionalism*, p. 108.

6. Bernard Barber, "Some Problems in the Sociology of the Professions," *Daedalus*, vol. 92, no. 4 (fall 1963), p. 686.

7. Hughes, "Professions," p. 666.

is thin. The engineer may be faced with a problem which had not been anticipated and for which a new solution must be found. The statistician may have to find new sources of information. The community organizer may find that old techniques fail to work and have to figure out new approaches: if they can do these things, these men are acting as professionals.

A man's own skills and knowledge, and the ethical standards of his group, define the *substance* of his behavior and thus make him a professional. (On the other hand, it is the *organizational* relationships to which the term "bureaucracy" is properly applied.) Within the organizational framework of bureaucracy (for instance, municipal government), goals may be set up by the professional's superiors, men who may in reality be nonprofessionals. The conflict in this relationship, between the presumed independence of professionals and the authority of others over them, makes it difficult for some professionals to work contentedly in the governmental environment. If the professional is merely "applying established techniques to established programs and implicitly or explicitly abrogating the consequences of his actions, the professional is the eternal bureaucrat. These are the two faces of the public professional." [8]

The professional regards himself and is regarded by others, as the agent of the public interest. He abides by the code of ethics of his own peer group and knows that "unprofessional behavior" will reflect on the image of this group and he may lose its respect—and incidentally may threaten the public interest with which he is entrusted. Of course it is often not clear what the "public interest" consists of, and professionals may find their substantive opinions in conflict within their own peer group. They each wish to benefit the public but reach different conclusions depending on their background, approach, and value judgment.

The public official, for example, who is privy to freeway plans, which enables him to speculate in real estate, will lose public confidence whether or not his actions are in violation of the law. Wheaton, referring to municipal behavior, calls the standards of professional practice or procedure "a unifying element in the

8. Herbert V. Gamberg, "The Professional and Policy Choices in Middle-Sized Cities," *Journal of the American Institute of Planners,* May 1966, p. 175.

whole chain of decision making. To the extent that these standards are well grounded and are commonly accepted," [9] they will lead to the making of rational decisions in the metropolitan framework. For the Philadelphia professionals, ethics and standards took the place of the noblesse oblige attitude prevailing among members of the power structure. The standing of the professionals in the city was thus enhanced and brought closer to the needs of the population in the period of the renaissance.

The fact that a good professional is generally not assumed to be subject to direction by a political officeholder can be very useful to the politician. The appointment of a nonpolitical professional may be interpreted by the electorate as an indication that decisions will be made purely on the basis of merit. Moreover, the professional's role may be decisive in negotiating with professional colleagues in the federal government, provided the elected officials have delegated a great deal of discretion to him, as was the case in the Philadelphia reform. There, as in some other cities, professionals have risen to their top positions primarily because they can attract support among professionals elsewhere to their city's administration.

## Consensus and Middle-Class Values

One of the less understood consequences of greater emphasis on professionalization is the change it has brought about in the value system of communities, especially under reform governments. Old-line politicians and interest groups competing for power have given way to a new middle-class style of politics. While members of the old Main Line aristocracy in Philadelphia had shied away from political involvement before, now that city action seemed professionally oriented it could be embraced confidently by elite and other civic groups alike. More important, professionalism brought with it a gradually emerging consensus within the community, pointing to broad goals of city development. "Only the large cities," says James Coke, "are likely to be policy oriented towards growth and development. . . . The differences in the characteristics of voluntary organizations between

9. William Wheaton, "Agents of Change in Urban Expansion," in Webber et al. (eds.), *Explorations into Urban Structure* (University of Pennsylvania Press, 1964), p. 193.

large and small cities are a striking manifestation of the role of the professional in public affairs." [10]

In a city like Philadelphia in the reform period, directed at growth and development, the technical expertise of professionals can contribute to the solution of many problems; development needs fiscal and economic understanding as much as highway or bridge construction projects need engineering knowledge. Choices among alternative solutions can best be made by the trained expert—whether in transportation, education, or planning. The need is for professional judgment, not that of the technician, who is merely an implementer.

This is a new kind of politics, what Coke calls "Type II politics." [11] He shows that it encompasses a shifting of the public debate to general policies in the public interest. Where it is important to achieve a certain public purpose, the market mechanism cannot be relied upon. Rather, the coercion exercised only by the government is needed to accomplish municipal functions. The new politics is learning to provide the necessary mechanism for formulating and enforcing the rules for the efficient performance of public functions. To do this, innovative ideas are needed to adjust the political system to its environment—a function likely to be carried out only if the municipality has been professionalized.

The new politics is also compatible with the dominance of middle-class values. If goals are clearly defined, open conflict is not likely, but the new political ethos is likely to bring a discussion of values to the fore. "Middle class politics is most overt during reform movements, but its values remain." [12]

The fact that consensus is possible if professionals share a common outlook does not mean that professionals necessarily do more than point out the consequences of alternatives as objec-

10. James Coke, "The Lesser Metropolitan Areas of Illinois," *Illinois Government*, no. 15 (University of Illinois, 1962), p. 5.

11. James Coke, "Ways and Means for Urban Universities to Exercise a Unique Function in their Communities," in Robb Taylor (ed.), *University and Community*, Proceedings of a Conference sponsored by the Johnson Foundation and the University of Wisconsin-Milwaukee, April 1963, pp. 14, 15, 16.

12. Herbert V. Gambert, *The Escape from Politics: Power in Middle Sized Cities* (Office of Community Development, University of Illinois, 1965), pp. 66, 72.

tively as they can: the decisions are still made by the community. Where the professionals' values are not shared by many of the civic groups—as was the case in Philadelphia on many issues in the poverty war—consensus regarding community goals is not likely to prevail. But as long as professionals share the overall outlook with community forces they will obviously have an important impact on decisions. Once the need for expert policy determination is recognized, one can seriously hope that there will not be a reversion to purely political decisions. That is the reason for the belief that the process of professionalization is usually irreversible.

## Is Professionalism Compatible with Democracy?

Even in a modern large city, consensus does not usually embrace fundamental changes in community mores or accepted approaches. This raises the question whether reaching consensus might imply disregarding the democratic will. Is decision-making by professionals (even when they advise duly elected officials) in contradiction to democratic self-determination? Are technical experts, as has been claimed, remote from the people and their needs? And if so, do means exist which might bridge this dichotomy by granting a voice to grass-roots desires, while assigning a role to professionals in the bargaining thus made necessary?

The clearest example is presented by racial or ethnic minorities. They may find it hard to believe that they could influence professionals. Excluded from professional associations, they are distrustful of solutions put forth by professionals. This is especially true, if, as happens frequently, the professionals' proposals are tailored to long-term objectives, while the disadvantaged have to carry the burden of immediate consequences. And often there is no viable public review of such decisions which would give minorities a realistic chance of changing them.

This question has recently become more important with the increasing demand for greater participation by those affected. If a forum for public discussion of community needs were to be established, it would become necessary to obtain professionals who could present adequately the issues raised by different groups. It would then be best if "advocate" professionals could be found to speak for organizations needing help, who could easily communicate their wishes to the Establishment professionals. Such advocates, however, must face the question how effectively they themselves can communicate with the groups whose interest they are to defend. A segment of the black community, for instance, may prefer to have its own black spokesman.

In helping those who might otherwise lose in a competitive struggle, the advocacy professional furthers his democratic ideals, based on a specific value judgment about the "oughts" of society. This is a different approach from that of the independent professional, who can advise either governmental bodies or civic groups, or both, by presenting alternatives objectively, irrespective of their philosophy.

President Kennedy was in the habit of listening to a number of different experts, preferably of diametrically opposed viewpoints, before making up his mind. Joseph Clark did the same thing, sometimes going out of his way to call in those he suspected of holding a viewpoint different than that presented by his advisers, so that he could have the benefit of both opinions. At the metropolitan level it might be an advisable procedure to systematically expose the chief executive to experts with different viewpoints. Could the concept of countervailing professionals in the local governmental setup be instituted so that the case for the neighborhood association or for an ethnic group would be presented by a professional in terms which his counterpart in the executive branch would understand and to which he would respond? There clearly is need for both kinds of professionals at the municipal level, those following objective principles, and those identifying with the values of specific groups.

This question, however, was not usually raised in the Philadelphia of the reform period. In this era the existence of professionals filling positions at the municipal level was itself novel enough. Consensus on middle-class values among public and civic professionals characterizes this period much more than the participatory voice of the grass roots. Their influence did not become an issue until the end of the period.

## The Role of Professionals in the Philadelphia Reform

Innovative activity is not always confined to the top professional level, in spite of the theoretical distinction made earlier between professionals and technicians. The opportunity to innovate may depend upon the position the public employee finds himself in. In judging administrative organization at any government level, the potential importance of civil servants at lower levels is often overlooked. In line with the increasing need for experts at all levels in Philadelphia during the reform, many decisions had to be made effectively by lower-level civil servants, who had to deal with problems as they arose. Such decisions, though usually routine, occasionally called for new interpretations.

Many problems in a city are entirely noncontroversial, though technical (for instance, questions about fire protection, sewer construction, airport design), so that decisions concerning them are made by "routine" bureaucrats. Where citizens lack any direct interest or an opinion of their own, the decision is likely to stand. If, on the other hand, enough citizens were concerned about a decision, did the matter become one of "policy" rather than routine?

The technician may make the decision in the first place; his superiors may not question it (or may not have either knowledge or interest to question it), and a precedent will have been created. He may, for instance, have a great deal of leeway in preparing the agenda for lower-level coordinating meetings, which can be decisive for the final result. It may be that the technician down the line prepares data and information for a decision to be made by his superior; the way he has prepared the case, however, makes the superior's decision a foregone conclusion, whether or not the superior is aware of it. Such influence of civil servants beyond their officially assigned role is apt to be exercised at all governmental levels.

Below those who made the top-level policy decisions, and above those concerned with routine problems, were a large number of professionals who laid the foundations for new policy through research or preparatory documentation. The standards for policy implementation had to be defined by professionals a few steps below the top level. It is this group that put meat on the bones of the policy, lend meaning to the policy decision itself, and perhaps indicate that a new policy is called for. From the question of "whether," they have moved on to the question of "how."

At the top of the city hierarchy were practical experts in different fields who had sufficient expertise to command the respect of the professionals within city departments, as well as of those working for civic groups. Only a few of the commissioners were political appointees, and sometimes they too proved competent or even expert in their fields. But the concern of the commissioners had to reach beyond the influence of experts: their policy decisions had to take into account a variety of ramifications and the impact on different groups of citizens; and they had to consider practical reality and political repercussions, including the likely reactions of the city council. In other words, in Philadelphia the commissioners were often policy-makers who had both political savvy and professional training. The professionals in the departments, not concerned with political implications, had to learn to think in terms of alternatives and of interrelationships between the problems under discussion and other policy areas beyond their immediate concern. On this difficult task hangs much of an administration's ability to shape policy based on priority thinking. And to confine such considerations to the cabinet or commissioner level will not accomplish the job as well.

When in Philadelphia a question of administration policy was involved, the top professionals concerned, representing both the city and civic groups, would jointly hammer out a policy position. Before it was made public, the position was likely to reflect consensus; but getting to that point consumed a considerable amount of time. Policy statements were prepared for the areas of transportation, port-related activities, urban renewal, code enforcement, and, in a way, Center City, but not (at least formally) for many other areas.

One cabinet member interviewed felt that new ideas were likely to originate from the new, bright young professionals in the administration. It mattered little at what precise spot within the city administration new proposals were advanced, or by whom. What did make some difference to the originators was whether their ideas were seriously considered and discussed. To have them disregarded caused a much greater morale problem than to have them finally discarded.

While the question of succession to the chief executive's job was a political problem, the difficulty of how the "best brains in the country," brought in by the mayor, could be persuaded to stay was an administrative one. This became clear when Clark stepped down, and even clearer when Dilworth did and some of the top-level professionals and "bright young men" moved to greener pastures. Why were successors not ready? How many professional levels were there below the department heads? In some cases there was only the deputy; in others there were division heads or section heads, but rarely more than these, and even these men had been there too long to be expected to have many new ideas. Neither Clark nor Dilworth was inclined to have close relations with professionals within the departments; some of the commissioners complained that even they had too little contact with the mayor. There was, in fact, no systematic effort to solicit ideas through division and section chiefs. The commissioners would have liked to meet regularly with the mayor, as the cabinet did, to discuss their problems. But the formal "Quarterly Commissioners' Meeting" of approximately seventy-five members of the mayor's "official family" was the only regular meeting. Sufficient backstopping existed only in areas where technical competence was primarily needed (such as civil service administration, accounting, and fiscal details).

Vernon Northrop, who had been both finance director and managing director under Clark, complained that the reform spirit caused the administrators to be so afraid of the possibility that political influence might be used, that they did not use imagination in recruiting. The rule was that promotions had to be decided by competitive examination, so that the bright young newcomer could be promised nothing beyond the level at which he entered. Naturally, this method failed to provide for new leadership.

Richard McConnell, former director of finance, was more benevolent in his judgment. While he agreed that there were too few city staff members ready to assume leadership in the city departments, he felt that middle management in the city administration had improved significantly through the years of the reform.

## The Bridge to Civic Professionals

If professionals were the key to making the reform work, it was primarily because there were positions for professionals parallel to public officials among the executives in the civic Establishment. A close relationship between the two sets of professionals developed. In addition to these executives, many of the board members of the civic groups were also professionals. Many "movers and shakers" acted as their own professional assistants and civic aides. This made the line between civic leaders and professional executives a very thin one. The direct line of communication between them and some city officials made the line even thinner.

Informality and easy understanding across organizational and even class lines became characteristic of Philadelphia in the reform period, contrasting sharply with a rather staid and self-conscious prior tradition. The new relationship was based in part on the increasing concern of both city and civic groups with the substance of the development and the changes being wrought, and in part on the growing confidence of each group in the other's integrity and competence.

The momentum may have started with amateurs, but staff were soon needed to undergird their efforts and to pull together in a common purpose. Almost every Philadelphia civic association (at least those concerned with citywide issues) employed one or more full-time professionals, ensuring continuous action on which they could rely—a feature in which Philadelphia was ahead of most other cities. Thus, the volunteer boards were permitted to be twice as effective and to go much deeper into policy questions. Obviously, the full-time staff exerted a good deal of influence on board members and on the activities the group undertook. But the board members tried to keep abreast of the area of the association's interests, and they thought about policy matters before they received the reports from their staff.

Staff influence was particularly visible in the nonprofit corporations, whose executives were bearing the brunt of daily operations and contacts, and were thus in a position to know what kinds of policy decisions were needed. Most of these executives were official members of their boards, and thus policy-makers for their corporations. This implied backing from their own board, giving them the strength also to make policy for the other committees and agencies on which they served.

Perhaps the most important function of these civic groups was the knowledge of city officials that they were serving as watchdogs. They were the conscience of the government, if the government forgot that it had a conscience. On the other hand, for those professionals in the city who wanted to maintain the cause of public welfare, it meant a great deal to know that the civic groups would lend support.

But there was another side to this coin. Rafsky as housing coordinator could not have accomplished as much if Dorothy Montgomery had not supported him on at least some of his policies before the board of the Housing Association. He often got support for city programs by consciously using the pressures generated by civic groups, for example, the Fellowship Commission on race questions, the Chamber of Commerce on priorities for industry, or the Philadelphia Housing Association for low-income housing. If a city professional could not persuade his superior (or even his department head) of the advisability of changing a certain policy, he might speak privately to the executive of a civic agency who was willing to persuade a powerful man on his board of a new idea (which the latter, incidentally, might be quite willing to claim as his own). The board member would put pressure on the mayor or a councilman to institute this new policy.

Whether Philadelphia's professionals worked for the city or for civic groups, there was a natural bond between them. There were a great number of interchanges of personnel between these groups, in both directions. Three of Mayor Clark's cabinet members came from civic groups, and Mayor Dilworth's managing director, Donald Wagner, had earlier been the executive of the GPM. High city officials left city employment to become executive vice-presidents of nonprofit corporations (Rafsky, McConnell, Northrop) and in effect continued some of the same tasks.

The boundaries between private and public activities in the sphere of developing urban areas are fluid and largely unexplored. This is what makes the investigation of the Philadelphia experience so fascinating. The relationship seems to have worked well though it is possible that one of the reasons was its novelty. Innovations were needed to reshape the city; once accomplished, nobody seemed to care whether the ideas were initiated by civic groups or by administration policy-makers. Moreover, the spirit of civic-city collaboration seemed to remain intact so long as the overriding need for new ideas and new solutions to difficult problems was recognized. There "are still very few professionals occupying positions on the boundary of public and private action," writes Coke. "Therefore, a strategic move is to nurture the professional growth of those now acting in this creative capacity, and to help create a climate in which more professionals will be employed by both government and quasi-public agencies." [13]

13. James Coke, "Ways and Means," p. 16.

# 11    Some Economic Policies

## Developmental Planning and the Economist

The professionals in the Philadelphia reform administration were not only experts in their fields of specialization, but also generalists in broader areas, trained and experienced in public administration or law or political science. Some of them guided administrative analysts in the managing director's office, others supervised statisticians and engineers on the Urban Traffic and Transportation Board, or environmentalists in the departments of health, welfare, and recreation.

In the federal government, economic techniques have been used for a long time, and many economists work for a variety of federal agencies. At the local level, however, the application of economic analysis is in a very rudimentary state. Local governments have been rather slow in recognizing that social science professionals could help evaluate broad policy decisions. The belief that local and regional development measures could be effective came only over time. It has begun to be appreciated only recently that the economist can make a contribution to metropolitan policies by helping to explain urban phenomena and to influence long-term regional development decisions. It was a novelty when economists were asked to help influence these decisions and to aid the municipal government in contributing to regional growth.

This field of expertise plays a unique role in the operation of any local government concerned with development. Underlying all decisions on development, all decisions affecting the program of the departments, authorities, and the public-private organizations described earlier, are economic factors which indicate the wisdom of one course of action over another, the cost to be calculated in order to project the desired benefits in both short-range and long-run terms. At the time the reform administration in Philadelphia took office, few cities in the United States had perceived the need for the public administrator-economist. And it is interesting that as late as 1971 Anthony Downs found it worthwhile to write a short article, "How Cities Could Use Economists."

Philadelphia's reform administration emerged at about the time when cities were beginning to realize that they could use the skills of economists in arriving at policy decisions. In groping for solutions to problems arising over time, the new regime had to make use of all available experts for a variety of purposes rather than assign each of them to a pigeonhole. This was particularly true of the economists, whose position in the local governmental structure was not yet clearly defined. Below, only a few examples are discussed of the methods in which the economist's expertise could be and has been actually used in Philadelphia. They were singled out because they seemed more interesting than others and of potential use to other cities.

The first economist joined the city government of Philadelphia during Mayor Clark's term. Examples of the way in which this background specialty was used, referred to in part II, include evaluation of the capital program, feasibility of the projected Food Distribution Center, and the desirability of attracting specific industries. The economic consequences of different kinds of renewal programs, the significance of Center City priorities, the multiplier effects of a university-centered R and D program, and the relationship of national unemployment figures to those of Philadelphia in order to maintain perspective on the health of the city's economy are further examples of the use to which the "dismal science" was put and the degree to which it affected all areas of the city's activity. It was only one—and by no means the most important—part of the economist's role to advise on the tax structure, so as to spread the burden fairly while raising the necessary revenue.

The importance of basing city policy decisions on clear goals was emphasized in chapter 5. The mayor's Economic Advisory Committee was specifically charged with "developing criteria so that the goals could be more precisely specified" and with recognizing that "there are many possible alternative growth patterns for Philadelphia." [1] The professionals in the reform administration soon learned that solutions to social problems would not be found without the imaginative application of social science tools, and hence the expertise of the social scientists was applied to a wide variety of urban problems. Efforts were made to apply benefit-cost analysis, long a tool of the economist, to social factors. In the absence of direct quantifiable data on which to base the analysis, social analysis was used to identify the source of the costs in human terms as well as the ultimate beneficiaries of some of the programs, for example, renewal or industrial development.

In addition to the problems for the economists discussed before, there were some broad problems they specifically had to face. A few were statistical, but the major ones were questions of human resources and what remedies could be found for them.

## The Problem of Unemployment

Throughout the period of the reform, the outstanding human as well as economic problem was unemployment. This problem first prompted Mayor Clark to add an economist to his staff.

Philadelphia had a larger-than-average share of manufacturing at a time when the volume of manufacturing activities had declined nationally. In addition, new technology in manufacturing increased its capital-to-labor ratio more than nationally, thus cutting employment while producing the same output, which especially affected the less skilled occupations. Philadelphia failed to participate as much as other urban areas in the national shift from the production of goods to the provision of services—an area where the use of capital at the expense of labor was less likely. Had Philadelphia's service industry grown at the national rate, the job loss in the manufacturing sector would have been more than made up. [2]

At the same time, the location of industry shifted toward markets and other population concentrations and thus away from the

1. Statement to the mayor's Economic Advisory Committee by David Melnicoff, president, Fels Naptha Company (now senior vice-president, Philadelphia Federal Reserve Bank), October 3, 1959.
2. Elizabeth Deutermann, *Economic Development*, CRP Technical Report, no. 13 (December 1964). Also *Overall Economic Development Program*, June 1964, issued for the U.S. Department of Commerce by the Philadelphia Economic Development Committee.

East Coast. This made the region in which Philadelphia was located the slowest-growing one in the nation. Philadelphia turned out to be too weak in fast-growing final industries, while it was too concentrated in slow-growing intermediate industries. With each new cycle of the economy, Philadelphia's employment level took a new dip, which was only partially erased by the next upswing. In the 1952–62 decade the "gross city product" showed an annual growth in output of $1\frac{1}{2}$ percent, while the national rate was 3 percent.[3] This situation meant considerably more than a large number of unemployed and underemployed; it implied low levels of spending and income throughout the area, and thus a low multiplier effect, wasted economic resources, underutilized public investment, and the absence of growth. (Underemployment refers not only to those employed below their potential, which is hard to measure, but also to those only employed irregularly during the year. The 1960 Census indicates that about 12 percent of male white workers in Philadelphia and over 16 percent of male nonwhites worked less than forty weeks, with the bulk in each case, 24 percent, falling in the 20–24 age group.)

Much of Philadelphia's public policy was thus concentrated on creating (or preserving) job opportunities. The question in each case which had to be raised, however, was the skill level involved in a new job: if the skills needed were not available among Philadelphia's unemployed—and could not be easily acquired through training—it was necessary to import workers from elsewhere, which amounted to an undiminished level of unemployment in spite of increased employment; it also meant either a greater daytime population, or else an increased city population with all that implies in terms of the use of schools, public utilities, and pressure on housing.

It was thus necessary to survey the unemployed, and their skills and potentials. They turned out to be concentrated in the same groups which are most prone to be hit by poverty: the young, the old, and the nonwhite. Before remedial measures could be suggested, the causes for the existing unemployment situation had to be analyzed in much more detail than has been possible in these pages. Philadelphia's industry mix resulted in less employ-

3. National Analysts, Inc., *Philadelphia's Position in the Regional and National Economy,* CRP Technical Report, no. 10 (May 1964).

ment and income than in other major cities. Both the reasons and possible policy strategies to counteract the problem were discussed in different issues of the economic report to the mayor.[4]

One prerequisite for meaningful suggestions was to forecast the potential demand for workers. Past data on manpower demand by different industries and occupations was collected, and past trends were determined, as soon as the use of computers became available to the economists. Toward the end of the reform period it became possible to predict the future demand for workers by industry and occupation, and thus engage in manpower planning.[5]

## Unemployment Figures

The most important figures for the formulation of economic policy were those dealing with unemployment, and both mayors wanted up-to-date information on unemployment in the city. Providing figures was difficult because the Employment Service produced data for the entire labor market and refused to give out that portion of the sample which pertained only to the city, claiming it was not representative for that portion of the total area. The problem was finally solved, however, so that the mayor received regular figures on the progress made in combating unemployment in the city. (Annual bench marks linked together provided a historical record of employment and unemployment from which it was possible to derive the figures for the city bimonthly from those which the Employment Service calculated for the area. A second method was to relate the unemployment compensation claims for the city to those for the area. This ratio was then applied to the official estimate of the total unemployed in the metropolitan area, thus giving a second source for an estimate of city unemployment.)

The problem was that official state and federal figures failed to disclose the central city's heavy burden of unemployment. In addition, the figures also obscured the importance of commuting.

4. Starting July and November 1955, unemployment was discussed throughout subsequent reports, but in especially great detail in March 1957 and May 1959.
5. *Philadelphia SMSA Labor Demand Projection,* Economic Development Unit, Technical Report V.F. This work was done with the help of the EDA grant and newly hired staff under the newest city economist.

Traditionally, employment figures are collected at the place of work, while unemployment figures are collected at the worker's residence. This naturally gives a lopsided picture of the relation between these magnitudes, if data for only a part of the metropolitan area are of interest. It thus became necessary to measure the rate of unemployment for the city differently: it was expressed as a ratio of those presently unemployed to that part of the labor force residing in the city, rather than to the entire labor force of the area. (The proposed ratio would thus compare the city's unemployed not to those who were working in the city wherever they may live, but to those living in the city whether or not they work there.) This novel way of calculating the rate of unemployment produced a much higher unemployment rate for the city of Philadelphia than the one for the labor market area as a whole: even so, this figure may have been understood, for it was believed that more residents of the central city than of the suburbs had quit the labor force because they had given up hope of finding a job, and thus were no longer counted in census enumerations or in surveys. This way of measuring unemployment was accepted only after many discussions, including extensive arguments with the U.S. Department of Labor before a committee of the U.S. Senate. In his testimony, Mayor Dilworth refuted each argument of the Bureau of Labor Statistics in turn. Though he did not prevail at the time, his viewpoint became important later when the applicability of the Area Redevelopment legislation to central cities was discussed.

## Indicators

The economic report to the mayor had to include statistical indicators of the city's economic condition. The city economist believed that the best possible indicator would be a measure of personal income. If such a measure could be obtained regularly on a current basis, it would indicate change in the economy and could be used in evaluating city policies on combating unemployment and other economic problems. A study to arrive at such a measure was thus undertaken for the office of the city economist.[6]

6. Louis R. Salkever, "Personal Income in Philadelphia: A Method of Community Income Estimation," December 1955 (mimeo).

Making personal income figures for city residents available was a challenging job, which had been undertaken only in a few communities. However, the city economist felt that "municipal administrators should have continuous data on employment, personal income," and gross output of the area.[7] Normally, personal income is estimated between census years only at the national and state levels. But the influence of changes at the national level of economic activity varies from state to state, let alone between local economies. The sources of income in a state, which includes farming and mining and small towns, are quite different from those in a large municipality, which includes large financial operations, wholesale and retail trade, and major government installations. Since the difference is considerably more than one of size, transferring measures from state to city would be meaningless. An indirect method of estimating income had to be devised.

Moreover, personal income is counted where it is received—the place of work—rather than where the recipient lives, a major factor in estimating the income of the city residents. The amount of the difference between those coming into the city to work and those leaving it for that purpose—the "situs" question—had to be separately estimated *after* personal income had been figured out without consideration of this factor. This added an additional calculation at the end, and not a simple one at that.

Annually, state income figures are available from the U.S. Department of Commerce (and, if requested, broken down by income components). To obtain local figures of personal income, each component of state income (such as wages and salaries, proprietory income, and transfer payments) had to be allocated to the city by constructing a state-to-local ratio for each specific subdivision (for example, proprietory income from each small sector of manufacturing, construction, and transportation). Then it was possible to use this ratio, obtained for periods when both state and local data were available, to estimate the local figure for times when only the annual state figure could be obtained.

After all these ratios had been figured out, it was decided that wage and salary information, which constituted three-fourths of all local income, would be a more reliable indicator of move-

7. Ibid., Foreword by city economist.

ments of the local economy than would total personal income, if that had to be derived from the necessarily arbitrary allocators for each subdivision of income generated. Wage and salary figures were annually made available by the State Employment Service, as were also quarterly estimates. The movement of the local economy from one period to the next was thus judged on the basis of the change in wage and salary data.

The next most important indicators were the employment as well as unemployment figures for the city. The fact that a city income tax was collected from all those living and working in the city made it also possible to obtain current unemployment data from the revenue department by industry and occupation for both residents and in-commuters, especially after the assembling of information was computerized, though much time-consuming rearranging of the data was necessary. Other indicators, collected and submitted to mayor and cabinet, included average work week and average earnings in manufacturing, data which qualified the city employment figures. In combination with electricity consumed during production, a rough indicator of gross manufacturing output could be obtained. Such a figure is a substantial portion of "gross city product" (the local counterpart to GNP), which could have served as an ideal companion figure for personal income, or for the figures just described serving as proxy for it, though the latter were available at best only on a quarterly basis.

When it later became possible to find out (with the aid of computers) which indicators would have predictive value for the movement of the economy, it turned out that manufacturing earnings and work week figures as well as those on initial unemployment claims and extended consumer credit were among those indicators forecasting future movements of unemployment because they were leading an upturn or downturn in the business cycle. To make that determination the strengthened economic unit of the late 1960s (under the EDA grant, see below) tested all indicators over past cycles in terms of the extent to which they had been leading cyclical movements of unemployment data in the past. This set of determinations made it possible to merge these predictive indicators into a single index, from which the subsequent movement of unemployment could be forecast on a monthly basis. Once this index was established, other relationships could be derived from it.[8]

## Depressed Area Legislation and Manpower Problems

The need for training and other help for unemployment in hard-hit communities had been discussed increasingly by the economists in the city ever since the mayor became aware of the rising unemployment rate and the reasons for it. The fact that many central cities needed help badly, even where the overall metropolitan area was in better shape, had also become very clear. Joseph S. Clark made the argument in correspondence with Senator Paul Douglas. Hence by the time Clark became a United States senator, he was ready to introduce an amendment to the "Douglas Bill." The amendment's provisions would have permitted, first, *portions* of metropolitan areas (if they could be clearly defined) to qualify for federal help for depressed areas under the bill, and, second, for areas such as central cities to be eligible even if the entire area was not. One version of this "depressed area" bill after another was vetoed by President Eisenhower. Mayor Dilworth testified for the different (but similar) versions at public hearings in 1957, 1958, 1959, and finally in 1961. He showed clearly how the grants for building additional public facilities, the loans to small (for example, incubator) industries, the provisions for training needed by the unskilled in the ghettoes, and so forth, would all prove especially helpful to central cities. He argued that the provisions of the bill, clause by clause, were tailor-made for the city's ills. Contradicting point for point the arguments advanced by the federal government, Dilworth pointed out forcefully that data for establishing the eligibility of such an area were indeed available, and scientifically verifiable statistics could be furnished.

The Area Redevelopment Act was finally passed in 1961. In deference to the objections by the U.S. Department of Labor, Senator Clark's amendment *as such* was removed from the law itself, though the "legislative materials" contained language which

8. Overall Economic Development Program for the City of Philadelphia: Wilford Grover, *Economic Indicators of the Philadelphia Economy*, Technical Report, no. 2 (October 1969).

permitted the administrator of this law to honor the amendment in the law's implementation. In spite of Philadelphia's pleading, however, the administrator refused to do so at the time, contending that if all central cities were aided, no money could be left for more seriously depressed areas, including rural ones.

It was not until 1964 that the eligibility of a few cities was established. Philadelphia's city economist then had submitted a tightly reasoned technical presentation to the Area Redevelopment Administration, which argued conclusively that a portion of a metropolitan area could be singled out for treatment as a "depressed area." The data collected for Philadelphia's economic indicators provided the factual basis for this point for Philadelphia.

In 1965, the ARA was replaced by the Economic Development Administration. The new act provided explicitly for designation of economic redevelopment areas *within* metropolitan areas or even within cities to provide remedial programs aimed at the most acute economic problems. Eventually the new agency awarded Philadelphia a "technical aid" grant, given its bad unemployment picture, which permitted setting up a more elaborate economic unit within the city administration with four additional economic specialists under a new city economist, and the money for using computers for its calculations; some benefits derived from their use were mentioned earlier.

One of the main benefits looked for in this new law was that money became available to train some of the unemployed. The Manpower Development and Training Act (MDTA) was passed soon after. Both pieces of legislation were found unsatisfactory especially in the case of the disadvantaged. A voluminous literature, pointing out all the shortcomings of the legislation, led to its amendments and the enactment of a series of new pieces of legislation. The Philadelphia experience has also been severely criticized by those investigating its training performance.[9]

On-the-job training was then only beginning to be tried. Aside

9. Leonardo Rico, "Urban Manpower and the MDTA: The Philadelphia Story," December 1964 (mimeo), p. 53. See also Norma W. Carlson and Patricia L. Mallory, *Federally Funded Manpower Development Programs in Philadelphia: An Evaluation*, Economic Development Unit, July 1967 (see n. 5, above).

from being cheaper than institutional training, it had the advantage that once the minority worker was accepted for training, the mutual adjustment to the work force could be accomplished during the training period, so that he should not have to overcome any further barriers. But it was found that the unwillingness of fellow employees to accept a trainee often stemmed from the fact that they could not get over their feeling that his different "culture" conflicted with their belief in the "work ethos." This experience indicated that we have much to learn about what needs to be done to assimilate disadvantaged workers.[10]

A program that eventually became commonplace but was tried early in Philadelphia was "pre-vocational" training for those not used to an industrial environment. Trainees were instructed not only in the three Rs but in handling their appearance, developing personal work habits, and learning how to apply for employment. Improved self-image and motivation were also part of this kind of training (it was later specifically recognized as an important part of training in the 1966 amendments to the MDTA), and it was therefore suggested that it be carried out by indigenous workers.

This was in fact part of the reason for the success of the "Opportunities Industrialization Center," started in North Philadelphia by the Reverend Leon Sullivan. He had become nationally known through the selective boycotts by a group of churches to force large firms to employ Negroes. Having won his case, he found that it could only be helpful if Negroes had the necessary skills, and therefore he started his training centers. His charisma enabled him to reach many of the 300,000 unemployed or underemployed in that part of the city. This kind of program, which included pre-vocational training of Negroes by Negroes, as well as emphasis on motivation of trainees, was carried on in many other cities but continued to be more successful in Philadelphia than elsewhere. The reason was not only Sullivan's ability to motivate both staff and trainees with the program's philosophy of self-help, indigenous recruiting and teaching, and pre-vocational training, but especially the fact that the Philadelphia business community

10. For a general discussion of this problem, see Kirk R. Petshek, "Barriers to Employability of Negroes in White-Collar Jobs," *Proceedings* (Industrial Relations Research Association, 1967 meetings), pp. 105 ff.

supported the undertaking wholeheartedly through funds and equipment, and donated buildings.[11] Needs of the cooperating firms for trained workers were kept continuously in mind during training by the center's job specialists, as well as in periodic follow-up; in the Philadelphia center a vast majority of trainees were placed, many more than in some of the ninety other centers. The 1970 manpower bill, passed by Congress in a period of severe unemployment, but vetoed by President Nixon, recognized the usefulness of OIC centers nationwide. They were among the few private training institutions to which substantial public funds were to be allocated.

## Economic Development Strategy

Seemingly unrelated activities of private organizations and public agencies can only be dovetailed into a meaningful strategy if policy-makers consciously try to influence the city's development in a specific direction. The goals for the city which cabinet and professionals were groping for can only be implemented if they are kept in mind every time a decision is made, especially if the decision-makers are continuously aware of the interrelationship of all public and private decisions. This is especially true of those which deal with economic development.

The capital program expressed the competition for public resources. Among the projects crying for priority were those public facilities which would lay the groundwork for private investment decisions—the infrastructure—which would thus influence those goals for the area's development which it was within the reach of the city to approach. This means that both public and private decisions were important for long-term development and had to be woven into any overall plan; mutual confidence made influence among the parties possible. Among the professionals, it was the economist who could point to both the advantages for the private firm and the benefits for the area as a whole, and could help the

11. More details on this organization in Michael Baran, Flourney Coles, John Harris, Alfred Parcell, and Carol Smith, *OIC-Philadelphia*. Final Report of the Task Force of the System Development Corporation, February 1966; and Herbert Striner, "The Opportunities Industrialization Center: A Successful Demonstration of Minority Self-Help, Training and Education" (University of Wisconsin Conference on Education and Training of Racial Minorities, May 1967.)

private investor to evaluate those alternative choices open to him which would help the region as such; he could appraise the importance of the strategy decided upon, and would be less likely to overstate the city government's influence on the local economy as compared to that of national economic forces.[12]

Such a strategy was in the minds of the professionals during the reform, though no official plan was ever made public. The method of joint public-private decision-making clearly helped. The Annual Development Program proposed by the CRP would have formalized such a plan, if it had been carried out. The "project packages" in the CRP's proposals, however, linked jobs and income and housing and education into an overall plan, which went further in showing the interrelationships of these apparently unrelated activities than the professionals of the period had yet been able to make clear to a larger audience.

12. See Kirk R. Petshek, "Issues in Metropolitan Economic Development," *Journal of the American Institute of Planners,* July 1966, pp. 241–46.

# 12    *Reform Politics*

The reform government did not reach its objectives primarily because they were endorsed by the Democratic party, but because it was able to form a coalition of diverse groups: those individual citizens and citizen groups who had worked hard to write the new City Charter and even harder to see that it was passed by the electorate; the business groups and the members of the elite (many living on the Main Line and therefore outside the city limits), who had realized the need for a new honest city government and increasingly liked the direction the new government was taking with regard to developmental programs. Included in the coalition were professionals affiliated with the city, civic groups, or universities, who agreed with the principles of the reform endeavors; some special groups, like minorities or downtown businessmen, who felt that they were benefiting from what the new government undertook; and finally, private individuals, primarily organized around the local ADA chapter.

Clark and Dilworth provided the political leadership which molded these diverse groups into an informal coalition. Through a series of committees, boards, and commissions these groups and the city officials concerned in each case were able to reach a basis for accommodation to formulate the various developmental programs. It was then up to the mayors to "sell" these programs, or as large a part of them as possible, to the members of the city council. Disagreement with the political party could spell life or death for a program, since most councilmen were much more closely tied to the party than were the mayors.

## City Council

Whether at public hearings, at committee meetings, or at a formal session, the city council was the legislative body through which individuals, groups of citizens, or their representatives could exercise the accepted democratic privilege of making their objections heard. This exercise of the democratic process was often used to register protest to a plan proposed for a neighborhood by the city's planners, to express the wish of an ethnic enclave to remain undisturbed by plans or programs designed to further the ends of progress for the city at large, or to express an individual's reluctance to become part of the community's "cost" in order to maximize long-run "benefits" which would, he was told, accrue to the greatest number.

Where plans and programs were endorsed by powerful civic groups or by individuals who were numbered among the community's "movers and shakers," the council chamber became the backdrop against which the covert class warfare which is latent in all large cities was carried on. Identifying closely with the Democratic City Committee, the majority of the council (especially after 1956) felt no kinship to the influential civic groups, whose members they saw—not entirely correctly—as representing only "big business," the financial fraternity, and the eggheads. The fact that the city council saw itself as the countervailing force to the reform administration probably contributed to the long hiatus which occurred between the presentation and the adoption of some of the city's most creative plans. The council felt the need to acknowledge that more had to be done for the "little man" who would be dispossessed. Is the generalization justified which points to the reformer-intellectual's impersonal desire to do the greatest good for the greatest number, in contrast to the politician's concern for the welfare of each individual for whom he has assumed responsibility and from whom he expects unquestioning loyalty and devotion, especially at the polls?

Members of the council saw it as the proper function of that body to make certain that no large numbers of individuals would be adversely affected by any plans promulgated by the administration, no matter how strongly the mayor may have felt that one or other program would be in the city's best interests. Negotiations with members of the city council (usually in the Democratic caucus) to reach the necessary accommodation were part of the overall political process. After all, at each level of government the executive and the legislative branches often take opposing positions, not only when the legislative majority is from a different party from the executive, or from a different faction of the same party, but because they see themselves as representing the interests of different constituencies. This held true in Philadelphia even in the case of the councilmen elected at large.

Clark and Dilworth had to constantly be on guard for ulterior motives of the party, which could be hidden by a councilman's publicly voicing opposition to a program on the basis of one of his constituents' opposition—a reason which the councilman was reluctant to admit openly. A contractor or a real estate operator, for example, in the good graces of the political party, might expect to be more successful in his bid for one project rather than for a different one the administration proposed. Councilmen might therefore favor the project not given highest priority by the administration; this would be even more likely to happen if the alternative project were state-financed, which in Pennsylvania meant that it would be awarded on a strict patronage basis. Clark and Dilworth tried to avoid having a project changed in order to contribute to someone's personal gain. But when they seemed to fail to convince councilmen of the merits of a certain proposal, they could not always be certain that the expressed reasons for the objections raised were the only ones motivating them.

## Could Reformers Forge Their Own Political Mechanism?

"The reform politician always has the problem of how to hold the independents without losing the vote of the regular party organization, which he also needs to be elected. He knows that political machines, like it or not, are an unavoidable part of our democratic system and that even though they are not necessarily corrupt, they inevitably consume as well as generate power." [1]

In looking at past reform governments, the complaint usually can be heard that the reformers were too deeply immersed in tinkering with the city's administrative machinery to be concerned about building their own political organization to keep themselves in power. This is true, though the reasons are not usually understood. In fact, of the twentieth-century municipal reforms I recall, only DeLesseps Morrison of New Orleans accom-

1. Hannah Lees, *The Reporter*, October 20, 1955.

plished it for a while. Both Clark and Dilworth were keenly aware of the need for setting up their own political organizations —if only because they knew the poor staying power of reform movements elsewhere. Every reform leader has faced the problem of how to cope with this issue. Clark's personality and coolness might have enabled him to start his own organization, but he was not willing to do so. Although his continual battles with the party slowed him down, he was in office only one term and was able to leave untarnished. Dilworth had a clearer perception of the advantages of offering a modicum of inducements to the party in power. He was widely accused of compromising his principles but was able to hold the line where it counted most.

### Might Early Action Have Succeeded?

Soon after the start of the reform government, the Democratic party politicians found out that patronage had now become a very feeble tool. Still, with the Republican organization discredited, fragmented, and unwilling to do battle—least of all on the side of reformers—there might have been a chance for the reformers to take over what Democratic forces existed. But could the reformers have been successful even then, given their lack of organizational experience and Mayor Clark's peculiar difficulty in gaining the confidence of committeemen and ward leaders? Moreover, this was just the time when James Finnegan had been made party chairman, the man who firmly believed that good government made good political sense, and hence helped all he could to let the reformers win their main causes. Council gave all the appearances at first of having also seen the light—at least as long as it was sure that everybody agreed from which side the sun was shining! (When later this illumination seemed to dim a bit, it appeared that they had taken advantage of the shadows to slink away.) Clark thus was able to get his way a number of times, even against the wishes of many of the party's stalwarts—after all, it was the goals of the reform he was elected for.

From time to time, in moments of discouragement, Clark spoke of his desire to resign and run again as an independent. Some of his close associates at the time believe he was prepared to do it and could win. Others believe that he was never serious about it or that, even if he had been, he could never have been successful, since he would have been succeeded immediately by the president of the city council and would have had to wait for the next regular election before being able to run. Even if he had won this election, the city council would probably have been much more hostile in this situation. One associate believes that he could indeed have run as an independent and won during the first few months of his administration. Another has pointed out the amazingly small number of people who were really responsible for the reform—although the reform was carried out with the help and moral support of many. Still another has stated that Clark never had a chance to control the Democratic machinery.

Throughout his term (and even later) Clark seemed determined to free the party from too many dealings with the boys in the back room. He felt that one good fight would teach the party to accept his ideas. But it was difficult to decide what was the good fight! For a while he still seemed determined (though with decreasing hopes) that the party would see matters through his eyes. But as he needed the party more to be effective in the Senate and to be reelected, he was forced increasingly to "play ball." The practical school of national politics modified his approach.

*Geographical Distribution*

A point which is often overlooked is the simple one of geography. In order to build an organization of its own (or take over an existing one) a reform group must have a comparatively large number of men willing to put a lot of time into detailed election work. A reasonable number of such people might have been found in the Philadelphia of the early 1950s—although many "did not have the fortitude for it," as one participant believes. Also, many members of the reform army, having one professional competence or another, had been absorbed into city service. The strictness with which the rule against partisan political activity by city employees was enforced was reminiscent of the Puritan forefathers of the reform leaders. The real barrier for reformers as politicians, however, was the rule (not accidentally enacted by the council!) that not only people elected to public office, but also political activists down to committeemen, had to be residents of the division or ward in which they served. This presented a real problem, because most members of the reform group, if they were residents of the city proper, lived near Center City, or in Chestnut Hill, the northwestern (suburban-type) district, or in West Philadelphia near the University of Pennsylvania. These are middle-income areas, comprising some five wards out of fifty-nine in the city. For reformers to move and spread out into the remaining fifty-odd wards would have been difficult; this would have cut their roots—roots which were important in political work! Also, many members were intellectuals and professional people, who might have felt ill at ease and been unsuccessful in influencing the men and women whose vote they wanted to capture and whose loyalty they needed to inspire. Recruiting a different kind of party worker by promising jobs and advancement was exceedingly difficult in a movement firmly committed to the merit system.

In contrast, the amateurs and intellectuals working on the national scene for Adlai Stevenson were able to maintain a modicum of group coherence, and it was always assumed that a call to arms could reach them easily. How much simpler should it have been with the greater visibility of local elections! Enough exciting things happened during the Philadelphia renaissance to keep any group of people who viewed themselves as part of the reform sufficiently excited and committed, if they were properly organized once the election was over. But they were unable to overcome their personal, professional, and geographical obstacles, though they continued to be enthusiastically committed to the goals of the reform.

*Labor in Politics*

Where, then, could these "new" party workers be obtained? What about labor, which had helped to win the election, whose members were benefiting greatly from a sympathetic government, and whose residence pattern was spread geographically all over the city?

First, labor leaders exerted a weak influence in Philadelphia. Unions bought tables at the Democratic party's fund-raising dinners and the reformers' Roosevelt Day dinner—and most of the leaders came to neither. The distinction between reformers and regulars for them became increasingly blurred. The two councilmen from labor's ranks were less responsive to the city chairman because labor's bread-and-butter issues were closer to their hearts, making them more independent. In addition, the unification of the AFL and the CIO nationally was not glued together firmly in Philadelphia. The CIO leader, Kelly, while clearly junior to the AFL's Blumberg, nonetheless insisted on his (basically meaningless) independence. But, while labor was generally in favor of broad developmental programs, its main concern seemed to be that labor be duly represented on all official boards and commissions and on the boards of the various nonprofit corporations—often by two separate representatives. Hence labor was so represented, invariably through its top officials, whose attentions, however, were much too thinly spread to allow them to exert any appreciable influence.

Second, unions are often reluctant to get involved in partisan political activity, unless they start from a strong and secure position, as, for instance, in Detroit. Labor leaders may support candidates, but to be the backbone of a political movement is a risk they prefer not to run. The strength of their political bargaining power would be impaired if they could be held responsible for a losing battle.

Third, labor was soon so satisfied with the treatment it received at the hands of the Democratic party that it rarely threatened to support Republicans, which of course weakened its own political bargaining power. In 1957, for instance, the unions strove hard to stop an increase in the wage tax but were turned down out of hand. Had they relied only on the forces of the reform and their own effort in it, they might have antagonized members of both political parties—and that is unhealthy for union officials hoping to be reelected.

Finally, much of the labor leaders' reluctance stemmed from the fact that they were able to work on their political chores only in off-duty hours. To support a third party and to stand for political elective office themselves is apt to be repugnant to union officials; if they are elected but later defeated for public office, they may find that they have been cut off from their base in the union, a union leader said, and there may be no place for them when they want to return to be a union officer again.

Business was in an even more precarious position, although its representatives were increasingly on the side of the reformers. Business leaders were ready to support a person but not a party, particularly since that party's philosophy was nationally at odds with their own (ticket splitting was only beginning to become acceptable). Civic groups, which many businessmen supported and belonged to, were of the greatest help to the reformers—but not in working on the party mechanism.

## Negroes and Third Party Strategy

The reform had opened to Negroes many civil service jobs, which were easier to obtain, in spite of the tests, than were jobs in private employment. The reform mayors also had backed the City Commission on Human Relations and other organizations trying to integrate more housing developments and keep the whites from fleeing to the suburbs. And in the early years of the reform, Negroes were staunch allies of the reform mayors. But as the Democratic party gained strength, and when a Democratic governor was elected, the Democrats were able to give out patronage jobs at the state level which included a large number in the unskilled and semiskilled categories. It was thus ever harder to tell whether Negroes were voting for the party or for the reform when they cast their ballots. In the 1958 congressional primary, for example, a clear-cut fight developed between a Negro backed by the Democratic party and another supported by all elements of the reform, including Clark, Dilworth, the ADA, and other civic groups. But Negro voters lined up two to one behind the Democratic organization candidate.

Part of the reason for this may have been the enormous chasm between the low-income Negro with few potential skills and the middle-class Negro professional with entirely different ideology and aspirations. Some of the latter became public officials and were more likely to be consulted by the reform administration than others. They were able to take advantage of increasingly available integrated housing and to move into well-kept middle-class neighborhoods. Many of their physical and medical needs were taken care of in newly established health and recreation centers. They had clearly benefited from the reform.

The low-income Negro, on the other hand, on whom the burden of the high level of unemployment fell, could scarcely avail himself of many of these benefits. He had little hope for employment, let alone for advancement. He could not benefit from new integrated housing as his income was too low, and dislocation hit him hard. He was living in the increasing clusters of slum housing in North Philadelphia or in some areas of West Philadelphia. Therefore his interest in politics was purely personal, and his vote was apt to be committed where he could see the greatest benefit for himself. If there was a distinction between party and reform, he was apt to vote for the party which might give him jobs or other benefits. For this group (a large part of the black population) it could probably be said that the reform administration had made little difference as far as the quality of life was concerned.

Negroes as a group had been unable, at least during the major part of the period discussed in this book, to muster any political bargaining power. The larger masses of potential black voters seemed to have no influence on the slating of candidates. Nor were they able to mount a strong attack on the problem of relocation in general, by which they were hurt worse than others, although the council served continuously as the forum for complaints against the dislocation of the few. There was really no black constituency whose threats of defection would be taken seriously and whose votes could be thrown in the scale to obtain a concession. The general political impotence of Negroes, although they constituted over a quarter of the population, was the more surprising if compared to the power of other ethnic groups with many fewer members. But at that time Negroes were not aware of their potential political power, nor were they organized to take advantage of it.

It was thus unlikely that black groups could be persuaded to join any reform coalition. Aside from anything else, this might have cut them off from possible sources of patronage. In addition, even though they had spread into different districts, the main body of their population was still concentrated in a few areas, so they had the same kind of handicap of geographical distribution as the reformers themselves had.

No reform organization was thus created, nor attempts made by the reform leaders to assure the continuance of this movement.

If it was to be saved, the initiative would have to come from another quarter.

## Reform or Political Organization

There was never any doubt among the reformers that they had not solved the problem of continuity for the reform. But they appeared to give little thought to the difficulty: they seemed to rely on the ingenuity of the many bright young lawyers and other professionals, active in and around the reform, to help them perform a miracle when the time came. James Reichley, a talented journalist-politician, asked in a 1958 pamphlet whether "these two most fascinating individuals [were] capable of building an organization that might carry on the good-government ideal? . . . Both possess great natural talents . . . which might well have suited them for the gigantic task of creating a permanent reform movement in the city." [2] Reichley predicted the imminent end of the reform. "The reform's objectives," he said, "seem finally to be reducible to an economic view of the nature of man. . . . The economic view . . . which insists that government must limit itself to removing the obstacles to fulfillment of the economic needs of the population . . . makes difficult if not impossible any sustained, large-scale political effort dedicated to the objective of 'reform.' The declared purpose of reform is the solution of this or that economic problem; when the problem is solved or when it has turned into a bore, the whole reason for the effort has collapsed." [3]

Reichley seems to have overlooked the broad, long-range progress envisaged by the reformers as their goal, and the achievement of part of this goal—enough to maintain it for a decade and longer. In the present book, the Philadelphia reform movement is seen as geared toward practicable sociopolitical goals, rather than, as Reichley suggests, "economic repair work." Reichley says that "if the motive for political participation is strictly an economic one, then it must take its place within the hierarchy of

2. James Reichley, *The Art of Government* (Fund for the Republic, 1959), pp. 113 ff. Reichley's pamphlet was quickly written during a few weeks of the summer of 1958, even before Dilworth was reelected for his second term. Being the only printed report on this period with scholarly pretensions, it has been widely quoted.
3. Ibid., pp. 114–15.

similar economic motives and concerns. Inevitably, the place that it enjoys there cannot be a very high one." [4] Economic self-interest alone could hardly have guided the action of the civic groups supporting the reform, for many of the social measures taken—the houses built for low-income families, the health centers constructed, the Skid Row clinic established, the historic areas renewed, the university redeveloped—increased their taxes. But in fact, these men and their businesses incidentally benefited from the improved social climate over the long run: thus, their action has been called "enlightened self-interest." The tradition of noblesse oblige is so strong in Philadelphia that it too is partly responsible for civic attitudes. Further, it is often necessary to present moral goals in an economic guise. The fear of appearing to be an impractical dreamer among practical men of affairs is endemic in twentieth-century America and has done considerable damage nationally.

The goals of the reform mayors were thus geared to what they considered to be in the public interest, and most of the time they were aimed at whatever they felt were social improvements which had a hope of becoming reality. No conflict of interest was likely, given their small personal fortunes, and their own political future was tied to success in what they were doing for Philadelphia. (The fact that during the war oil was found on the property of Joseph Clark's family, which rendered him moderately wealthy, had no bearing on his attitude in the city. For that matter, when he got to the U.S. Senate, he deliberately took a stand against the entrenched oil interests—a position for which some members of his own family never forgave him.) This author observed for years the reform mayors' meticulous care to deny information about public decisions in the making (for example, the route of an expressway) to those whom they suspected of wishing to turn a personal profit from these programs; their success in preventing appointment to boards and commissions of those who may have wanted to serve for reasons of personal gain; and even their insistence on returning *any* gift of more than nominal value. There is no question that what constitutes "public interest" is seen differently by different individuals. It can

4. Ibid., p. 122.

be asserted, however, that the reform government in Philadelphia tried to serve the interests of the largest number of citizens.

The increasing rise of the "public-regarding, Anglo-Saxon, Protestant, middle-class ethos" as against the "private-regarding, lower-class," boss-oriented one is discussed by Banfield and Wilson. As the lower class is increasingly absorbed into the middle class, its members accept middle-class political ideals—the search for "a more or less objective public interest, and interest of the 'community as a whole,'" as well as honesty, efficiency, and so forth. The consequence is a "deepening popular hostility toward everything that has about it the odor of the smoke-filled room. . . . To regard politics as contrary to the public interest is consistent with the middle-class ideal; reformers have always taken this view." [5] In the "non-partisan apolitics" of Washington, D.C., as Martha Derthick sees it,[6] the absence of competition for public jobs makes debate on issues and programmatic goals more important (see the discussion of Type II politics in chapter 10).

Even with "public interest" as the motive force, however, objectivity may lead to awarding contracts to honest but inept contractors, or to promoting governmental innovations which reflect the needs of the new, larger middle class, such as increased parking or health care facilities for preventive medicine, because this is the dominant group. At the same time, the needs of the lower socioeconomic group may become submerged because this group is smaller and less articulate. Good intentions do not necessarily lead to better government.

Given the kind of machine the Philadelphia reform government had to defeat to come to power, it is understandable that it continued to feel that any kind of machine was dangerous to good government. But such an approach is not necessarily correct.

If we look to the writings of political scientists, the answer is by no means unequivocal. The worst aspect of partisan machine

5. Edward Banfield and James Q. Wilson, *City Politics* (Harvard-M.I.T. Press, 1963), pp. 329–30. Banfield and Wilson elsewhere put it differently: "The reformers assumed that there existed an interest ('the public interest') that pertained to the city 'as a whole' and that should always prevail over competing, partial (and usually private) interests" (ibid., p. 139).

6. Martha Derthick, "Politics in Voteless Washington," *Journal of Politics*, 1963, pp. 101 ff.

government to those in favor of reform ethos was that it capitalized on socioeconomic cleavages, class differences, and ethnic antagonisms in order to keep the reins of government in the machine's hands.[7] The opposite view emphasizes the parties as managers of conflict, crystallizing opinions into manageable groups framing alternatives, and thus bringing order into politics.[8]

The elimination of parties might thus intensify the conflict between the socioeconomic cleavages within a city, for without party affiliation ethnic and other divisions are emphasized, while the role of social conflict may be minimized in governments changed in line with reform ideas. Those concerned with giving the poor and the working-class population a voice find machine politics doing just that, while the "sterilized" nonpartisan government, which disperses power to a wide range of civic associations and bureaucracies, contributes to middle-class domination of city politics. When investigating "community action programs" under antipoverty legislation in four large cities, Greenstone and Peterson found that machine politics are apt to solve "the economic dimensions of poverty" rather than to distribute political power to the groups representing them, while governments with reformed institutions are more likely to "concentrate their attack on the political conditions associated with poverty." [9] It is thus possible to argue that under today's conditions machine politics may prove less favorable to the lower-income classes in the long run. But machine politics has always functioned to respond quickly, certainly before the next election, whereas the rationale of reform has been building for the future.

The political science literature identifies "reform" with the institutional changes introduced by most reform governments (nonpartisan elections, office of city manager, at-large election, civil service) and discusses the consequences of these changes for democratic government. The changes which the Philadelphia government introduced, however, were less a matter of changing

7. See Georgije Ostrogorski, *Democracy and the Organization of Political Parties*, vol. 2 (Doubleday, 1964).

8. Frank J. Sorauf, *Political Parties in the American System* (Little, Brown & Co., 1964), pp. 165–66.

9. J. David Greenstone and Paul E. Peterson, "Reformers, Machines, and the War on Poverty," in James Q. Wilson (ed.), *City Politics and Public Policy*, p. 289.

the nature of democratic institutions (which the charter had already done) than of shifting the priorities which would affect the development of the city—often, but not necessarily, to the advantage of the poor—for a long time to come. That is the reason why this volume has maintained that much of what the reform achieved might prove irreversible by subsequent administrations.

# 13      *Epilogue:*
## The Impact of Civic Groups

Active middle-class groups forming the civic Establishment and professionals practicing the art and science of public administration under the leadership of dynamic mayors: this was the combination responsible for Philadelphia's renaissance. Neither the war on poverty nor the law-and-order issue was part of the reform era. The undertakings of the reform administration must be judged as successes or failures depending on whether they came to grips with the current problems at the time, not whether they solved them forever. It is especially important that this be kept in mind because the pace as well as the scope of change has accelerated so sharply on the urban scene since the mid-sixties.

Joseph S. Clark was elected mayor of Philadelphia in 1951. Dwight D. Eisenhower was elected president of the United States in 1952. The mayor was elected on a platform of "sweeping the rascals out, restoring honesty to City Hall, and getting Philadelphia moving again." The president was elected on a platform which promised to slow the forces of change, limit innovation, and curb governmental intervention in the lives of its citizens. Mayor Clark's election was the response to a long period of apathy which, at best, maintained the status quo and left Philadelphia ever farther behind as the social forces of the twentieth century gathered momentum. President Eisenhower's election reflected the mood of a nation which, within recent memory of its voters, had survived a depression, a world war, and adjustment to a peacetime economy, and now had assumed an unsought-after role as the dominant world power. Philadelphia was ready for some radical change; the administration in Washington was ready to consolidate gains and slow the pace of experimentation and innovation.

In 1951, in most other cities politics was being carried on as usual. Joseph Clark's victory as the Democratic reform candidate, therefore, drew the national spotlight to Philadelphia, and it stayed there as the city became a laboratory for much of the social innovation and economic experimentation which followed. Many programs for combating urban problems first saw the light of day in Philadelphia as a result of the alliance of many concerned citizen groups with the professionals in both civic groups and the city. Philadelphia professionals maintained a relationship with Washington civil servants that made the latter more responsive to many of the ideas emanating from Philadelphia. Mayor Lee of New Haven also found a good relationship with Washington to be fertile soil and, beginning with his fervent belief that urban renewal was good politics, started many new programs in the 1950s. Some of New Haven's innovative programs in the area of human resources later had an influence on federal antipoverty legislation, just as some of Philadelphia's ferment in the area of urban renewal influenced later housing legislation.

The 1960s brought a greater awareness and concern for the problems of the cities: legislation such as that for depressed areas, many new remedies in various Housing Act amendments, the start of a cabinet department for urban problems, or manpower training. Many legislative enactments were beginning to be designed to help the cities, though lagging appropriations slowed their implementation. The Kennedy-Johnson administrations were acutely aware of the needs of underprivileged citizens and began to respond to the growing insistence of the poor, the disillusioned, and the alienated to be heard and heeded. The big city mayors, being closer, heard these voices even more clearly. Mayor Cavanaugh of Detroit, for example, said in 1969: "You had the interest of the officials in Washington. You had the problems locally that were beginning to surface, and then you had new men in the cities who decided to try and do something about them. A lot of the federal programs then were the products of some of these new mayors." [1] It was by then easier for the cities to get response from Washington, though the problems had increased. More thoughtful, concerned, and imaginative mayors were being

1. Interview with Fred Powledge, in "The Flight from City Hall," *Harper's Magazine*, November 1969, p. 84.

elected, beginning with the Kennedy period—Arthur Naftalin of Minneapolis, Ivan Allen of Atlanta, Jerome Cavanaugh of Detroit, Raymond Tucker of Saint Louis, and others. They all could have used—and undoubtedly often did—some of the ideas and methods of Clark and Dilworth. In many ways they carried into the 1960s what Philadelphia (and New Haven) had started in the 1950s. At the end of the sixties many of these mayors refused to run for reelection and were replaced by men with entirely different goals (Charles Stenvig in Minneapolis, Roman Gribbs in Detroit, Alfonso Cervantes in Saint Louis), though men like Peter Flaherty in Pittsburgh, Carl Stokes in Cleveland, and John Lindsay in New York maintained or initiated reform-style administrations in their respective cities.

## The Changed Climate in the 1960s

What made the problems of 1969 different from those of 1962? The first change was a different approach to minority problems. The ratio of Negroes to the total population had increased sharply in most northern cities. Antipoverty legislation had given them more chance for participation in local decision-making. The introduction of "model cities" further increased black people's power in determining what should be done with their neighborhood, and the grass-roots organizations of different minority groups played an ever greater role.

The officials of Philadelphia's reform administration had shown their concern for neighborhood sentiment in urban renewal problems, especially in the "leadership program" and in their increasing attention to problems of relocation. They had helped to organize neighborhood organizations, for instance, in Haddington and the University City area. The Community Renewal Program professionals emphasized choice of housing sites, equality of opportunity, and mobility, as well as the need to take care of the inner city first. With the "human resources" grant from the Ford Foundation, a nonprofit corporation for self-help activities of the poor was started—a forerunner of the war on poverty, which, however, unlike the New Haven experience, was not one of Philadelphia's greatest successes.[2] Some, like Paul

2. Peter Marris and Martin Rein, *Dilemmas of Social Reform* (Atherton Press, 1967), chap. 4, esp. pp. 119 ff.

Davidoff, wanted to go even further by suggesting that professional planners should become "advocates" to represent neighborhood groups, particularly from disadvantaged areas. The problems of the poor and the disadvantaged were present in the thinking of the officials of the reform administration long before the antipoverty legislation. When the Philadelphia reformers spoke of citizen participation, however, they did not mean that of grass-roots organizations but that of civic associations which had matured over decades and seemingly came to full fruition after World War II, such as the Philadelphia Housing Association or the Citizens' Council on City Planning (which in turn considered neighborhood groups as its component organizations), and the comparative newcomers, the Greater Philadelphia Movement and the Citizens' Committee on Public Education.

Along with these civic associations, groups recruited from the poor and the minorities also began to play their part during the latter part of the reform. The professionals working for the poverty program were often able to persuade the poverty representatives on their boards to vote for the programs they had worked out. Similarly, minority groups were beginning to be assimilated into the mores of the community, especially as they became upwardly mobile and fitted into the philosophy of the "work ethos."

Still, while response to the demands by minority groups was gradual, it was a different method than the reform leaders were used to. Their need to express their own value systems and have them recognized and accepted made it more difficult at first to make organized minority groups and their different cultures part of the total community. It was only the inner security of Philadelphia's civic leaders, who had dealt successfully with a large variety of groups, which enabled them to help the minorities to act more quickly the way other civic associations did and thus be accepted and listened to. Hence, at least in the initial phase of the war on poverty, the minorities seemed less inclined in Philadelphia than elsewhere to attack the system as such. They found it more responsive to their needs and more willing to accommodate them than was the case in many other cities.

Community Action programs and Model Cities agencies at first appeared to be an onslaught on the power of City Hall.

When dislocation of the poor and the Negroes in West Philadelphia led to sit-ins in Mayor Tate's office, he lost the services of the executive director of the Human Relations Commission because Tate failed to support his position. But gradually Tate realized that a political accommodation with these new forces was possible by paying some attention to their valid demands and, more important, by allocating positions to their spokesmen. Since the spokesmen's salaries were paid by the Office of Equality of Opportunity, the U.S. Department of Housing and Urban Development, or the U.S. Department of Health, Education, and Welfare, and were not city appointments subject to city civil service, Tate saw them as a new source of patronage. This swing toward City Hall power was emphasized by the amendment to the antipoverty act sponsored by Congresswoman Edith Green in 1967 and by the express change in the intent of the model cities under the new Nixon HUD appointees. Deputy Assistant Secretary Robert Baida had written to the Philadelphia Model Cities' Administration on June 5, 1969: "In the model cities program, projects and activities should be operated by existing public and private institutions, whenever possible. . . . [They] must be strengthened and become more responsible for, and more responsive to, the needs of the model neighborhood." Floyd Hyde, HUD assistant secretary in charge of model cities, put an even stronger emphasis on this matter: "The fundamental purpose of the model cities program—and one to which I am totally committed—is strengthening the capacity of local government." [3] In an HUD-commissioned study in 1968 the authors emphasized that cities such as Philadelphia saw model cities "as surprisingly sensitive and responsive political instruments. [These cities] have to cater to the needs of a multitude of constituencies with totally inadequate resources. Their practice of allocating scarcity among an abundance of varied citizen organizations . . . is not untypical of the big-city politics of redistribution." [4] This was not the way of Philadelphia's reform, which usually attempted to bring about

3. Both quotations from Michelle Osborn, "Postscript: The Conflict in Context: An Overview of the Philadelphia Struggle," *City*, October–November 1970, pp. 40, 43.

4. Ibid., p. 42. Quoted from the 1968 study of neighborhood power and control by Hans B. Spiegel and Stephen D. Mittenthal, contracted for by U.S. Department of Housing and Urban Development.

some kind of consensus, an agreement on common objectives, among the parties involved. By the late 1960s, however, the adjustment that had to be made was between the organizations of the poor and the dominant political forces in the city. And the fact that at the time this still took place without a major confrontation is probably due to the tradition of accommodation among civic groups.

The second thread of the change from the early to the late sixties had been much less explored until rather recently. It is the somewhat parallel problem of the white ethnics encompassed by their own subculture. The majority of them are blue-collar workers, though a number have found their way into modest white-collar or service jobs.

Their problem is that they are trapped between the "haves" and the "have-nots"—too rich to receive scholarships for their children or subsidized medical care, but too poor to finance major illnesses or send their children to college without undue hardships. Meaningful promotion is barred by the fact that supervisory positions are firmly held by better educated WASPs, while the security of their jobs is threatened by the upgrading of lower skilled workers, who are often Negroes. This feeling of "going down an up escalator" is aggravated by the belief that their work has no "status" in the eyes of society or even their own children. They perceive their inability to effectively influence public decisions which could have great impact on their lives. Nor has technology actually removed, as it seemed to promise, the drudgery from manual or service work. The resulting dissatisfaction, discouragement, and alienation are evident, and those affected attribute these feelings to a variety of reasons.

The middle-class ethnics are reluctant to give up their ethnic identities and increasingly emphasize the differences that distinguish one group from the others, partly in reaction to the growing militancy of black Americans. A sort of class warfare results, in which the middle-class ethnics find their groups championed by the police. Hence they are apt to believe deeply in a "law-and-order" approach to society, even though they are not likely to be able to afford legal redress if they are in need of help. Though they share many problems with their black neighbors, they are unwilling to acknowledge any bond, as they fear that Negroes

might be usurping their jobs, encroaching upon their neighborhoods, and deflating the value of their properties. "Like a significant number of their fellow Americans, white ethnics today
attribute poverty to the failing of the individual and not to dislocation in society," writes Henry Goldstein. "White ethnic community leaders charge that government has ignored the pockets of
poverty in their neighborhoods. . . . The welfare state and the
reform of city government brought about the demise of the
machines which provided the white ethnics with access to city
hall. . . . [The bosses] had ameliorated group conflict in their
bailiwicks. The present level of conflict in our cities is in no small
part attributable to the reformers' confusing administration with
politics, which is another word for conflict control. The frustra-
tion of these groups of workers, proud of their 'work ethos,' is as
yet a poorly defined malaise, a protest against how things in
general are shaping up, against Negro and other groups who
might increase their insecurity, a protest against their own anger
and bewilderment,[5] and against the existing institutions in general. Though their philosophy has not been clearly enunciated,
these groups and their frustrations have become an important
new force in the late sixties and early seventies, only partially
explained by the Vietnam War. Wilson called it "a sense of the
failure of community and the nostalgia of the lower middle-class
for security, order and proper behavior in public places." [6]

During the 1960s confrontations among these groups were
avoided in Philadelphia. Nor did as large numbers vote for
George Wallace for president in 1968 as they did in some other
cities. It is too early to tell whether the election of Frank Rizzo
as mayor in 1971, certainly a "law-and-order" candidate and himself a conscious member of an ethnic group, should be interpreted as a break in Philadelphia's civic tradition. But more
than a twenty-year history of civic involvement may well warrant
instead a note of long-term optimism regarding the ability of a
flexible civic Establishment to adjust new minority and ethnic
organizations to the existing civic groups and their attitudes. This

5. Henry Goldstein, "The White Ethnics: Who Are They and Where
Are They Going?" *City*, May–June 1971, pp. 28–29.
6. James Q. Wilson, "The Urban Unease," *The Public Interest*, Summer
1968, pp. 26–28.

author believes—as will be discussed further below—that the Philadelphia reform engendered the kind of vital change in structure and behavior of civic groups to make Philadelphia citizens in the long run inclined toward accepting peaceful changes and adjusting to them.

## Why Were Civic Groups So Important?

The new charter in 1951 gave a clear-cut mandate to the executive branch under a strong mayor plan. This "represented a recognition that leadership is the key factor in governing . . . and the vesting of unmistakable responsibility in the mayor . . . [and] continuous citizen action in public affairs." [7] In defining the legislative function, the Charter Commission stated: "The Council is not to interfere in any way with administration, but . . . is to have complete and adequate means for checking on the performance of the administrative branch." [8]

Civic groups whose efforts were responsible for this basic law were to continue to play an official role under the charter in the several independent boards and nominating panels. But it was the virtually unbridled power of the mayor, both in appointments and substantive programs, combined with the expressed limit on the duties of the city council, that made civic groups feel themselves to be an influential part of the reform. Conflicts were avoided because generally these groups were driven by what they—and the reform administration—considered to be in the public interest, rather than by more narrow group interests. In other words, charter provisions, the personalities of the mayors, and the attitude of civic leaders made it possible that open ideological conflict with elected political representatives was avoided. The reform period was thus dominated by the administration and the professionals who joined them from far and wide on the one hand, and, on the other, by the civic groups from both the power structure and the middle class, and the nonprofit corporations set up by them. Policies were determined jointly by all of these.

7. Joseph D. Crumlish, *A City Finds Itself* (Wayne State University Press, 1959), p. 82.
8. Philadelphia Charter Commission, *Comments on the Proposed Home Rule Charter*, February 25, 1951, p. 5.

How can conclusions be drawn for other cities from the Philadelphia reform experience? It is doubtful that any of these elements was expendable—the leaders, the professional experts, the dedicated civic groups and their followers, the public-private partnership, or the apparatus of joint policy-making. The only clear lesson is that the Philadelphia reform was brought about and continually sustained by the varied civic associations, emanating from different groups and sharing a purpose they had in common with the reform government, and the impact on both by a dedicated group of professionals who laid the substantive groundwork to the development programs of the reform.

There were not only many professional experts in city government (see chapter 10), but a surprising number of "professional citizens" outside of it, the "indispensible one-hundredths of one percent" who worked as an informal pressure group for developmental programs. This "'fourth power' in a new sense [is] a largely self-selected minority of citizens wielding tremendous influence over the affairs of government. . . . [It is] a new wrinkle in government, an involvement that bypasses the entrenched political parties as a new countervailing power." [9] These different civic groups had learned to compromise with each other to reach some measure of the consensus they seriously desired. This was possible because they shared their basic values with both professionals and with the city administration. "The goals they have urged . . . have reflected their class bias," says Martin Meyerson. "They have not advanced policies and programs in their own self-interest; they have merely assumed that all people view the world, or ought to view the world, as they do." [10]

The most interesting aspect of including civic groups in the determination of reform decisions lay in the process of policy-making: Philadelphia's unique creation—which other cities could well imitate—was the quasi-public corporations created by civic groups, sometimes in collaboration with the city administration, who met with representatives of the city and other levels of government to decide on how developmental programs were to be

9. David Wallace, "Renaissancemanship," *Journal of the American Institute of Planners*, August 1960, p. 176.

10. Martin Meyerson, "Urban Policy: Reforming Reform," *Daedalus*, vol. 97, no. 4 (Fall 1968).

carried out. Formal meetings and informal discussions guaranteed that all public, civic, and private voices were heard. Even the numerical relationship between private and public members was established in the Articles of Incorporation of some of these bodies—but the relative numbers were not really important, because Philadelphia got early into the habit of joint public-private policy-making.

"A great many lessons can be learned by other cities from Philadelphia's experience," claimed an article in the Philadelphia *Bulletin* in 1968. "No other city has a process as complete, as sensitive to real policy changes, and yet as resistant to arbitrary or capricious manipulation. . . . It is tough to develop explicit policy and to make decisions in this way. It is tough, but it is the most democratic device which any city has yet achieved to ensure that the end product really reflects the aspirations and wishes of those involved." [11]

Over the time of the reform period the relationship between public and private "partners" changed substantially, as we have observed. The city learned a lesson from its powerlessness to influence the Pennsylvania Railroad (Penn Center). By the time the Food Distribution Center was devised, it was seen that if the city's financial stake was substantial, the city should be able to call the tune. Consciously planned partnerships followed (for example, in industrial development). Eventually no formal agreement seemed to be necessary, and private corporations such as the West Philadelphia Corporation were inclined to act as if the city were a full-fledged partner.

## How Firm Was Civic Determination?

Throughout the period under discussion, well into Tate's first term, civic groups maintained a close liaison with the city's developmental programs. At the end of 1964, however, an editorial appeared in the Philadelphia *Bulletin* entitled: "End of the Renaissance?" Its tenor is pertinent here: "The truth is that the renaissance *has* run down; but that it has not come to a halt. . . . Just before and during the renaissance, Philadelphia developed an unusually gifted—and endowed—group of civic and business agencies. These are still hale and hearty and continuing

11. Philadelphia *Bulletin,* July 29, 1968.

to function. . . . The vitality of assorted citizen groups . . . attests to the fact that the old city is still bursting with new energy. . . . The renaissance has merely hit a downcurve, with every reason to think that it will start up again. . . . And, after all, it wasn't City Hall alone that created the renaissance—it was also the civic minded citizenry." [12]

In the mid-sixties it seemed worthwhile to inquire of many involved in these civic groups and watchdog organizations whether they were ready to defend what they had helped to bring about. The answers this author received sounded hopeful. Business and civic groups indicated that they were fully committed to a renewed Philadelphia and would act when they felt that it was necessary. They might be older and sparkle less than they did in the forties and fifties, they said, but that did not make their commitment any less deep. "We have been at it too long, we just can't let City Hall fall apart again." "This impetus takes a long time to lose. Things are still happening." Another statement was even more specific: "If things get worse, GPM is prepared to stand up any time and be counted. It was born out of necessity, and would not now want to accept the evils which it was founded to avoid." Virtually everybody from within the civic Establishment who was asked sounded certain. Emphasis seemed to be on consolidating gains rather than blazing new trails. In the mid-sixties, this author came away with the clear impression that the civic concern was very much alive, and that the groups knew that any inroads against the reform programs had to be fought vigorously.

Although this author gained the impression that civic groups were willing to do battle if the situation warranted it, external changes raised some questions about this conclusion. By the time of the next election some changes had taken place in the business structure of Philadelphia, and hence in the civic power that business was able to exert. A number of firms had been merged or acquired by out-of-town concerns. Philadelphia had lost corporate headquarters. Top personnel had been transferred. And those leaders who were still in top positions in Philadelphia had been

12. Philadelphia *Bulletin,* December 29, 1964, p. 24.

there a long time—in other words, not enough new leadership was visible.[13]

## The Persistence of the Reform Spirit

The question whether or not the civic spirit was still alive seemed to be answered when the tickets for the 1967 mayoral election were known: Tate was opposed by a Republican ticket, on which many of the candidates were clearly reform-minded. Civic groups were ready to unite behind a new reform administration. Many of their top leaders endorsed the ticket in a full-page advertisement, much as they had done for Dilworth in 1959. Though this was a blow to Tate, the action seemed to prove the general belief that the spirit of reform was still alive.

As if to confirm this point, a Philadelphia *Bulletin* editorial explained, just before the election, that the real legacy of the renaissance had been the ability of Clark and Dilworth to work in partnership with most segments of the community, especially the civic and business groups. The *Bulletin* faulted Tate for his inability "to marshall the talents, energies, and resources of all sectors of the community in team work to deal with Philadelphia's problems." [14]

Though Tate's narrow victory was a disappointment for them, a group of prominent civic and business leaders arranged, a few months later, a meeting with him to discuss cooperation on important developmental programs. A small liaison group was formed under the chairmanship of the head of the Pennsylvania Railroad, on which the chairmen of the OPDC, the Philadelphia Port Corporation, the Science Center Corporation, and the Chamber of Commerce served, as well as the president of the Board of Education, Richardson Dilworth. The chairman of OPDC, William Day, mentioned afterward that the mayor had agreed that "redevelopment of center city has been the real economic prop of the city." Others quoted Tate as sharing the group's concerns "in the field of jobs, education and housing—the things confronting a lot of big cities." [15]

13. Charles McNamara, "The Power Crisis," *Philadelphia Magazine*, November 1971, p. 92.
14. Philadelphia *Bulletin*, October 29, 1967.
15. Philadelphia *Bulletin*, July 29, 1968.

These groups were obviously not able, in the next four years, to prevent the massive reentry of political considerations into the city's business, the appointment of the mayor's friends to the most influential boards and commissions, or the activities of some of them which led to their indictments by a grand jury. But although such politization made close cooperation with Tate even harder than it had been in his first few years in office—when he still spoke of himself as a reform mayor—the civic groups apparently succeeded in having at least some of the developmental programs continued: expansion of the Center City business area, extension of the transportation network under SEPTA, urban renewal especially of the inner city, continuation of industrial attraction, the creation of job opportunities, and so forth. Whatever cooperation with civic groups was still feasible during this period had an important influence on this direction. It is in this sense of having started on the path of substantive developmental programs with the aid and support of civic groups, that the gains of the reform have been called "irreversible."

The renaissance was the first reform movement in Philadelphia which exhibited staying power, as a result of the wide variety of substantive changes it introduced, resting on broad-based civic initiative and professional expertise. The Quaker tradition of consensus prevailed, and agreement on broad goals was based on shared values. Philadelphia became a mature, sophisticated, and pluralistic city.

Some of the changes discussed earlier in this chapter seemed to have their full effect: in 1971 Frank Rizzo was elected mayor, a person quite unlike any of the other postwar chief executives. His campaign rhetoric promised radical changes. How completely he intended to turn the direction of the city away from what it had been during the reform period depends partly to which of the national or local changes he attributes his election success. The time lapsed since then has been too short to evaluate what was actually decisive, let alone to judge what his goals as mayor will turn out to be. These questions are obviously beyond the scope of this volume. However, it may be pertinent that in 1972 the Philadelphia *Bulletin* arranged a panel discussion of civic leaders on "How to Get Philadelphia Moving Again." Among the participants were Thacher Longstreth, Lennox Moak, Martin Meyerson, the deputy mayor, the executive director of the Urban Coalition, and the chairman of the GPM.

New problems, new challenges, new potentialities face cities today. Yet if a new city administration wants to build for the best interests of the majority of Philadelphia's citizens, it is difficult to believe that the issues encountered would be totally different from those faced by the reform government, no matter how much the environment has changed. Unless the new mayor's purpose is to break entirely with the aims for Philadelphia's development followed by the city for twenty years, he will have to subscribe to at least some of the developmental goals pointed to during the reform period, and some of the tools tried by the reformers. On the other hand, if he breaks with this tradition and refuses to work with professionals or civic groups, this author believes that a firm basis has been laid for the pendulum to swing back within the foreseeable future.

# Appendixes

Appendixes

# 1    *Chronology*

1683     William Penn founds Philadelphia.

1752     Benjamin Franklin starts "Philadelphia Contributionship."

1880     Mugwump movement and Committee of One Hundred started by Quakers.

1881     Samuel King elected mayor, serves one term as weak reform mayor.

1885     Charter reform (Bullitt), giving mayoral power over department heads.

1904     Committee of Seventy started.

1908     Bureau of Municipal Research started.

1909     Philadelphia Housing Association started.

1910     Progressive movement starts reform party in Philadelphia.

1912     Rudolph Blankenburg elected reform mayor.

1915     First City Housing Code passed, drafted by Philadelphia Housing Association.

1919     Charter reform establishes unicameral system as well as pro forma civil service.

1939     Charter change attempted, but fails.

1940     City Policy Committee started.

1942     City Planning ordinance passed.

1943     City Planning Commission started, with Robert Mitchell executive director.

          Citizens' Council on City Planning started.

1945     State law passed establishing Redevelopment Authority.

1946     Robert K. Sawyer becomes director of the Bureau of Municipal Research.

1947     "Better Philadelphia Exhibition" shown at Gimbel's department store.

          Richardson Dilworth runs unsuccessfully for mayor against Samuels.

1948     Report of Committee of Fifteen presented.

          Greater Philadelphia Movement started.

Edmund Bacon becomes executive director of City Planning Commission.

Congress creates Independence National Historical Park.

1949    Home Rule bill passed by legislature, giving city the right to draft its own charter.

Clark and Dilworth run successfully for controller and treasurer, respectively.

Citizens' Charter Commission started.

Citizens' Charter Committee started by GPM.

1950    Dilworth runs unsuccessfully for governor.

1951    Home Rule Charter passes.

Clark elected mayor, Dilworth district attorney.

Constitutional amendment on city-county consolidation passed by voters.

1952    Development Committee of Redevelopment Authority started.

1953    James Finnegan resigns as Democratic party chairman; Congressman William Green succeeds him.

Urban Traffic and Transportation Board appointed. Robert Mitchell becomes executive director.

1954    Clark defeats charter "ripping" amendments.

City economist appointed.

William L. Rafsky appointed housing coordinator.

Interagency Committee on Housing started.

"Leadership Program" grant approved.

George Leader, Democrat, elected governor.

1955    Food Distribution Center Corporation started.

Eleven prominent citizens urge a new Housing and Urban Renewal policy on the city.

Urban Traffic and Transportation Board report presented.

Dilworth runs for mayor and defeats Thacher Longstreth.

1956    Charter amendments defeated in spite of Dilworth's support.

Central Urban Renewal Area study completed.

Center City Coordinating Committee started.

Rafsky appointed development coordinator.

John A. Bailey appointed deputy managing director and transportation coordinator.

Old Philadelphia Development Corporation started.

Second Urban Traffic and Transportation Board appointed, with Bailey as executive director.

Joseph S. Clark elected to U.S. Senate.

Gaylord Harnwell appointed president of the University of Pennsylvania.

**1957**    New renewal policy announced by development coordi-**nator.**

Philadelphia Housing Association publishes "Let's Speed the Pace of Urban Renewal."

PTC agreement renegotiated. Service Standard Board started.

Public Housing Committee established by Philadelphia Housing Association and Citizens' Council on City Planning to mark twenty years of public housing, suggests "used house" program.

"Washington Square East Urban Renewal Area" approved by federal government.

Pennsylvania, New Jersey, Delaware, Inc. (Penjerdel) incorporated.

**1958**    Comprehensive Plan completed by City Planning Commission.

Mayor's Economic Advisory Committee appointed.

Philadelphia Industrial Development Corporation started.

Interagency Committee on Industry and Commerce started.

David Lawrence, Democrat, elected governor.

**1959**    West Philadelphia Corporation started.

Dilworth runs for reelection as mayor and defeats Harold Stassen.

Penjerdel regional study becomes active.

Penn-Jersey Transportation Study contract signed.

**1960**    Leo Molinaro appointed executive director of West Philadelphia Corporation.

**1961**    Community Renewal Program committee appointed on basis of approval of federal grant.

Passenger Service Improvement Corporation started.

**1962**    Southeastern Pennsylvania Transportation Compact started.

"Used house" program started, held up by lawsuit.

Dilworth resigns to run for governor and is defeated.

James H. J. Tate becomes mayor.

William Scranton, Republican, elected governor.

Building starts in "Washington Square East Urban Renewal Area."

GPM publishes report on public education.

Add Anderson, business manager of Board of Education, dies.

Richard Graves resigns from PIDC. Richard McConnell succeeds him. PIDC merged with FDC.

1963    Appointment of Educational Home Rule Charter Commission.

Tate elected mayor, appoints small Development Council.

Congressman William Green dies and is succeeded as party chairman by Francis Smith.

PIDC and West Philadelphia Corporation form the University City Science Corporation.

Sit-in in Mayor Tate's office. George Schermer resigns as executive director of Human Relations Commission.

Law establishing Southeastern Pennsylvania Transportation Authority passed.

1964    SEPTA begins operation.

Philadelphia Housing Development Corporation started.

1965    Paul Anderson appointed president of Temple University.

Educational Home Rule Charter passes. New board appointed, with Dilworth as president.

1967    CRP Final Report released.

Tate runs for mayor and defeats Arlen Specter by narrow margin.

# 2 *Persons Interviewed*

*The positions shown below are the positions held during the period discussed in the book or at the time of the interviews. Most of the interviews took place in 1964 and 1965, with some, however, as late as 1967.*

Alhart, Clarence: deputy director, Philadelphia Redevelopment Authority.

Amsterdam, Gustave: president, Bankers' Security Corporation; chairman, Philadelphia Redevelopment Authority.

Arnett, Keeton: executive director, Chamber of Commerce of Greater Philadelphia.

Bacon, Edmund: executive director, Philadelphia City Planning Commission.

Bailey, John A.: deputy managing director, city of Philadelphia; executive director, Philadelphia Passenger Service Improvement Corporation; deputy managing director, Southeast Pennsylvania Passenger Transport Authority.

Baltzell, E. Digby: professor, Department of Sociology, University of Pennsylvania.

Batten, Harry: chairman of the board, N. W. Ayers and Company; cochairman, Greater Philadelphia Movement.

Beatty, Edward: staff, Philadelphia Industrial Development Corporation.

Beerits, Henry: lawyer; past president, Philadelphia Housing Association.

Berger, David: city solicitor, city of Philadelphia (Dilworth administration).

Blackburn, Robert: Citizens' Council on Public Education; staff, Philadelphia Board of Education.

Bonnell, Alan: vice-president, Drexel Institute of Technology; president, Philadelphia Community College.

Buford, Richard: deputy development coordinator; commissioner of licenses and inspections, city of Philadelphia.

Burns, Lilian: assistant to the vice-president, University of Pennsylvania.

Byrne, Michael: deputy to the mayor (Clark administration).

Childs, Damon: chief, Urban Renewal Division, City Planning Commission.

Chisholm, Terence: director, Commission on Human Relations.

Clark, Dennis: staff, Philadelphia Commission on Human Relations; Temple University.

Clark, Joseph S.: mayor, city of Philadelphia, 1952–56; U.S. Senator, 1956–68.

Coughlin, Robert: chief, Division of Long Term Planning, Philadelphia City Planning Commission; Regional Science Institute, University of Pennsylvania.

Croley, Paul: assistant executive director, Philadelphia City Planning Commission; executive vice-president, Philadelphia Industrial Development Corporation.

Culp, John: city economist, Philadelphia.

Dash, Samuel: district attorney (Dilworth administration); executive director, Philadelphia Council for Community Advancement.

Davidoff, Paul: Department of City Planning, University of Pennsylvania.

Davis, David: assistant director of commerce for port development, city of Philadelphia.

Deutermann, Elizabeth: staff, Penn-Jersey Transportation Study; Philadelphia Community Renewal Program; economist, Federal Reserve Bank, Philadelphia.

Dexter, Sidney: banker; chairman, Philadelphia Civil Service Commission.

Di Angelo, Anthony: administrative assistant, Philadelphia City Planning Commission.

Dilworth, Richardson: mayor, 1956–62; president, Philadelphia Board of Education, 1965–71.

Dolbeare, Cushing: assistant managing director, managing director, Philadelphia Housing Association.

D'Ortona, Paul: president, Philadelphia City Council.

Dougherty, Michael: staff, Philadelphia Industrial Development Corporation.

Duane, Morris: lawyer, civic leader.

Duckrey, Marjorie: staff, Philadelphia Urban League.

Eisenberg, Warren: assistant editor, *Greater Philadelphia Magazine*.

Evans, Samuel: executive director, Philadelphia Area Action Committee.

Fagan, Maurice: executive director, Philadelphia Fellowship Commission.

Ferleger, Harry: executive director, Trade and Convention Center, Philadelphia.

Finney, Graham: assistant executive director, Philadelphia City Planning Commission; deputy superintendent for planning, Philadelphia Board of Education.

Folk, Edward: executive director, Citizens' Council on City Planning.

Frazier, Charles: former commissioner of procurement, city of Philadelphia; chief engineer, Philadelphia Gas Company; chairman, Urban Traffic and Transportation Board.

Freedman, Abraham: city solicitor (Clark administration); federal judge.

Freeman, Andrew: executive director, Urban League, Philadelphia.

Gerenbeck, George, Jr.: executive director, Friends' Guild Rehabilitation Program.

Gladfelter, Millard: president, Temple University.

Gluckman, Ivan: office of the deputy managing director for housing.

Greenfield, Albert M.: chairman, City Planning Commission; real estate developer.

Grigsby, William: professor, Institute of Urban Studies, University of Pennsylvania.

Gruenberg, Frederick: civic leader.

Guess, Joseph M.: reporter, Philadelphia *Bulletin;* administrative assistant, Philadelphia City Council.

Harnwell, Gaylord: president, University of Pennsylvania.

Hetherston, John: vice-president, University of Pennsylvania.

Hemphill, Alexander: comptroller, city of Philadelphia.

Hoeber, Johannes: deputy commissioner of welfare, city of Philadelphia.

Hopkinson, Edward: president, Drexel and Company; civic leader; former chairman, Philadelphia City Planning Commission.

Hyman, Allan: deputy personnel director, city of Philadelphia.

Karabell, Milton: executive director, West Philadelphia Corporation.

Karras, Mead Smith: assistant development coordinator, city of Philadelphia.

Kaufman, Manuel: deputy commissioner of welfare, Philadelphia.

Klein, Phillip: president, Junta (adult education college), Philadelphia; member, City Planning Commission.

Knapp, Edward: chief, Comprehensive Planning Division, City Planning Commission.

Kurtz, William Fulton: banker; co-chairman, Greater Philadelphia Movement.

Lamason, Marshall: executive vice-president, Food Distribution Center Corporation.

Lieberman, Barnet: deputy managing director, city of Philadelphia; executive director, Philadelphia Housing Development Corporation.

Longstreth, Thacher: executive director, Chamber of Commerce of Greater Philadelphia; mayoral candidate 1967, 1971.

McConnell, Richard: director of finance, city of Philadelphia (Clark and Dilworth administrations); executive vice-president, Philadelphia Industrial Development Corporation.

Marshall, John: University of Pennsylvania; chairman, Citizens' Committee on Public Education.

Mitchell, Allen: vice-president, Philadelphia Electric Company.

Mitchell, Robert: director, Institute of Urban Studies, chairman, Department of City Planning, University of Pennsylvania.

Moak, Lennox: director of finance (Clark administration); executive director, Pennsylvania Economy League–Bureau of Municipal Research.

Molinaro, Leo: executive vice-president; president, West Philadelphia Corporation.

Montgomery, Dorothy: managing director, Philadelphia Housing Association.

Murphy, James: staff, Old Philadelphia Development Corporation.

Nathan, Jason: Philadelphia regional director, U.S. Housing and Home Finance Agency.

Niebuhr, Herman, Jr.: director, Center for Community Studies, Temple University.

Northrop, Vernon: finance director; managing director, city of Philadelphia (Clark administration); executive vice-president, Food Distribution Center Corporation; federal representative to the Delaware River Basin Commission.

Norwitch, Harry: member, Philadelphia City Council.

Oberman, Joseph: staff, City Planning Commission; staff, Philadelphia Industrial Development Corporation; city economist, Philadelphia.

Patterson, John: civic leader.

Perkins, G. Holmes: dean, School of Architecture, University of Pennsylvania; chairman, City Planning Commission.

Phillips, Walter M.: lawyer; civic leader; director of commerce, city of Philadelphia (Clark administration); consultant, Penjerdel.

Rafsky, William L.: former executive secretary to Joseph S. Clark; housing coordinator, development coordinator, city of Philadelphia; executive vice-president, Old Philadelphia Development Corporation.

Rapkin, Chester: Institute of Urban Studies, University of Pennsylvania; Institute of Environmental Studies, Columbia University.

Rauch, Stewart, Jr.: president, Philadelphia Savings Fund Society; member, City Planning Commission; co-chairman, Greater Philadelphia Movement.

Rogers, Thomas: staff, Philadelphia City Council; executive secretary to Mayor James H. J. Tate.

Rubel, Donald: member, Philadelphia City Council.

Russell, Edward: executive director, Committee of Seventy.

Sass, Frederick: economist, Pennsylvania Railroad Company.

Sawyer, Henry III: lawyer; former member, Philadelphia City Council.

Schauffler, Peter: former executive secretary to Mayor Joseph S. Clark; assistant director of commerce for port development; associate executive director, Greater Philadelphia Movement.

Schermer, George: executive director, Human Relations Commission, Philadelphia (1952–63).

Schraga, Saul: reporter, Philadelphia *Inquirer;* chief, public relations, Redevelopment Authority.

Schwartz, George: member, Philadelphia City Council.

Short, Frank: staff, Department of Commerce.

Short, Raymond: professor, Department of Political Science, Temple University.

Shull, Leon: executive director, Southeastern Pennsylvania chapter, Americans for Democratic Action; executive director, national office, Americans for Democratic Action.

Shusterman, Murray: assistant city solicitor.

Smith, L. M. S.: lawyer; chairman, Board of Trade and Convention Center.

Somers, Herman: professor of political science, Haverford College; consultant to Mayor Joseph S. Clark; professor of political science, Woodrow Wilson School of Public Administration, Princeton.

Staebler, Jan: assistant vice-president, Philadelphia Industrial Development Corporation.

Standish, Miles: director, International Council, Chamber of Commerce of Greater Philadelphia.

Stonorov, Oscar: architect; civic leader.

Sullivan, Leon: clergyman; president, Opportunities Industrialization Center.

Sweeney, Stephen: director, Fels Institute of State and Local Government, University of Pennsylvania.

Tate, James H. J.: mayor, city of Philadelphia, 1962–71.

Taylor, George: professor, Department of Industry and Geography, University of Pennsylvania.

Tucker, George: staff, City Planning Commission, Community Renewal Program.

Turchi, Joseph: assistant development coordinator; assistant executive director, Redevelopment Authority.

Uhlig, Richard: staff, Health and Welfare Council, Philadelphia.

Vaughan, Pastelle: assistant director, Manpower Commission, city of Philadelphia.

Wagner, Donald: managing director, city of Philadelphia (Dilworth administration).

Wallace, David: director of planning, Redevelopment Authority; Department of City Planning, University of Pennsylvania.

Weintraub, Tina: deputy managing director, city of Philadelphia.

Wheaton, William: director, Institute of Urban Studies, University of Pennsylvania.

Wilcox, William: executive director, Greater Philadelphia Movement.

Wilhelm, Paul: assistant director of commerce, city of Philadelphia;

Philadelphia Industrial Development Corporation; executive director, Greater Wilmington Committee.

Winett, Nochem: judge; civic leader.

Wise, Harold: planning consultant; Philadelphia Industrial Development Corporation.

Wise, Randolph: commissioner, Department of Welfare.

Young, Andrew: chairman, Philadelphia Industrial Development Corporation.

Zucker, William: executive vice-president, Southeastern Pennsylvania Economic Development Corporation and Southeastern Pennsylvania Development Fund.

# 3  Reports of the Community Renewal Program

City of Philadelphia, Community Renewal Program, *Major Policies and Proposals*, 1967 (final report).

## Technical Reports

1. CRP staff, *Initial Six Month Work Program and Budget*, May 1962.
2. CRP, *Second Six Month Work Program and Budget*, 1962.
3. Philadelphia City Planning Commission, *West Philadelphia District Plan and Program*, 1962.
4. CRP staff, *Community Renewal Programming*, December 1962.
5. Health and Welfare Council, Inc., *A Study of the Social Aspects of the Community Renewal Program*, 1963.
6. Marcia Rogers, CRP staff, *The Redevelopment Authority Program 1945–1962, Dollars, Acres, and Dwelling Units*, September 1963.
7. Mauchly Associates, *The Application of Network Scheduling to the CRP Program: Consultants Report on the Critical-Path Method: Resources Planning and Scheduling*, July 1963.
8. Robert Shawn, CRP staff, *Development Programming as Applied to West Philadelphia*, February 1964.
9. Mary W. Herman, Health and Welfare Council, Inc., *Comparative Studies of Identifiable Areas in Philadelphia*, April 1964.
10. National Analysts, Inc., *Philadelphia's Position in the Regional and National Economy*, May 1964.
11. Donna M. McGough, Health and Welfare Council, Inc., *Social Factor Analysis*, October 1964.
12. CRP staff, *Philadelphia's Living Pattern*, October 1964.
13. Elizabeth Deutermann, CRP staff, *Economic Development*, December 1964.
14. Robert Gladstone and Associates, *Philadelphia Housing Analysis, Trends and Outlook*, February 1965.
15. George Tucker, CRP staff, *Phase I, Months 1–30, Progress Report*, July 1965.

16. Richard H. Uhlig, Health and Welfare Council, Inc., *Planning in the Urban Environment: Next Steps in Social Research and in Social Planning, City of Philadelphia,* July 1965.

17. Elizabeth Wood, Management Services Associates, *The Needs of People Affected by Relocation,* October 1965.

18. Charles Abrams, "The Negro Housing Problem: A Program for Philadelphia," *Equal Opportunity in Housing: A Consultant's Report,* December 1966.

19. Redevelopment Authority, city of Philadelphia, *Relocation of Business and Industrial Firms,* 1966.
    Unnumbered. Harold Wise, *Industrial Renewal: Requirements and Outlook for Philadelphia,* December 1964.

## Staff Papers and Consultants' Reports

CRP staff, *Development Program, 1965–1970* (illustrative), n.d.

———, *Dispersal of Relocated Cases, 1958–1962,* 1963.

———, *Future Relocation Caseloads: Problem Cases and Services Needed,* 1965.

Health and Welfare Council, Inc., *Inventory of Social Resources:* vol. 1. *West Philadelphia,* 1964; vol. 2, *Germantown–Chestnut Hill–Roxborough–Manyunk,* 1964; vol. 3, *South Philadelphia–Southwest Philadelphia,* 1964; vol. 4, *Far Northeast–Near Northeast–Olney–Oak Lane,* 1965; vol. 5, *North Philadelphia,* 1965; vol. 6, *Center City,* 1965.

Robert I. McMullin, CRP staff (in cooperation with the Health and Welfare Council, Inc.), *Neighborhood Associations in Philadelphia,* 1963.

Office of the Development Coordinator, "Targets for Low-Income Housing Programs," 1966.

Office of the Director of Finance, *Funds Available for Renewal,* 1966.

———, Economic Development Unit, "Philadelphia's Job Potentials in Specific Renewal Areas for the Next Ten Years," 1966.

Marcia Rogers, CRP staff, *Analyzing the Renewal Strategy Impact,* 1965.

Robert Shawn, CRP staff, *Possible Administrative Arrangements for Renewal and Development,* April 1965.

# Index

# Index